AF564644

Housekeeping and Laundry Operations

Housekeeping and Laundry Operations

Rajendra Kumar Khatan

RANDOM PUBLICATIONS
NEW DELHI (INDIA)

Housekeeping and Laundry Operations

ISBN 978-93-5111-547-2

Published in 2015 in India by

RANDOM PUBLICATIONS

4376-A/4B, Gali Murari Lal, Ansari Road
New Delhi-110 002
Phone : +9111-43580356, 011-23289044, 011-43142548
e-mail: sales@randompublications.com,
info@randompublications.com, randomexports@gmail.com

Type Setting by : Friends Media, Delhi-110089

Printed at Thomson Press(India) Limited

Preface

Housekeeping refers to the management of duties and chores involved in the running of a household, such as cleaning, cooking, home maintenance, shopping and bill pay. These tasks may be performed by the household members, or by other persons hired to perform these tasks. The term is also used to refer to the money allocated for such use. Laundry is the washing of clothing and linens. Laundry processes are often done in a business, room or area in a home or apartment building, reserved for that purpose; this is referred to as a laundry room. The material that is being washed, or has been laundered is also generally referred to as laundry. Much of a guest's overall impression of the hotel relates to its cleanliness; therefore Housekeeping associates play a crucial role in ensuring an exceptional guest experience. The Housekeeping department is typically the largest in the hotel in terms of both the number of associates and annual operating budget. Ideal Housekeeping and Laundry associates are extremely detail-oriented. They strive to provide guests with clean and comfortable accommodations while away from home. From fresh bed linens to spotless bathrooms and immaculate lobbies, our associates are committed to upholding Starwood's quality and cleanliness standards at all times.

I would like to thank my team for standing beside me throughout my career and writing this book. My special thanks go to "Random Publications" who have published the book.

– Rajendra Kumar Khatan

Contents

1

Fundamentals of Housekeeping

An uncluttered workplace is fundamental to any plant's safety programme. In addition to cleanliness, industrial housekeeping must include other factors, such as orderliness and proper arrangement of materials. It is important to know the benefits of good industrial housekeeping. Let's review the importance and meaning of order in achieving good housekeeping, and discuss some guides for checking your own work area. Sloppy working conditions can lead to a lack of pride in your work. We should not overlook slippery floors, obstacles in aisles, tools on the floors, floors and platforms that are not in proper condition, or other housekeeping hazards.

In addition to encouraging poor attitudes, bad industrial housekeeping can lead to:

- Slips from slick or wet floors, platforms, and other walking and working surfaces.
- Trips from objects or materials that are left in walkways and work areas.
- Falls from holes in walking and working surfaces, uneven flooring, uncovered pits or drains, and boxes and pallets that are used instead of adequate platforms.
- Collisions caused by poorly stored materials, overhanging or protruding objects, haphazard spotting of pallets, and use of aisles for storing materials and equipment.

Poor industrial housekeeping creates hazards for all employees in the immediate area.

Good industrial housekeeping:

- Eliminates accident and fire causes
- Saves energy by eliminating the need to work "around" congested areas and "deadwood" stored in the work area.
- Provides the best use of space
- Keeps inventory of materials to a minimum
- Helps control property damage
- Guarantees a good workplace appearance

- Encourages better working habits
- Reflects an image of a well-run operation
- Reduces the amount of cleanup and janitorial work

Housekeeping is more than just sweeping the floor and wiping dust off machines and equipment. Cleanliness is only a part of housekeeping. The most critical and most overlooked part of housekeeping is order. A work area is in order when there are no unnecessary objects in the area and when all necessary items are in their proper places.No in this definition means none—not any—not even one!

A workplace is not considered to be in order simply because "there is a place for everything and everything is in its place." Do you use your production area for storage? Do you keep supplies in the area because "they'll be needed one of these days?"

If there is one item in an area that is unnecessary or not in its proper place, then you do not have order. Order is maintained, not achieved. You cannot put an area in order and then forget about it. A daily conscious effort by everyone working in the area is necessary to maintain order. Order also must be obtained throughout the day. If you wait until the end of the day and then place everything in order, what good did it do you during the day? Disorder wastes time, energy and materials.

A good housekeeping programme must include careful planning, a clean-up schedule or policy, effective inspection, and continuous supervision and enforcement of house-keeping rules. Inspect your area for unnecessary tools, equipment, parts, materials and supplies; items that are not needed should be sent to the storage room or used for salvage. Reorganize the storage area in your workplace.

Establish one or more storage areas for holding finished products and daily quantities of raw materials and supplies; storage areas should not obstruct aisles and work areas.

Create a daily clean-up policy and programme. Periodically review the housekeeping rules, clean-up policies and procedures.

Housekeeping rules

- Walking and working surfaces should be clean, dry and unobstructed.
- Aisleways and exits should be clearly marked and unobstructed.
- Approved trash receptacles should be provided to assure proper waste disposal.
- Splash guards and oil pans should be available for machinery as needed.
- Work area floors should be kept free of pallets, parts, equipment, extension cords and hoses.
- Floors, platforms and stairways should be kept in good repair.

- Adequate platforms should be provided; never use additional platforms or boxes and pallets as substitutes.
- Walls and ceilings should be free of hangings and temporary wiring.
- Materials should be stacked in a stable manner; limit height as necessary to maintain stability.
- Overhanging or protruding storage should be eliminated.
- Storage areas in and around buildings should be free of refuse and debris.
- Stock should be stored in a manner that will not obstruct sprinklers (18-inch clearance for ordinary combustibles, 36-inch clearance for flammable liquids).

Combustible materials should never be stored on radiators, steam coils, ovens or other heat sources; in transformer vaults; or around electrical switch gear.

- Production equipment should be arranged to prevent overcrowding.
- Storage areas should be placed in a convenient location to encourage their use.
- Adequate lighting, both natural and artificial, should be provided to assure good visibility for work activities and to reveal dirt, obstructions and poor housekeeping conditions.
- Leaks from hoses, pipelines and valves should be repaired immediately.
- Racks, shelves and lockers should be maintained for tools, personal protective equipment and personal items.
- Lunch facilities, locker rooms and toilet areas should be clean, orderly and sanitary.
- Order results in greater and safer production of better products at lower costs. Improved production and costs mean increased business and prosperity for our company and you, its employees.

Hotel Housekeeping

What Can Happen

Cuts, bruises, sprains, strains, electrocution, Chemical-related injuries, infections etc.

What we Can Do

Watch for things that may cause accidents and report them immediately to your supervisor. Place mops, buckets and other equipment where no one can fall over them.

Practise safe lifting techniques, lift with your legs, not your back. Be careful with cleaning solutions or chemicals read product labels. Store cigarette butts and sharp objects in a separate, metal container. Roll up all linen, rugs and spreads before putting them in the soiled laundry bundle. Wear rubber gloves when using strong cleaning solutions. Push tall or heavy pieces of furniture get help if necessary.

Do not touch light switches or handle electrical equipment when your hands are wet or you are standing on a damp floor Do not stand on the edge of bathroom tubs

Do not mix ammonia and chlorine-based cleaners together, poisonous gas is produced. Do not run up or down stairs, always walk and use the handrail. Do not try to repair machines or equipment, report problems to your supervisor. Do not run your hands along or inside objects unless you have checked first for razor blades, needles, broken glass, etc.

Do not use your hands to compress garbage in a bag, use a stick or plunger. Do not unplug the vacuum cleaner by pulling on the cord, pull on the plug.

Housekeeping in a hotel is a very physically demanding job that includes many, varied tasks. Typically, in this case study, housekeepers were responsible for cleaning 16 rooms per shift. The actual amount of work depends on the size of the room and the number of beds. A housekeeper needs between fifteen and thirty minutes to do one room.

A housekeeper carries out the following tasks:

- Making beds
- Tidying rooms
- Cleaning and polishing toilets, taps, sinks, bathtubs and mirrors
- Washing floors,
- Removing stains, and
- Vacuuming

Housekeeping in a hotel is a very physically demanding job that includes many, varied tasks. Typically, in this case study, housekeepers were responsible for cleaning 16 rooms per shift. The actual amount of work depends on the size of the room and the number of beds. A housekeeper needs between fifteen and thirty minutes to do one room.

The main risk factors for repetitive motion injuries (RMIs) in housekeeping are:

Heavy physical workload and excessive bodily motions which are a high risk for back injuries and forceful upper limb motions in awkward positions which are a high risk for neck or shoulder and arm injuries. Space limitations require workers to use many uncomfortable postures.

These are:

- Standing or walking,
- Stooping,
- Squatting,
- Kneeling,

- Stretching,
- Reaching,
- Bending,
- Twisting, and
- Crouching.

A housekeeper changes body position every three seconds while cleaning a room. If we assume that the average cleaning time for each room is twenty-five minutes, we can estimate that a housekeeper assumes 8,000 different body postures every shift.

In addition, forceful movements while using awkward body positions include lifting mattresses, cleaning tiles, and vacuuming every shift. Housekeeping is a physically demanding and very tiring job. It can be classified as "moderately heavy" to "heavy" work because the energy required is approximately 4 kilocalories per minute (4 kcal/min.)

Hotel housekeepers work in a unique place. Hotels are usually designed for the comfort of their guests rather than their housekeeping staff. This fact makes it very difficult to improve working conditions for housekeepers by means of better engineering.

However, some improvements can be made by selecting more appropriate equipment. Lighter vacuum cleaners (preferably the self-propelling type), and lighter service carts with wheels designed for carpeted floors would ease the workload for their operators providing this equipment is always kept in good repair. When new vacuum cleaners are purchased, low noise emissions should be one of the criteria.

Improving the body postures that pose a major risk for musculoskeletal disorders seems an unachievable task. Again, this fact results from the peculiarity of hotels as a workplace. To attract guests and remain competitive, hotel management pursues a policy that everything should be "so clean it sparkles".

Floors, walls, windows, mirrors, and bathroom fixtures might be adequately cleaned with some form of an extension tool to reduce bending and over-stretching.

However, the demand for spotless cleanliness and hygiene, management often requires their cleaning staff to spend extra time and effort cleaning by kneeling, leaning, squatting, crouching, slouching and stretching. These postures will in time contribute to new musculoskeletal injuries and aggravate old ones.

New approaches, other than strictly ergonomic ones, need to be investigated. For example, action can be taken from the administrative level.

Options for improvement include:

- Job rotation,
- Job enrichment and job enlargement,

- Team work, and
- Education and training on work practices.

Job rotation is one possible approach. It requires workers to move between different tasks, at fixed or irregular periods. However, it must be a rotation where workers do something completely different. Different tasks must use different muscle groups to allow muscles already stressed to recover.

Another approach is job enlargement. This increases the variety of tasks built into the job. It breaks the monotony of the job and avoids overloading one part of the body. Job enrichment involves more autonomy and control for the worker.

Team work can provide greater variety and more evenly distributed muscular work. The whole team is involved in the planning of the work. Each team member carries out a set of operations to complete the whole product, allowing the worker to alternate between tasks. This reduces the risk of RMI.

A well-designed job, supported by a well-designed workplace and proper tools, allows the worker to avoid unnecessary motion of the neck, shoulders and upper limbs. However, the actual performance of the tasks depends on individuals.

Training should be provided for workers who are involved with housekeeping activities. It is important that housekeeping staff be informed about hazards in the workplace, including the risk of injuries to the musculoskeletal system. Therefore, identification of the hazards for such injury at any given hotel is fundamental.

Individual work practices, including lifting habits, are shaped by proper training. Training should encourage employers and workers to adopt methods that reduce fatigue. For example, it is advisable to plan one's workload and do the heavier tasks at the beginning of the workshift, rather than at the end, when fatigue is at its maximum. When a person is tired, the risk of injuring a muscle is higher.

Training should also explain the health hazards of improper lifting and give recommendations on what a worker can do to improve lifting positions. Training should also emphasize the importance of rest periods for the workers' health and explain how active rest can do more for keeping workers healthy than passive rest. The effect of such training can reach far beyond occupational situations because the workers can apply this knowledge also in their off-job lives.

The Housekeeping department must be the most important. It has the greatest proportion of staffing hours to cover, the most staff, the most hours to cover and it is a cost centre. Unlike the restaurant and bar, which are revenue centres, and as long as they are not overstaffed, the more staff you have the more revenue is generated. The housekeeping department is also the one the customers notice most if anything is wrong. You have to have the right number of staff on duty, or it shows. The housekeeping department can have the following staff depending on the size of hotel.

Housekeeper and assistant housekeepers, room maids, cleaners, staffmaids, cloakroom attendants, houseporters, valets, laundry and linen keeper. The staff hours of cover depend on the hotel and type of customer, business people require different time schedules to people on holiday with children. The staff need to be scheduled accordingly and in a ratio to the number of guests staying in the hotel. Fortunately, most people book ahead and the workload is known well in advance, especially during peak periods.

Your staffing requirement will depend on the occupancy of your hotel. It is possible to get quite good estimates of staff numbers based on average times to do tasks, such as cleaning a room. Then you can allocate 10, or 15, or even 20 rooms to each room maid. It is also quite easy to estimate the total number of staff needed in a year for a task. We have a page about annual hours.

For example, cleaning an occupied room takes 30mins/day, en-suite bathroom 6mins/day, therefore a maid for every 13 occupied rooms. A hotel with 100 rooms(all occupied) needs 8 maids. Then we can sum this up for a year of 365 days, which comes to 2900 maid days per year. We can then divide this by the number of days a maid works per year, say 240, and arrive at a figure of 12 full time maids.

Hence we can recruit the 12 maids and start using them on the rooms. I haven't allowed for average occupancy, sickness rates, and a lot of other things which readily come to mind, because at this point, the difficult thing is to find a way of sharing the yearly workload on a day by day basis. This is the difficult part, just how do you allocate the maids so that you have just the right number on every day.

Well, the answer depends on where you are at the moment. An existing hotel staffed, is different to a new hotel unstaffed. If I first deal with a new hotel, then the resultant method is easier. First, don't start from the above yearly totals, use the daily hour totals to tell you how many staff are needed each day.

Start Visual Rota, set it up for, say 13 4week periods and name the staff, as RM1, RM2, etc. Then start to allocate shifts according to your occupancy rates(anticipated). At this stage you can use full time or part time staff, working full shifts, half shifts and split shifts. Give the staff days off, usually in the ratio of for every 5 days they work, they have 2 off. Try to use full time staff as much as possible if they are cheaper, and fill in the blanks with part time staff. Then you can recruit the staff in accordance with your requirements and allocate shifts to the staff weeks in advance, possibly months.

At some stage you need to deal with holidays and staff turnover. All staff take holidays but it is difficult to know in advance when this is going to be. That's why we invented dice. If you look back at your records(difficult if you are a new hotel, I know, then you have to guess) you will see the pattern of absenteeism, sickness and holidays, and even staff turnover. This pattern can be replicated by throwing dice. For instance, if you employ 12 maids and your staff turnover is 50 per cent, then six of your maids leave every year, or one every 2 months. You won't know when exactly and it is difficult for us to be random in our decisions, so throw a dice for each month. If the number is even, a 2, 4,or 6, then a maid leaves that month, if the number is odd, no one leaves that month. Then you can arrange for a new maid to be recruited in line with the throw of the dice. Perhaps not, perhaps what you will do is to include into your budgets the cost of hiring a new recruit and the cost of using an employment agency.

You can use Visual Rota to allocate training days for new staff and existing, or keep records of sickness, absenteeism, lateness, frequency of requests and holidays.

An existing hotel will be using their established working practice for staffing. Visual Rota enables you to analyse this and see if improvements can be made and how much you can save by changing your working practice. Staff need an incentive to change and if you offer part of your savings as a pay increase, that goes a long way to getting the changes accepted. We have regularly improved the way we work by incorporating new pay deals for existing staff and hiring new staff as and when we replaced the staff due to natural wastage on our new terms.

Visual Rota enables you to move your staff around to minimise the effects of peaks and troughs in occupancy levels. You can bring in more staff when needed and give them days off during slack periods. The programme keeps track of their hours and shifts, so everyone gets exactly the right number of hours of work, but your costs are minimised.

Other departments are equally capable of being analysed and scheduled by Visual Rota. It is possible to have one file for the entire hotel, or several files to cover each area, floor or department. Whichever method you use at the moment, you can do the same on the computer, but faster.

There is always a compromise between the number of staff doing a particular job and the cover they provide. If there is only one housekeeper, then the maximum cover would be 40 hours/week, whilst the staff rota would be providing up to 168 hours of cover a week, hence one of the main management functions is to determine how much staffing is provided and at what grade of staff. Fortunately, hoteliers are not subject to staffing levels determined by legislation, and can decide for themselves.

HOSPITALITY SERVICE

The concept of Hospitality Services, also known as "accommodation sharing", "hospitality exchange", and "home stay networks", refers to centrally organized social networks of individuals who trade accommodation without monetary exchange. While this concept could also include house swapping or even time share plans, it has come to be associated mostly with travellers and tourists staying with one another free of charge. Since the 1990s, these services have increasingly moved away from using printed catalogs and phone trees to connect users towards Internet web sites. These have grown exponentially since 2000 and today it is estimated that well over 100,000 people are registered users of these networks.

These vary in operational structure, place different emphasis on graphical vs. textual formatting, and cater disproportionately to specific geographic regions.

In 1949, Bob Luitweiler founded the first hospitality service called Servas Open Doors as a cross national, non-profit, volunteer run organization advocating interracial and international peace. The next earliest began in 1965 when John Wilcock set up the Traveller's Directory, originally as a listing of his mutual friends willing to host each other when traveling. This later became the Hospitality Exchange in 1988 when Joy Lily rescued the organization from imminent demise.

Hospitality Club is the direct successor Hospex, the first Internet-based service, operating out of Poland since 1992. It is currently the largest hospitality exchange network, growing rapidly. CouchSurfing is a newer but also rapidly growing hospitality exchange organization founded in 2004. Just as all the individual services have their own individual creation stories and organizational histories (often including demise and resurrection), many also have specific niche markets that they cater to including students, activists, religious pilgrims, and even occupational groups like police officers. However, the trend in recent years points to a greater consolidation of users in networks without a specific group, value, or lifestyle affiliation.

In essence, these systems employ reciprocity – users gain access to other users' information only by posting their own. Required fields normally include name and contact information, though newer services encourage users to include more detailed personal material, including likes and dislikes, hopes and dreams, and even photographs. Of course, more information included tends to improve the chances that someone will find them trustworthy enough to host or stay with while traveling. It is very much akin to online dating services.

Staying in private homes means that travellers can save lots of money on accommodation that they would usually be spending on hotels or hostels. Used over a long period of time (2 to 4 weeks), this strategy can cut overall travel budgets in half, or even more combined with hitchhiking. These savings can then be passed on towards more generously patronizing local establishments or simply staying abroad for longer periods of time.

Many tourist vacations today are sold in package form, often including flights, hotels, rental cars, sightseeing tours, and coupons for chain restaurants and bars. While this makes purchasing more convenient, it also puts more money in the hands of large multinational corporations exploiting the synergy strategy of marketing their products in the context of their subsidiary companies operating in other markets. Many years ago, this might have been termed collusion; today, however, it is the norm. This comes at the expense of locally owned independent businesses. Accommodation sharing helps to break apart this monopoly and hopefully redirects some of the tourist revenue back to the local or national economy.

While this is especially important in more rural travel venues where hotels are often built in very picturesque, though fragile environments, every night stayed at a local's home means that much less demand for such hotel rooms. Also, if accommodation sharing does in fact increase the length of average stays, it may reduce the amount of trips to and from different locations and back home again, thus reducing the overall fuel expenditures in the process.

Ostensibly, one of the primary reasons we travel is to experience what life is like for people living in other countries. Making interpersonal connections and fostering understanding of different cultures may in the long run also be important to international relations.

However, even in our increasingly globalized world supposedly rife with diversity, in many popular travel destinations we find tourists milling around "tourist enclaves" where the companies they patronize back home have set up shop to cater to their desires while they are abroad. Sociologist George Ritzer has referred to this phenomenon as the "McDonaldisation of society" and the more recently, the "globalization of nothing". The location of hotels near these centres only fosters more convenient envelopment of the tourist dollar. During hospitality exchanges, hosts want to show off their local knowledge and exciting "off the map" venues. Not only may travellers get a distinctly different experience, but they will also get a feel for the everyday lives of local residents.

These systems foster richer and more convenient travel experiences not so much on the premise of altruism, but on the basis of social exchange theory. Implicit in the agreement to host travellers is the ability to ask to be hosted by them in the future. If one enjoys having interesting guests in their home, this works out well for both parties. It works comparatively better if you are visited by travellers from a locale you find particularly attractive. Thus, hosting someone from New York City in Gainesville, FL seems to be an unbelievable opportunity. Moreover, if you are a Westerner visiting someone in a developing nation, your stay might be the only way that this individual or family could afford a trip to a rich nation. This may mean more than just a relaxing vacation for such disadvantaged parties.

Tourism has always searched for these two qualities, but much like Midas and his golden touch, the reach of tourism has to a large extent destroyed the opportunity to encounter them in most places. Unluckily, the experience has been thoroughly commodified by everyone who wanted to secure their opportunity to make a buck in the process. Accommodation sharing offers a way out of this bind and a viable alternative to having one's desires manipulated by corporate conglomerates who never had the best interests of the place or the people foremost in their minds.

There is no contractual agreement between users in these systems. Reservations are made, but if they are for some reason broken, there is no higher authority to which one could plead for a refund or other compensation. The only repercussion will be the poor rating you give that user and your only consolation will be that your warning will deter others from visiting or hosting them. For those who feel insecure unless their travel arrangements are written in stone before departure, this system will not be comforting.

There is a chance that guest and host will not get along. Perhaps there will be scheduling or ideological conflicts. Maybe you will find that hosts or visitors have misrepresented themselves. Perhaps the experience will not live up to your expectations. Intense interpersonal communications in advance and a flexibility once you have arrived is your best bet. These experiences require additional planning and courtesy towards the demands of your host. Thus, your living conditions, length of stay, and overall experience will be circumscribed by the living conditions you enter into.

The average user is a young white person who speaks English and lives in a developed nation. While there are many users who do not fit this description, the more different they are, the less likely they will be involved. This is especially true for persons living in the developing world who likely do not have easy access to the fundamental prerequisite for using these services: computers and the Internet. Thus, the sample population found in searches of these databases are really much less diverse than a geographical representation of worldwide users might suggest.

There is a distinct possibility that someone will abuse the system and that innocent users (especially women) will get hurt. All services include disclaimers that require users to waive their rights to hold anyone but themselves responsible for any harm that may come to them in using the system. They advise that the best defence mechanism is to only involve oneself with users that have extensive personal information and interpersonal networks within the system that have been verified by others.

It does seem entirely plausible that someone clever and patient enough might be able to invent an entire group of complex user identities and build histories convincing enough to fool even more cautious patrons. Still, the difference between these systems and the other social networking platforms popular nowadays on the web (such as MySpace, Tribe, Orkut, LiveJournal and Ebay) is that any agreement reached through the accommodation sharing medium is contingent on actually meeting other people face-to-face. Other web scams are easier because interpersonal interactions rely so much on putative identities that are never actually verified in the real world. However, this does not diminish the greater risk to physical well being that this kind of traveling by definition must entertain. The best advice is to meet unknown persons in public spaces first, and try to meet some of their acquaintances in person before agreeing to a hospitality exchange.

2

Changing Trends in Housekeeping

Over a period of time with advancements in technology and modernisation, housekeeping in hotels has undergone changes. Technology has brought a significant change in efficiency and product quality in the housekeeping department.

When we speak about housekeeping, we think about high staff turnover caused by a repetitive and physically demanding job and pressure to deliver clean rooms quickly at the lowest possible cost. Technology has brought some relief to the executive housekeepers to monitor guest floor operations. A housekeeping software called The Optii keeper is a housekeeping solution that unites the department to enhance the guest experience while increasing net profits and reducing stress levels in hotels overseas. It is interfaced with PMS of the hotel property.

How does it work? Each room attendant and floor supervisor carries a PDA which is connected via wireless technology and interfaced with the hotel PMS system. Room attendants can see in real time the next room to be cleaned and how long it will take.

Duration for cleaning is calculated based on the guest and room profile created through ever changing history. Savings in productivity can be made on actual room cleaning times rather than the current inaccurate room credit system.

Other features include an in-built quality control checklist tool on the supervisors' PDA's allowing them to record inspection results.

Monthly statistics on average room cleaning time and average quality scores can then be used for focused individual training and counseling. A spring cleaning or special jobs list is also included, ensuring weekly or monthly tasks are in the system and allocated onto the daily cleaning checklist for the Room Attendants to follow.

At front office, the dashboard enables front office to see at a glance where the room attendants are and when the rooms will be ready. Integration with the PMS also alerts front office if the room is not going to be ready for the guest's arrival so quick action can be taken.

Advantages of this software are: Improving room attendant productivity by up to 20 per cent:

- Saving up to 40 per cent of floor supervisor's time
- Eliminating 80 per cent of phone calls between front office and housekeeping
- Ongoing optimisation of cleaning schedules throughout the day.
- Allowing a fairly spread workload among housekeeping team members.
- Improved quality and staff morale.
- Savings of at least two hours every morning by automating the room allocation process at the push of a button.

TRADITION IN HOUSEKEEPING

With their roles covering several different aspects, from cleaning rooms and making beds to laundry and floristry, housekeepers are play an essential role in the efficient operation of a hotel.

"Housekeeping is one of the most difficult jobs in a hotel and one of the most important. If you don't have clean rooms or you have issues with cleanliness, our guests are not going to come back," stresses Daniel Kingston, director of rooms at the W Doha Hotel and Residences in Qatar.

KEY CONCERNS

However, as important as the housekeeping department is, it also has one of the highest staff turnover rates in the industry.

To tackle issues with staff retention, executive housekeepers have to make sure their teams are constantly motivated to perform and come up with new ways to foster loyalty.

It all begins with recruiting the right people, explains Naser Mohamed, executive housekeeper at Jumeirah Zabeel Saray in Dubai. He says: "You need to be very selective during recruitment; you recruit people based not on their talent, but based on their attitude.

You can hire someone who has a lot of knowledge of housekeeping, but if the willingness is not there, nothing gets done. So the first thing is selecting the right candidate, bringing in the right people".

According to Mohamed, most new members also don't realise how demanding the job is. "Sometimes people think room attending is an easier job, but it's not. So I try to paint a real picture and ask them if they think they can handle it," he says.

Staff empowerment also plays a big role in fostering loyalty among housekeeping staff. Nicholas Daoud, executive housekeeper at the Chedi Muscat in Oman comments: "A team member should always feel that they have an ability to make a decision that will help to assist a guest.

"This is also a key tool in helping the team members to develop their own skill set. The only wrong decision is to not make a decision at all."

Kingston adds: "Empowerment encourages our staff to gain new skills and knowledge and therefore helps in supporting their development, ultimately providing staff who are confident in their abilities and who can make decisions for our guests, without the old saying of "Let me check with my manager". You need to build a culture of support for staff so that they know if they make a decision, you will back them up."

However, according to Mohamed, the freedom to make decisions comes with a limit. "Housekeeping is a very bureaucratic system," he argues, "You need to have certain systems put in place for work to be done in a homogenised way.

If you leave it up to the people, they will like things done their own way and at the end of the day, there won't be any uniformity and the discipline that you're looking for." Douglas Matthew, executive housekeeper at Qasr Al Sarab Desert Resort by Anantara in Abu Dhabi agrees: "I give the freedom of empowerment to the staff within their limits. Obviously they cannot abuse the empowerment; it is within their boundaries. I empower the supervisors and my assistant to make decisions if I am not around. I think empowerment is very important in the hospitality industry."

Furthermore, staff empowerment alone is not sufficient to build a strong housekeeping team; communication and training are essential to develop skills and boost morale.

"We have many different internal Starwood and W trainings that we offer staff, as well as external trainings from some of the different suppliers and contractors that help develop staff to be better at what they do.

We also encourage cross training in other departments. This enables staff to develop new skill sets in areas that they may never have been exposed to, whilst also providing the hotel with a bigger pool of staff to utilise throughout the hotel," says the W's Daniel Kingston.

And although training programmes can be an added expense for the department, Mohamed believes the returns are worth the investment.

"Empowerment alone will not work if staff don't have the knowledge. You need to invest in their future and teach them and investing in the learning and development of colleagues is not cheap, it's very expensive. Sometimes management thinks this is a burden on the company, but it's not a burden, it's an investment. The rate of return is much higher than what you had allocated," he urges.

Claudia Arnhardt, executive housekeeper at The Address Dubai Mall, believes management plays a vital role in retaining staff and combating the problem of high turnover in the housekeeping department. "I think it depends on you and the management has a huge influence on this factor. When you are able to build a good relationship with your employees, they are working for you and not only for the property," she says.

In Muscat, The Chedi's Daoud adds: "Respect is key in helping to develop loyalty and commitment. The work that is carried out by a housekeeping team is often overlooked".

IN HOUSE STAFF VS. OUTSOURCED

While training staff and fostering loyalty are one part of the equation, limited budgets also mean executive housekeepers have to hire outsourced staff when the department needs extra hands during busy months, a situation that is less than ideal for most executive housekeepers who have to deal with issues such as lack of training, communication problems, and staff rotation by the contracting company.

"The discipline is not there, the communication skills are lacking, the talent is not there, the hygiene that you are looking for is not there, you cannot train them properly. And then there are rotations – you train someone for five days at the hotel and on the sixth day, they move them to different hotels... those are some of the issues you have so it's difficult," laments Mohamed.

At Qasr Al Sarab, Douglas Matthew says they have introduced a trainee programme, where they bring in inexperienced staff and train them in housekeeping duties, following which, the trainees are absorbed by the department. It's a solution that seems to be working and that Matthew is quite happy with.

"What we are actually doing now at the hotel is getting a lot of six-month trainees. So if you're looking at saving costs, casual staff will save costs, yes, but trainees are the same; you invest the money in them and you get it back in terms of their performance. The trainees we have here are superb.

Within two months, they are as good as any professional room attendants or professional housekeeping attendants. So instead of casual staff, I prefer trainees and full time staff," he says.

According to The Chedi's Daoud, outsourced staff provides the flexibility required to deal with the seasonal nature of the hotel industry. "Outsourced staff helps us to maintain a dynamic in the team and also helps us to ensure that we are continually developing the team. This also provides us with the flexibility to respond to the shifting nature of the business demands," he observes.

All things considered, it all comes down to how the management deals with outsourced staff, believes Kingston: "It is important that the outsourced staff we have are treated equally and are involved in the department, such as in the morning departmental briefing.

"Ultimately, it is our responsibility, not the outsourced company's, to ensure that the outsourced staff we have perform and do the job to the high standards that we set, and this is only done through the correct supervision from our side," he explains.

GOING GREEN

With hotels becoming increasingly conscious about their carbon footprint, the housekeeping department plays an enormous role in supporting a property's green initiatives.

"We have a policy whereby we leave it to the individual guest to determine when they would like to have their sheets and towels changed. We also try to ensure that we maximise the capacity and increase efficiency in our laundry facility. We also take steps to reduce the costs of the hotel such as AC and electricity as much as possible.

This is done by relocating guests to specific areas of the hotel and closing other areas of the hotel to our guests," says Daoud at The Chedi Muscat.

The W Doha adopts similar practices through Starwood's Make a Green Choice programme, which gives guests an option to choose how frequently they would like to have their linen and towels changed.

"The Make a Green Choice programme gave us a great opportunity to re-enforce the sustainability message with our team. We also have our internal green committee that consists of staff from different departments, who meet on a monthly basis," says Kingston.

QUALITY COUNTS

In the current economic climate, hotels have to maintain standards while also ensuring the properties are profitable. With room amenities proving to be one of the biggest expenses for the hotel, housekeepers have to work with the purchasing department to strike a balance between costs and quality, and source suppliers who meet the criteria.

At Qasr Al Sarab, Matthew says he can choose suppliers as long as they meet Anantara's brand standards and are cost effective.

"We have the same brand standards across all the Anantara properties, the same amenities and the same products in each category of rooms. If I want to make a change, I will get five or six suppliers in, where they can give me the best products, and I decide the quality I need for Qasr Al Sarab.

Once they give me the price, I compare every single option and I get the best price and best quality, and then I tell the purchasing department which company I want to order from. Anantara has a standard for linens and towels. I cannot choose what the standard is; the standard has been set. I just need to find the suppliers where I can get the best price," he explains.

In some cases, executive housekeepers are not required to be as involved. At Jumeirah, where the purchasing department is centralised, the system is less flexible. "We do not approach the suppliers directly, but they approach us and if they have a product we like, we ask them to approach our supply chain and logistics department, which looks after the purchasing," explains Mohamed.

"The great thing is, there are more and more suppliers coming in the market, so you can find more options for the hotel for a more competitive price," adds Kingston.

Whatever the issues may be, the fact is that the housekeeping department is the backbone of the hotel. With the role of the department constantly developing, executive housekeepers have to keep up with changing trends to run an efficient and motivated team while ensuring guest satisfaction at all times. Not an easy task by any means, but someone's got to do it.

HOUSEKEEPING TRENDS AND BEST PRACTICES

Housekeepers do their bit by emphasising environmental policies in daily briefings. Local crafts are creatively used in amenities and turn down, bring tourism dollars to local traders. Carbon footprints are reduced by supporting local businesses and encouraging them to go green as well. Suppliers are discouraged from using plastic in packaging, all chemicals and guest amenities are eco-friendly..

We recruit actively team members from local areas and train in housekeeping skills, this goes a long way in the progress of the individual and supporting the local township.

Guests are also encouraged to contribute by participating in towel reuse programmes. Parents are cajoled into being green by their children as schools drive home this message. More and more guests choose to stay in Eco friendly hotels, companies are careful, Green Companies would put up their Employees only in Green Hotels.

So it looks as if Going Green is the only way!

- *Microfibre:* Traditional cleaning rags are being replaced by this wonder fabric "microfibre". This fabric consists of really tiny charged fibres, as dust is negatively charged, it is attracted to the fabric like a magnet, oils are also easily absorbed. Microfibre can absorb eight times its own weight in water. This miracle fabric is also exceptionally soft and highly durable. A combination of all these characteristics makes it a very good cleaning material, currently highly priced but being more effective in the long run due to its durability and efficiency. Now all that is needed is to convince the Financial Manager to invest!One word of warning: never to tumble dry this fabric, no bleach or softener to be used.
- *Creative Turndowns:* Turndown Service in Hotels (at least in India) is getting more competitive and therefore standards are rising. Just when you think "it can't get any better" somebody turns up with

something new! ViP and long stays are wooed with turndown trays, free internet, meal vochurs and other value addons, that can have anything from a teddy bear to a simple good night quote, Chocolates (now old hat), scented candles by the tub, beautiful satin gowns. Herbal teas by the bed stand. Whatever happened to thatgood old simple "Good night sir "?

- *Weddings:* The wedding industry is a whopping 71 billion dollars worldwide and growing by 25 per cent annually (this is not an industry hit by recession!). Housekeepers cannot choose to ignore this, earlier we were very strict about not allowing any heavy decorations in rooms, it has now been tackled by clever use of textured and coloured sheets, floral arrangements, on extra props, romantically folded towels. Newlyweds are offered special up grade packages turndowns with champagne, quotes on love and red roses.
- *Ergonomics:* This is the science of making things comfortable. Housekeepers want suitably designed furniture (and operating equipment) so that the team will not have to suffer from any long term health hazards. It was very common for room attendants to complain about back aches. However you can now get light weight furniture that is appreciated by both the guest and team. Ergonomically designed mattresses are so popular that guests often want to buy it from the Hotel. Hilton has a programme called Hilton to Home where the guests can buy the "Hilton Bed " and have introduced amazing beds in their Garden Hotels in which you can choose the hardness/softness. It is essential for all new comers to Housekeeping to be shown the ergonomically correct way to make beds, clean Bathrooms etc. It's a great motivational tool and they will always be thankful for the timely advice. For me the prize will go to the cobbler who designs comfortable shoes that with stand 14 hours of hard labour and still look stylish!
- *Outsourcing:* In India Guest rooms are still mainly done by permanent Hotel employees, but Public areas, Horticulture and even laundry is being out sourced to contractors. This may be cost effective in some ways but brings new challenges-Housekeepers need to strike a balance and think up of innovative ways to keep the outsourced teams motivated. As this is a fast growing fledgling industry India faces a lack of quality service providers, an ever changing team, lack of ownership on the part of the contractor and their labour force. Like it or not "Outsourcing" is a reality we have to face.It is said to make a huge differrence to the bottom line,whether it really does is to be debated.

INNOVATION IN HOUSEKEEPING IMPROVES EFFICIENCY

New technology and innovation in materials have emerged in recent years to significantly increase housekeeping efficiency and effectiveness with proven bottom line benefits.

However, in general housekeeping has not seen any fundamental changes for a number of decades. As consultants, the Lycette and Associates team is working all over the globe and see a lot of stagnant housekeeping management.

While new technology has been introduced to increase efficiency in all other hotel departments, experienced housekeeping managers still rely on the same archaic procedures and tools as when they started their careers 20 or more years ago.

What's worse, the new generation of Executive Housekeepers is often promoted too quickly and the position itself is no longer in proportion to the core importance for the hotel.

The advent of the Rooms Division Manager, who is commonly from a front office background with little exposure to housekeeping management, aids in the de-sophistication of the position.

Who is left to drive the innovative processes to make efficiency and quality improvements? You can't blame the Executive Housekeepers. With constraints such as a high staff turnover caused by a repetitive and physically demanding job and pressure to deliver clean rooms quickly at the lowest possible cost, there is no room for reflection for the manager.

At the end of the day, the industry expects a better result, while doing the same thing over and over again. That is a clear case of insanity.

We now have a global shortage of skilled and well-trained Executive Housekeepers who are all-rounders in people management, financial management and practical housekeeping operational skills. But things are not as bleak as they sound. There have been noteworthy innovations in housekeeping over recent years, which are now gaining ground in hotels around the world.

Bamboo is an environmentally sustainable material for uniforms, towelling and sheeting and is gaining popularity as its cost is coming down. Nano technology used in surface coating makes it dirt and dust resistant. Used in Korea and Japan for years, they are now showing up on other continents.

Microfibre as a cleaning system has been in use in hospitals for years and is now slowly adopted into housekeeping departments around the world. Not only is microfibre cleaning environmentally friendly through the absence of chemicals and cost effective, but it also produces better cleaning results. The Professional Housekeeper's Association of New South Wales commissioned laboratory analysis of cleaning hygiene, comparing the effectiveness of 5 methods of cleaning bathroom glasses.

The tests showed that all 5 methods; using dishwashing liquid, microfibre, a sterilizing tablet, all purpose cleaner and using a dishwasher were effective in removing bacteria and mould present.

L&A, has been educating, coaching and training Housekeeping Managers worldwide for over 10 years and has recently become involved in assisting with the training of a new Housekeeping software system called Optii Keeper. Without doubt, this new technology will change the way Housekeeping operates in the future.

Productivity and quality improvements have hit the glass ceiling of what is possible with the trusted manual procedures and processes. Optii Keeper is by far the most exciting innovation because it breaks the ceiling down and allows housekeeping to go to the next level.

3

Housekeeping Control Desk

The housekeeping control desk is the central hub of the housekeeping department. This is the area in the department where all information is received and from where messages are conveyed to housekeeping and other staff present in various parts of the hotel. Thus, the control desk may be considered the nerve centre for to–and–fro communication in the housekeeping department. one of the main functions of the control desk is ensuring smooth coordination between housekeeping and other departments such as maintenance, front office, food and beverages, security, sales and marketing and so on. The location of control desk is normally adjacent to the Executive Housekeeper's office. This desk is manned 24-hours otherwise the lifeline of housekeeping communication would stop.

ROLE OF CONTROL DESK

- The role of the housekeeping control desk is to facilitate communication to various parts of hotel. this role can be exercised in many forms which are as follows;
- The control desk receives messages from in house guests over the telephone apart from maintaining the intra and inter–departmental channels of communication. Hotel room directories provide the control desk extension number to the guests which they can use if they require housekeeping services.
- The control desk attendant receives all the message of the guests such as a request for extra blankets, baby-sitter services, which she transmit to the concerned floor supervisor for further action.
- Front office also alerts the desk attendant about the expected and existing crews in the house. So that the rooms can be make ready for the new arriving crew after the departure of existing crew in a very short period of time.
- In most of the hotels, this is the area where housekeeping employees; report for work; collect keys and signing for them; persue the log book get their briefing and at the end of their shift, report back to.

- Its is the control room attendants who receives departure room numbers from the front office and transmits them to the appropriate floor supervisor.
- The floor supervisor informs the desk attendant once rooms are cleaned and ready for sale and this is updated in the computer so that front office can easily obtain the information o f the status of room.
- The main physical feature visible in most control desk is the key cabinet. On the wall, where all floor masters keys and store keys are kept under lock and key themselves.
- Another common feature here is a large notice board displaying notices like
  - Room numbers of the groups in the house
  - Room numbers of crews in the house
  - Night cleaning schedule
  - VIPs in the house
  - Weekly cleaning schedules
  - Daily roster of supervisors and staff
  - Any other significant information relating to in-house guest or the hotel staff.
- One of the most important roles of the control desk is maintaining various important records, registers, forms and formats so that they are available and easily accessible for reference to managers and supervisors.

COORDINATION WITH FRONT OFFICE

The control desk acts as the nerve centre for coordination with the other departments in the hotel. the control desk attendants receives the night report, the arrivals and departures list, VIP list, and the list of crews and groups in the house from the front office. Based on these documents, the housekeeping department schedules the workers for cleaning, maintenance and servicing of guestrooms and related areas.

- To ensure efficient rooming of guests, both housekeeping and front office must inform each other of changes in a room's status. Knowing whether a room is occupied, vacant, on change, out of order (OOO), under repair, or similar for proper room management
- There should be coordination to clean front office public areas
- There must be coordination between housekeeping and front office department to share information on occupancy levels which helps to forecast occupancy for the year and makes it easier to draw up a budget, establish par stock levels and estimate required staff strength.

- There should be coordination know about the daily room report and housekeeping discrepancy report.
- It also helps to gear renovations and spring cleaning to low occupancy periods there by preventing loss of revenue.
- The housekeeping and front office department also coordinate with each other for other important information which require special attention like
- 7. *Night report*: this report, prepared each night by front desk attendant, indicates the rooms occupied that night and ones that are to become check-outs the following day. Based on this report, the executive or assistant housekeeper schedules employees for servicing these rooms. Once the rooms have been cleaned and made ready, the floor supervisor calls the control desk or the front desk directly, releasing the room for sale.
- *VIPs in house*: this information is essential so that the staff can take a little extra care and keener precautions in cleaning and supervising VIP rooms.housekeeping can take extra care in cleaning the VIP rooms by equipping the rooms with additional amenities as per the policy of the management. These amenities can be; bathrobe; bath slippers; extra soaps; hangers; and glass tumblers.
- *Groups in the house*: the group rooming list must be provided before the group's arrival to the housekeeping as groups tends to move together in terms of arrival, departure, sightseeing tours and meals. Their rooms need to be readied together in view of strict time parameters. Group rooming lists enable the hk department to organize their work and have the group's room ready on time.
- *Crews in the house*: Sometimes the arrival of a crew and the departure of another crew from the same airline may overlap. In such circumstances, it is important for the allotted rooms to be cleaned within a short period of time. Thus for this there should be a effective coordination between front office and housekeeping.
- *Flowers*: sometimes the management extends its compliments to a guest with a special gesture of a flower arrangement in the room as recognition of the importance of a person. This requirement of flower arrangements for certain guests is conveyed to housekeeping by the front office on a daily basis.
- Apart from the communications the front office needs to depend on housekeeping for the provision of clean uniforms to its staff.

COORDINATION WITH ENGINEERING DEPARTMENT

The housekeeping control desk have to coordinate with the engineering department for maintenance request that the room attendants registers while servicing the guest room or in the floor.

- The housekeeping department depends on maintenance to keep things in order.
- While carrying out their scheduled work, housekeeping employees may find some deficiencies in the hotel facilities, such as faulty electrical plugs, dripping faucets, leaking pipes or malfunctioning air-conditioning units etc.
- A need for urgent repairs is reported to maintenance over telephone and these requests are usually taken into action immediately.
- There are various heads under which maintenance work is done they are:
- *Electrical work*: Air conditioning and heating; fused bulbs, lights and lamps that are not functioning; defective plugs and plug points; short circuits; and faulty geysers, refrigerators, and minibar fall under this category.
- *Boiler work*: This is necessary to maintain a supply of hot water to guestroom.
- *Mechanical work*: This entails repair or replacement of any faulty equipment, such as vacuum cleaners, ice-cube machines, and so on.
- *Plumbing work*: This deals with faulty faucets (taps), showers, drainage systems, water closets, and so on.

All maintenance requirements needed on floors are entered in the maintenance register kept in the control desk. The control desk attendant notes down the room number, the maintenance work required and the name of the GRA or the supervisor who called attention to the problem. The desk attendant prepares a maintenance slip in duplicate. She retains the second copy in her book and forwards the first copy to the engineering department. The engineering department then prepares a 'work order slip' and sends the concerned technician directly to the floor. When the job is completed, a copy of tradesperson's completed 'work order ' is sent to the executive housekeeper for acknowledgement of work completed satisfactorily. If this copy is not sent to the executive housekeeper within an appropriate amount of time, housekeeping issues another 'work order', which signals maintenance to provide a status report on the request repair.

FILES AND RECORDS OF THE DESK

Many important forms, formats, records, and registers are maintained at the control desk.

MAINTENANCE REGISTER

This register is used for recording all the maintenance work required in rooms. Based on the information contained in the register, the control desk attendant fills out the work order form to be sent to the maintenance department.

Table. Maintenance Register

Maintenance register Date:						
Room Number	Time Complaint Lodged	Nature of Complaints	Lodged By	Received by	Time of Completion	Signature

Table. Maintenance Slip

Maintenance slip Room Number Date: Time:
Nature of Complaint
Control Desk Supervisor Signature——————————————————

WORK ORDER FORMS

The work order forms are used by the control desk to initiate scheduled maintenance in guestrooms and public areas. A sample work order form is illustrated below:

Table. Work Order Slip

Work Order Room Number .... Date.................................. Time..........................							
Carpenter	Mechanic	Plumber	Electrician	A/C – Heating technician	AV/Audio technician	IT	Other
Nature of Complaint Name of Technician assigned..............................							
Date of Completion........................ Housekeeping Supervisor Signature.........................				Time of Completion................. Technician's Signature..............			

KEY CONTROL REGISTER

This is one of the most important registers maintained at the housekeeping control desk. It is a part of the key-security system to be followed by the housekeeping department.

Table. Format of a Sheet in the Key Control Register

Key Control Sheet Date:							
Key code	Name of staff	Signature	Time out	Issued by	Time in	Signature	Received

Each employee who is handed over a key, any key, from key cabinet is supposed to sign for it in a key control sheet in this register. The format of a key control sheet is illustrated below:

LOG BOOK

Another important register kept for reference at the housekeeping control desk is the log book. The log book is used to record all messages that staff from an earlier shift want to convey to the employees on the next shift.

All supervisors reporting for work should use the log book for any important messages left for them by the staff of the previous shift. The format of the log book is illustrated below:

Table. Format of a Page in the Housekeeping Log Book.

Housekeeping Log Book Shift..................... Time...................... Date..................
Log entries - - - -
Name an d signature of the desk attendant ....

ROOM CHECKLISTS FILE

A floor supervisor checks each room prepared by the room attendant, before the room is handed to front office for sale. She uses the room checklist to guide her to examine as per the standards set by the management during her inspection. She ticks the items found okay and makes comments on things which are not upto the standards.

Table. Room Checklist.

Room Checklist		
Floor...........Room No............Room Attendants Name.................Floor Supervisor's Name...........		
Room Items	**Tick Ok**	**Comments**
Wardrobe Hanger		
Laundry Lists		
Laundry Bags		
Shoe shine card		
Wardrobe under –lin ers		
Spare Pill ows		
Bed		
Side table		
Lamp bulb working		
Bible / Koran / Gita		
Pad and Pen		
Telephone Directories		
Date...................................... Signature of Floor Supervisor....................................		

The deficiencies have to be rectified by the room attendants immediately. The checklist reflects the performance of the room attendant as well as the supervisor. it is handy to refer to it in the event of a guest complaint. All room checklists are deposited by the floor supervisors at the control desk and filed for a month.

GUEST MESSAGE REGISTER

The housekeeping control desk also acts as a point of contact for in-house guests who require any housekeeping related services. The housekeeping control desk is responsible for taking these guest messages and passing them onto the concerned staff.

The message could be about the provision of certain guest loan items or a request to a second service additional blankets, fresh towels, maintenance requirements etc.A guest messages register is maintained for this purpose at the control desk.

The format is illustrated below:

Table. Guest Message Register

Guest Message Register Date :								
Room no	Time of request	Nature of request	Received by	Signature	Action taken	Time	Service completed	Time

BABY SITTER REGISTER

Babysitting is provided as a service by most hotels' housekeeping departments for guests who have small children.

The guests requiring the service contact the housekeeping control desk and the desk attendant enters the request in the babysitting register.

Table. Baby Sitting Registers

Baby Sitting Register								
Date	Room No	Name of Guest	Time from	Time to	Received by	Person Assigned	Sitter's signature and time-in	Sitter's signature and time out

LEAVE APPLICATION FROM

Leave application forms are stocked at the control desk so that they are easily accessible to employees who wish to take leave. The format of a leave application form is illustrated below:

Table. Leave Application Form

leave application form	
Employee Name............................	Date of Joining............................
Department...................................	Weekly Off..................................
Designation and Grade.....................	Date of Application....................
Sir / Madam, 1, ...wish to avail, casual / sick / earned / leave of ....days, from the date..............................to..........................	
Purpose..	
Signature of employee.. Signature of HOD: Approved /Refused... Signature of Personnel Manager..	

MEMO BOOK

This contains records of all the pending maintenance work for which the housekeeping department initiated work orders. This information is made in copies so as to alert the concerned housekeeping supervisor that work is incomplete. The format of sheet in the meme book is as illustrated below.

Table. Memo Book

Memo book						
Work Order No	**Date**	**Description of maintenance work**	**Location/Room No**	**Reported By**	**Job completed by**	**Signature of supervisor.**

LOST AND FOUND SLIP/LOST AND FOUND REGISTER

'Lost and Found' is a term used in hotel terms for those articles left by guests or misplaced by guests in a hotel.

Table. Lost and Found Slip

Lost and Found Valuable/Non valuable No	
Finder's Name................................. Location /Room no........................... Description of article .... Name of the guest................................... Address... Signature of depositor	Date.................... Time................. Signature of receiver
A. Received by owner Name................................ Address............................ Date..................................	 Telephone No:.............. Signature........................

B. Dispatched by Post, Postal receipt No.............	
Name	
Address..........................	Telephone No..............
Date.............................	Signature......................
C. Retrived by finder	
Name....................................	Signature..........................
Cloak No.................................	Gate pass No....................
Property handed over by	
Name...............................	Designation........................
Signature..........................	Date.........................

Table. Lost and Found Register

No. Lost and Found Record								
Date / time	Received be Owner			Received by Finder			Dispatched by	
	Name	Address	Signature	Name	Signature	Gate Pass No.	Name.	

Such articles can range from jewellery, costly electronic goods, and travel documents to simple garments. The hotel is obliged to protect such items and return them to the guests. Whenever such items are found by the room attendant or any staff of housekeeping they have to directly report to housekeeping control desk where lost and found is filled. The format of lost and found slip is illustrated below

ACCIDENT BOOK

This records all the accidents of any sort that employees or guest have met with at the hotel. The format is illustrated below,

Table. Accident Book

S.No	Date of Accident	Name of staff/ guest	Nature of Accident	Action Taken	Supervisor in charge

Other Files and Registers that are maintained by the housekeeping control desk are

ROOM OCCUPANCY REPORT FILE

All room occupancy reports are filed for the future reference. The room occupancy reports are important to Executive Housekeeper to determine the level of workload anticipated so as to provide the necessary staff to meet the efficiency each day.

DUTY ROASTER FILE

The duty roaster is filed for information, if required by any one in the department.

ROOM INSPECTION CHECKLIST FILE

All room inspection checklists are filed in the room inspection checklists file kept at the control desk. These reports may be referred to in case there are guest complaints on cleaning. The Executive housekeeper will be able to find the supervisor in charge inspecting the particular guestroom in this file and confirm whether he/she checked the particular surface in question.

STORE INDENT BOOK

The stores indent book is kept at the control desk so that the supervisors may indent for housekeeping supplies that are required by GRA's.the supervisors fill up the indent sheet in the book and the desk supervisor forwards it. It stores after approval for the issue of supplies. The format of store indent sheet in the store indent book is illustrated below

stores indent book Date..........................			
S No	Indented Items	Quantity Indented	Quantity Issued with Remarks
Made By................................... Approved By............................... Storekeeper....................................			

4

Operations in Housekeeping Management

INTRODUCTION

The development of the Area Responsibility Plan and the House Breakout Plan before opening led to preparation of the Department Staffing Guide, which will be a major tool in determining the need for employees in various categories. The housekeeping manager and laundry manager should now be on board and assisting in the development of various job descriptions. The hotel human resources department would also have been preparing for the hiring event.

They would have advertised a mass hiring for all categories of personnel to begin on a certain date about two weeks before opening. Even though this chapter reflects a continuation of the executive housekeeper's planning for opening operations, the techniques described apply to any ongoing operation, except that the magnitude of selection, orientation, and training activities will not be as intense.

Also, the fourth activity—development of existing employees— is normally missing in opening operations but is highly visible in ongoing operations. Job Specifications Job specifications should be written as job descriptions are prepared. Job specifications are simple statements of what the various incumbents to positions will be expected to do. An example of a job specification for a housekeeper is as follows: Job Specification—Example Housekeeper (hotels).

The incumbent will work as a member of a housekeeping team, cleaning and servicing for occupancy of approximately 18 hotel guestrooms each day. Work will generally include the tasks of bed making, vacuuming, dusting, and bathroom cleaning. Incumbent will also be expected to maintain equipment provided for work and load housekeeper's cart before the end of each day's operation.

Housekeepers must be willing to work their share of weekends and be dependable in coming to work each day scheduled.

STAFFING HOUSEKEEPING POSITIONS

There are several activities involved in staffing a housekeeping operation.

Executive housekeepers must select and interview employees, participate in an orientation programme, train newly hired employees, and develop employees for future growth. Each of these activities will now be discussed.

EMPLOYEE REQUISITION

Once job specifications have been developed for every position, employee requisitions are prepared for first hirings (and for any follow-up needs for the human resources department). Note the designation as to whether the requisition is for a new or a replacement position and the number of employees required for a specific requisition number.

The human resources department will advertise, take applications, and screen to fill each requisition by number until all positions are filled.

For example, the first requisition for GRAs may be for 20 Staffing Housekeeping Positions. The human resources department will continue to advertise for, take applications, and screen employees for the housekeeping department and will provide candidates for interview by department managers until 20 GRAs are hired. Should any be hired and require replacing, a new employee requisition will be required.

SELECTING EMPLOYEES SOURCES OF EMPLOYEES

Each area of the United States has its own demographic situations that affect the availability of suitable employees for involvement in housekeeping or environmental service operations. For example, in one area, an exceptionally high response rate from people seeking food service work may occur and a low response rate from people seeking housekeeping positions may occur.

In another area, the reverse may be true, and people interested in housekeeping work may far outnumber those interested in food service. Surveys among hotels or hospitals in your area will indicate the best source for various classifications of employees. Advertising campaigns that will reach these employees are the best method of locating suitable people. Major classified ads associated with mass hirings will specify the need for food service personnel, front desk clerks, food servers, housekeeping personnel, and maintenance people. Such ads may yield surprising results.

If these sources do not produce the volume of applicants necessary to develop a staff, it may become necessary to search for employees in distant areas and to provide regular transportation for them to and from work. If aliens are hired, the department manager must take great care to ensure that they are legal residents of this country and that their green cards are valid.

More than one hotel department manager has had an entire staff swept away by the Department of Immigration after hiring people who were illegal aliens. Such unfortunate action has required the immediate assistance of all available employees (including management) to fill in.

PROCESSING APPLICANTS

Whether you are involved in a mass hiring or in the recruiting of a single employee, a systematic and courteous procedure for processing applicants is essential. For example, in the opening of the Los Angeles Airport Marriott, 11,000 applicants were processed to fill approximately 850 positions in a period of about two weeks. The magnitude of such an operation required a near assembly-line technique, but a personable and positive experience for the applicants still had to be maintained.

Employee requisition, used to ask for one or more employees for a specific job. The efficient handling of lines of employees, courteous attendance, personal concern for employee desires, and reference to suitable departments for those unfamiliar with what the hotel or hospital has to offer all become earmarks for how the company will treat its employees.

The key to proper handling of applicants is the use of a control system whereby employees are conducted through the steps of application, prescreening, and if qualified, reference to a department for interview. Note the opportunity for employees to express their desires for a specific type of employment.

Even though an employee may desire involvement in one classification of work, he or she may be hired for employment in a different department. Also, employees might not be aware of the possibilities available in a particular department at the time of application or may be unable to locate in desired departments at the time of mass hirings.

Employees who perform well should therefore be given the opportunity to transfer to other departments when the opportunities arise. According to laws regulated by federal and state Fair Employment Practices Agencies (FEPA), no person may be denied the opportunity to submit application for employment for a position of his or her choosing. Not only is the law strict on this point, but companies in any way benefiting from interstate commerce (such as hotels and hospitals) may not discriminate in the hiring of people based on race, colour, national origin, or religious preference.

Although specific hours and days of the week may be specified, it is a generally accepted fact that hotels and hospitals must maintain personnel operations that provide the opportunity for people to submit applications without prejudice.

PRESCREENING APPLICANTS

The prescreening interview is a staff function normally provided to all hotel or hospital departments by the human resources of the organization. Prescreening is a preliminary interview process in which unqualified applicants—those applicants who do not meet the criteria for a job as specified in the job specification–special qualifications—are selected (or screened) out.

For example, an applicant for a secretarial job that requires the incumbent to take shorthand and be able to type 60 words a minute may be screened out if the applicant is not able to pass a relevant typing and shorthand test.

The results of prescreening are usually coded for internal use and are indicated on the Applicant Processing Record. If a candidate is screened out by the personnel, he or she should be told the reason immediately and thanked for applying for employment.

THE INTERVIEW: MANAGER OF THE DEPARTMENT

An interview should be conducted by a manager of the department to which the applicant has been referred. In ongoing operations, it is often wise to also allow the supervisor for whom the new employee will work to visit with the candidate in order that the supervisor may gain a feel for how it would be to work together.

The supervisor's view should be considered, since a harmonious relationship at the working level is important. Although the acceptance of an employee remains a prerogative of management, it would be unwise to accept an employee into a position when the supervisor has reservations about the applicant.

Certain personal characteristics should be explored when interviewing an employee. Some of these characteristics are native skills, stability, reliability, experience, attitude towards employment, personality, physical traits, stamina, age, sex, education, previous training, initiative, alertness, appearance, and personal cleanliness.

Although employers may not discriminate against race, sex, age, religion, and nationality, overall considerations may involve the capability to lift heavy objects, enter men's or women's restrooms, and so on.

In a housekeeping (or environmental services) department, people should be employed who find enjoyment in housework at home. Remember that character and personality cannot be completely judged from a person's appearance. Also, it should be expected that a person's appearance will never be better than when that person is applying for a job. Letters of recommendation and references should be carefully considered. Seldom will a letter of recommendation be adverse, whereas a telephone call might be most revealing.

If it were necessary to select the most important step in the selection process, interviewing would be it. Interviewing is the step that separates those who will be employed from those who will not produce a result that can be both frustrating and damaging for both parties. In addition, inadequate interviewing will result in gaining incorrect information, being confused about what has been said, suppression of information, and, in some circumstances, complete withdrawal from the process by the candidate.

The following is a well-accepted list of the steps for a successful interview process:

1. *Be prepared:* Have a checklist of significant questions ready to ask the candidate. Such questions may be prepared from the body of the job description. This preparation will allow the interviewer to assume the initiative in the interview.
2. *Find a proper place to conduct the interview:* The applicant should be made to feel comfortable. The interview should be conducted in a quiet, relaxing atmosphere where there is privacy that will bring about a confidential conversation.
3. *Practice:* People who conduct interviews should practice interviewing skills periodically. Several managers may get together and discuss interviewing techniques that are to be used.
4. *Be tactful and courteous:* Put the applicant at ease, but also control the discussion and lead to important questions.
5. *Be knowledgeable:* Be thoroughly familiar with the position for which the applicant is interviewing in order that all of the applicant's questions may be answered. Also, have a significant background knowledge in order that general information about the company may be given.
6. *Listen:* Encourage the applicant to talk. This may be done by asking questions that are not likely to be answered by a yes or no. If people are comfortable and are asked questions about themselves, they will usually speak freely and give information that specific questions will not always bring out. Applicants will usually talk if there is a feeling that they are not being misunderstood.
7. *Observe:* Much can be learned about an applicant just by observing reactions to questions, attitudes about work, and, specifically, attitudes about providing service to others. Observation is a vital step in the interviewing process.

RESULTS OF THE INTERVIEW

If the results of an interview are negative and rejection is indicated, the candidate should be informed as soon as possible. A pleasant statement, such as "Others interviewed appear to be more qualified," is usually sufficient.

This information can be handled in a straightforward and courteous manner and in such a way that the candidate will appreciate the time that has been taken during the interview.

When the results of the interview are positive, a statement indicating a favourable impression is most encouraging. However, no commitment should be made until a reference check has been conducted.

REFERENCE CHECKS

In many cases, reference checks are made only to verify that what has been said in the application and interview is in fact true.

Many times applicants are reluctant to explain in detail why previous employment situations have come to an end. It is more important to hear the actual truth about a prior termination from the applicant than it is to hear that they simply have been terminated.

Reference checks, in order of desirability, are as follows:

1. Personal (face-to-face) meetings with previous employers are the least available but provide the most accurate information when they can be arranged.
2. Telephone discussions are the next best and most often used approach. For all positions, an in-depth conversation by telephone between the potential new manager and the prior manager is most desirable; otherwise a simple verification of data is sufficient to ensure honesty.
3. The least desirable reference is the written recommendation, because managers are extremely reluctant to state a frank and honest opinion that may later be used against them in court.

Applicants who are rated successful at an interview should be told that a check of their references will be conducted, and, pending favourable responses, they will be contacted by the personnel department within two days. Applicants who are currently employed normally ask that their current employer not be contacted for a reference check.

This request should be honoured at all times. Applicants who are currently working usually want to give proper notice to their current employers. If the applicant chooses not to give notice, chances are no notice will be given at the time he or she leaves your hotel.

In some cases, the applicant gives notice and, upon doing so, is "cut loose" immediately. If such is the case, the applicant should be told to contact the department manager immediately in order that the employee may be put to work as soon as possible.

INTERVIEW SKILLS VERSUS TURNOVER

There is no perfect interviewer, interviewee, or resultant hiring or rejection decision in regard to an applicant. We can only hope to improve our interviewing skills in order that the greatest degree of success in employee retention can be obtained.

The executive housekeeper should expect that 25 per cent of initial hires into a housekeeping department will not be employed for more than three months. (This is primarily because the housekeeping skills are easily learned and the position is paid at or near minimum wage.) Some new housekeeping departments have as much as a 75 per cent turnover rate in the first three months of operation. Certainly this figure can be improved upon with adequate attention to the interviewing and selection processes. However, regardless of the outcome of the interview, the processing record should be properly endorsed and returned to the personnel department for processing.

ORIENTATION

A carefully planned, concerned, and informational orientation programme is significant to the first impressions that a new employee will have about the hospital or hotel in general and the housekeeping department in particular.

Too often, a new employee is told where the work area and restroom are, given a cursory explanation of the job, then put to work.

It is not uncommon to find managers putting employees to work who have not even been processed into the organization, an unfortunate situation that is usually discovered on payday when there is no paycheck for the new employee. Such blatant disregard for the concerns of the employee can only lead to a poor perception of the company.

A planned orientation programme will eliminate this type of activity and will bring the employee into the company with personal concern and with a greater possibility for a successful relationship.

A good orientation programme is usually made up of four phases: employee acquisition, receipt of an cmployec's handbook, tour of the facility, and an orientation meeting.

INTERVIEW PITFILLS

Perhaps of equal importance to the interviewing technique are the following pitfalls, which should be avoided while interviewing:

1. Having a feeling that the employee will be just right based on a few outstanding characteristics rather than on the sum of all characteristics noted.
2. Being influenced by neatness, grooming, expensive clothes, and an extroverted personality—none of which has much to do with housekeeping competency.
3. Over generalizing, whereby interviewers assume too much from a single remark (for instance, an applicant's assurance that he or she "really wants to work").
4. Hiring the "boomer," that is, the person who always wants to work in a new property; unfortunately, this type of person changes jobs whenever a new property opens.
5. Projecting your own background and social status into the job requirement. Which school the applicant attended or whether the

applicant has the "proper look" is beside the point. It is job performance that is going to count.

6. Confusing strengths with weaknesses, and vice versa. What is construed by one person to be over aggressiveness might be interpreted by another as confidence, ambition, and potential for leadership, the last two traits being in chronic short supply in most housekeeping departments. These are the very characteristics that make it possible for management to promote from within and develop new supervisors and managers.
7. Being impressed by a smooth talker—or the reverse: assuming that silence reflects strength and wisdom. The interviewer should concentrate on what the applicant is saying rather than on how it is being said, then decide whether his or her personality will fit into the organization.
8. Being tempted by overqualified applicants. People with experience and education that far exceed the job requirements may be unable for some reason to get jobs commensurate with their backgrounds.

Even if such applicants are not concealing skeletons in the closet, they still tend to become frustrated and dissatisfied with jobs far their level of abilities. The application of the techniques and avoidance of the pitfalls will be valuable tools in the selection of competent personnel for the housekeeping and environmental service departments. For many years, the approach of many managers was to write a job description and then fill it by attempting to find the perfect person. This approach may overlook many qualified people, such as disadvantaged people or slow learners.

Job descriptions may be analysed in two ways when filling positions:

1. What is actually required to do the work, and
2. What is desirable. Is the ability to read or write really necessary for the job? Is the ability to learn quickly really necessary?

A person who does not read or write or who is a slow learner can be trained and can make an excellent employee. True, it may take additional time, but the reward will be a loyal employee as well as less turnover. It has been proven many times that those who are disadvantaged or slightly retarded, once trained, will perform consistently well for longer periods. There are agencies who seek out companies that will try to hire such people.

EMPLOYEE ACQUISITION

Once a person is accepted for employment, the applicant is told to report for work at a given time and place, and that place should be the personnel department. Pre-employment procedures can take as much as one-half day, and department managers eager to start new employees to work should allow time for a proper employee acquisition into the organization.

At this time it should be ensured that the application is complete and any additional information pertaining to employment history that may be necessary to obtain the necessary work permits and credentials is on hand.

Usually the security department records the entry of a new employee into the staff and provides instructions regarding use of employee entrances, removing parcels from the premises, and employee parking areas.

Application for work permits, and drug testing, will be scheduled where applicable. All documents required by the hotel's health and welfare insurer should be completed, and instructions should be given about immediately reporting accidents, no matter how slight, to supervisors.

The federal government requires that every employer submit a W-4 (withholding statement) for each employee on the payroll. The employee must complete this document and give it to the company. Mandatory deductions from pay should be explained (federal and state income tax and Social Security FICA), as should other deductions that may be required or desired. Note the permanent information that will be carried on file.

The PAF is serially numbered, is created from data stored on magnetic discs, and is maintained in the employee's personnel file. When a change has to be made, such as job title, marital status, or rate of pay, the PAF is retrieved from the employee's record, changes are made under the item to be changed, and the corrected PAF is used to change the data in the computer storage.

Once new information is stored, a new PAF is created and placed in the employee's record to await the next need for processing. A long-time employee might have many PAFs stored in the personnel file.

Once an applicant has been prescreened and interviewed, has had references checked, and has received an offer of employment, the checklist is used to ensure completion of data required to place the employee on the payroll.

When either regular or special performance appraisals are given, the last (most current) PAF will be used to record the appraisal.

These forms are usually found on the reverse side of the PAF. Since performance appraisals may signify a raise in pay, the appropriate pay increase information would be indicated on the front side of the PAF. All recordings on PAFs, whether on one side or both, require the submission of data, storage of information, and creation of a new PAF to be stored in the employee's record. The PAF and performance appraisal system should be thoroughly explained to the new employee, along with assignment of a payroll number. The employer should also explain how and when the staff is paid and when the first paycheck may be expected.

THE EMPLOYEE HANDBOOK

The new employee should be provided with a copy of the hotel or hospital employee's handbook and should be told to read it thoroughly. Since the new housekeeping employee is not working just for the housekeeping department but is to become integrated as a member of the entire staff, reading this handbook is extremely important to ensure that proper instructions in the rules and regulations of the hotel are presented.

The handbook should be developed in such a way as to inspire the new employee to become a fully participating member of the organization. Note the tone of the welcoming letter and the manner in which the rules and regulations are presented.

Upon completion of the acquisition phase, a facility tour should be conducted for one or all new employees. For new facilities, access to the property should be gained within about one week before opening, and many new employees can be taken on a tour simultaneously. It is possible for employees to work in the hotel housekeeping department for years and never to have visited the showroom, dining rooms, ballrooms, or even the executive office areas.

A tour of the complete facility melds employees into the total organization, and a complete informative tour should never be neglected. The reverse side of the PAF may be used to record performance appraisals, written warnings, or matters involving terminations.

For ongoing operations, after acquisition, the new employee may be turned over to a department supervisor, who becomes the tour director. An appreciation of the total involvement of each employee is strengthened when a facilities tour is complete and thorough. If necessary, the property tour might be postponed until after the orientation meeting; however, the orientation activity of staffing is not complete until a property tour is conducted.

ORIENTATION MEETING

The orientation meeting should not be conducted until the employee has had an opportunity to become at least partially familiar with the surroundings. After approximately two weeks, the employee will have many questions about experiences, the new job, training, and the rules and regulations listed in the Property and Department Handbooks.

Employee orientation meetings that are scheduled too soon fail to answer many questions that will develop within the first two weeks of employment. The meeting should be held in a comfortable setting, with refreshments provided.

It is usually conducted by the director of human resources and is attended by as many of the facility managers as possible. Most certainly, the general manager or hospital administration members of the executive committee, the security director, and the new employees' department heads should attend.

Each of these managers should have an opportunity to welcome the new employees and give them a chance to associate names with faces. All managers and new employees should wear name tags. In orientation meetings, a brief history of the company and company goals should be presented. A planned orientation meeting should not be concluded without someone stressing the importance of each position. Every position must have a purpose behind it and is therefore important to the overall functioning of the facility.

An excellent statement of this philosophy was once offered by a general manager who said, "The person mopping a floor in the kitchen at 3:00 A.M. is just as valuable to this operation as I am—we just do different things." The orientation meeting should be scheduled to allow for many questions. And there should be someone in attendance who can answer all of them. Although the new employee will be gaining confidence and security in the position as training ends and work is actually performed, informal orientation may continue for quite some time.

The formal orientation, however, ends with the orientation meeting (although the facility tour may be conducted after the meeting).

Finally, it should be remembered that good orientation procedures lead to worker satisfaction and help quiet the anxieties and fears that a new employee may have. When a good orientation is neglected, the seeds of dissatisfaction are planted. The efficiency and economy with which any department will operate will depend on the ability of each member of the organization to do his or her job. Such ability will depend in part on past experiences, but more commonly it can be credited to the type and quality of training offered. Employees, regardless of past experiences, always need some degree of training before starting a new job.

Small institutions may try to avoid training by hiring people who are already trained in the general functions with which they will be involved. However, most institutions recognize the need for training that is specifically oriented towards the new experience, and will have a documented training programme. Some employers of housekeeping personnel find it easier to train completely unskilled and untrained personnel.

In such cases, bad or undesirable practices do not have to be trained out of an employee. Previous experience and education should, however, be analysed and considered in the training of each new employee in order that efficiencies in training can be recognized.

If an understanding of department standards and policies can be demonstrated by a new employee, that portion of training may be shortened or modified. However, skill and ability must be demonstrated before training can be altered. Finally, training is the best method to communicate the company's way of doing things, without which the new employee may do work contrary to company policy.

FIRST TRAINING

First training of a new employee actually starts with a continuation of department orientation. When a new employee is turned over to the housekeeping or environmental services department, orientation usually continues by familiarizing the employee with department rules and regulations.

Many housekeeping departments have their own department employee handbooks. For an example, which contains the housekeeping department rules and regulations for Bally's Casino Resort in Las Vegas, Nevada. Compare this handbook with that of the generic handbook. Although these handbooks are for completely different types of organizations, the substance of their publications is essentially the same; both are designed to familiarize each new employee with his or her surroundings. Handbooks should be written in such a way as to inspire employees to become team members, committed to company objectives.

A SYSTEMATIC APPROACH TO TRAINING

Training may be defined as those activities that are designed to help an employee begin performing tasks for which he or she is hired or to help the employee improve performance in a job already assigned.

The purpose of training is to enable an employee to begin an assigned job or to improve upon techniques already in use. In hotel or hospital housekeeping operations, there are three basic areas in which training activity should take place: skills, attitudes, and knowledge.

AREAS OF KNOWLEDGE TRAINING IN HOUSEKEEPING

Areas of knowledge in which the employee needs to be trained are as follows:

1. Thorough knowledge of the hotel layout; employee must be able to give directions and to tell the guest about the hotel, restaurants, and other facilities
2. Knowledge of employee rights and benefits
3. Understanding of grievance procedure
4. Knowing top managers by sight and by name for all employees, regardless of how long they have been members of the department.

There are two instances when additional training is needed:

(1) The purchase of new equipment, and

(2) Change in or unusual employee behaviour while on the job. When new equipment is purchased, employees need to know how the new equipment differs from present equipment, what new skills or knowledge are required to operate the equipment, who will need this knowledge, and when. New equipment may also require new attitudes about work habits. Employee behaviour while on the job that is seen as an indicator for additional training may be divided into two categories: events that the manager witnesses and events that the manager is told about by the employees. Events that the manager witnesses that indicate a need for training are frequent employee

absence, considerable spoilage of products, carelessness, a high rate of accidents, and resisting direction by supervisors. Events that the manager might be told about that indicate a need for training are that something doesn't work right (product isn't any good), something is dangerous to work with, something is making work harder. Although training is vital for any organization to function at top efficiency, it is expensive.

The money and man-hours expended must therefore be worth the investment. There must be a balance between the dollars spent training employees and the benefits of productivity and high-efficiency performance.

A simple method of determining the need for training is to measure performance of workers: Find out what is going on at present on the job, and match this performance with what should be happening. The difference, if any, describes how much training is needed.

In conducting performance analysis, the following question should be asked: Could the employee do the job or task if his or her life depended on the result? If the employee could not do the job even if his or her life depended on the outcome, there is a deficiency of knowledge (DK).

If the employee could have done the job if his or her life depended on the outcome, but did not, there is a deficiency of execution (DE).

Some of the causes of deficiencies of execution include task interference, lack of feedback (employee doesn't know when the job is being performed correctly or incorrectly), and the balance of consequences (some employees like doing certain tasks better than others). If either deficiency of knowledge or deficiency of execution exists, training must be conducted. The approach or the method of training may differ, however.

Deficiencies of knowledge can be corrected by training the employee to do the job, then observing and correcting as necessary until the task is proficiently performed. Deficiency of execution is usually corrected by searching for the underlying cause of lack of performance, not by teaching the actual task.

TRAINING METHODS

There are numerous methods or ways to conduct training. Each method has its own advantages and disadvantages, which must be weighed in the light of benefits to be gained. Some methods are more expensive than others but are also more effective in terms of time required for comprehension and proficiency that must be developed. Several useful methods of training housekeeping personnel are listed and discussed.

ON-THE-JOB TRAINING

Using on-the-job training (OJT), a technique in which "learning by doing" is the advantage, the instructor demonstrates the procedure and then watches the students perform it. With this technique, one instructor can handle several students. In housekeeping operations, the instructor is usually a GRA who is doing the instructing in the rooms that have been assigned for cleaning that day. The OJT method is not operationally productive until the student is proficient enough in the training tasks to absorb part of the operational load.

SIMULATION TRAINING

With simulation training, a model room (unrented) is set up and used to train several employees. Whereas OJT requires progress towards daily production of ready rooms, simulation requires that the model room not be rented. In addition, the trainer is not productive in cleaning ready rooms.

The advantages of simulation training are that it allows the training process to be stopped, discussed, and repeated if necessary. Simulation is an excellent method, provided the trainer's time is paid for out of training funds, and clean room production is not necessary during the workday.

COACH-PUPIL METHOD

The coach-pupil method is similar to OJT except that each instructor has only one student (a one-to-one relationship). This method is desired, provided that there are enough qualified instructors to have several training units in progress at the same time.

LECTURES

The lecture method reaches the largest number of students per instructor. Practically all training programmes use this type of instruction for certain segments.

Unfortunately, the lecture method can be the dullest training technique, and therefore requires instructors who are gifted in presentation capabilities. In addition, space for lectures may be difficult to obtain and may require special facilities.

CONFERENCES

The conference method of instruction is often referred to as workshop training. This technique involves a group of students who formulate ideas, do problem solving, and report on projects. The conference or workshop technique is excellent for supervisory training.

DEMONSTRATIONS

When new products or equipment are being introduced, demonstrations are excellent. Many demonstrations may be conducted by vendors and purveyors as a part of the sale of equipment and products. Difficulties may arise when language barriers exist. It is also important that no more information be presented than can be absorbed in a reasonable period of time; otherwise misunderstandings may arise.

TRAINING AIDS

Many hotels use training aids in a conference room, or post messages on an employee bulletin board. Aside from the usual training aids such as chalkboards, bulletin boards, charts, graphs, and diagrams, photographs can supply clear and accurate references for how rooms should be set up, maids' carts loaded, and routines accomplished. Most housekeeping operations have films on guest contact and courtesy that may also be used in training. Motion pictures speak directly to many people who may not understand proper procedures from reading about them. Many training techniques may be combined to develop a well-rounded training plan.

DEVELOPMENT

It is possible to have two students sitting side by side in a classroom, with one being trained and the other being developed. Recall that the definition of training is preparing a person to do a job for which he or she is hired or to improve upon performance of a current job. Development is preparing a person for advancement or to assume greater responsibility. The techniques are the same, but the end result is quite different.

Whereas training begins after orientation of an employee who is hired to do a specific job, upon introduction of new equipment, or upon observation and communication with employees indicating a need for training, development begins with the identification of a specific employee who has shown potential for advancement. Training for promotion or to improve potential is in fact development and must always include a much neglected type of training—supervisory training.

Many forms of developmental training may be given on the property; other forms might include sending candidates to schools and seminars. Developmental training is associated primarily with supervisors and managerial development and may encompass many types of experiences.

Note the various developmental tasks that the trainee must perform over a period of 12 months. Development of individuals within the organization looks to future potential and promotion of employees. Specifically, those employees who demonstrate leadership potential should be developed through supervisory training for advancement to positions of greater responsibility.

Unfortunately, many outstanding workers have their performance rewarded by promotion but are given no development training. The excellent housekeeper who is advanced to the position of senior housekeeper without the benefit of supervisory training is quickly seen to be unhappy and frustrated and may possibly become a loss to the department.

It is therefore most essential that individual potential be developed in an orderly and systematic manner, or else this potential may never be recognized. While undergoing managerial development, student and management alike should not lose sight of the primary aim of the programme, which is the learning and potential development of the trainee, not departmental production.

Even though there will be times that the trainee may be given specific responsibilities to oversee operations, clean guestrooms, or service public areas, advantage should not be taken of the trainee or the situation to the detriment of the development function.

Development of new growth in the trainee becomes difficult when the training instructor or coordinator is not only developing a new manager but is also being held responsible for the production of some aspect of housekeeping operations.

RECORDS AND REPORTS

Whether you are conducting training or a development programme, suitable records of training progress should be maintained both by the training supervisor and the student. Periodic evaluations of the student's progress should be conducted, and successful completion of the programme should be recognized.

Public recognition of achievement will inspire the newly trained or developed employee to achieve standards of performance and to strive for advancement.

Once an employee is trained or developed and his or her satisfactory performance has been recognized and recorded, the person should perform satisfactorily to standards. Future performance may be based on beginning performance after training. If an employee's performance begins to fall short of standards and expectations, there has to be a reason other than lack of skills. The reason for unsatisfactory performance must then be sought out and addressed. This type of follow-up is not possible unless suitable records of training and development are maintained and used for comparison.

EVALUATION AND PERFORMANCE APPRAISAL

Although evaluation and performance appraisal for employees will occur as work progresses, it is not uncommon to find the design of systems for appraisal as part of organization and staffing functions. This is true because first appraisal and evaluation occurs during training, which is an activity of staffing.

Once trainees begin to have their performance appraised, the methods used will continue throughout employment. As a part of training, new employees should be told how, when, and by whom their performances will be evaluated, and should be advised that questions regarding their performance will be regularly answered.

PROBATIONARY PERIOD

Initial employment should be probationary in nature, allowing the new employee to improve efficiency to where the designated number of rooms cleaned per day can be achieved in a probationary period (about three months). Should a large number of employees be unable to achieve the standard within that time, the standard should be investigated.

Should only one or two employees be unable to meet the standard of rooms cleaned per day, an evaluation of the employee in training should either reveal the reason why or indicate the employee as unsuitable for further retention.

An employee who, after suitable training, cannot meet a reasonable performance standard should not be allowed to continue employment.

Similarly, an employee who has met required performance standards in the specified probationary period should be continued into regular employment status and thus achieve a reasonable degree of security in employment.

EVALUATION

Evaluation of personnel is an attempt to measure selected traits, characteristics, and productivity. Unfortunately, evaluations are generally objective in nature, and raters are seldom trained in the art of subjective evaluation. Initiative, self-control, and leadership ability do not used to cycle the trainee through the various functions involved in a hotel housekeeping department.

Note the position of the person who will coach the development in the various skills, and the time expected to be spent in each area lend themselves to measurement; therefore such characteristics are estimated. How well they are estimated depends to a great extent on the person doing the estimating. Two raters using the same form and rating the same person will probably arrive at different conclusions.

Certain policies on the use of evaluations should be established so that they are understood by both the person doing the evaluating and the person being evaluated. These policies must be established and disseminated by management. In order to establish such policies, the following questions, among others, must be answered and communicated to all those involved in the evaluation: What will evaluations be used for? Will evaluations influence promotions, become a part of the employee's record, be used as periodic checks, or be used for counselling and guidance? What qualities are going to be evaluated? Who is going to be evaluated? Who will do the evaluating? Reliable evaluations require careful planning and take considerable time, skill, and work. An evaluation must be understood by the employee.

Evaluation should be used at the end of a probationary period, and the employee must understand at the Staffing Housekeeping Positions beginning of the period that he or she will be observed and evaluated. Each item, as well as what impact the evaluation will have on future employment, should be explained to the employee.

People undergoing periodic evaluations, such as at the end of one year's employment, should also know why evaluations are being conducted and what may result from the evaluation. In both situations, the evaluation should be used for counselling and guidance so that performance may be improved.

Evaluations should be made for a purpose and not for the sake of an exercise. They should ultimately be used as management tools. Evaluations should be developed to fit the policies of the particular institution using it and the particular position being evaluated. The same evaluation may not be suitable for every position.

OUTSOURCING

In certain locales, such as isolated resorts, hotels are tempted to use contract labour because the local market does not support the necessary number of workers, particularly in housekeeping. Advocates of outsourcing are quick to point out the advantages of the practice. Scarce workers are provided to the property, and there is no need to provide expensive employee benefits.

The entire staffing function is assumed by the contractor. There are no worries regarding recruiting, selecting, hiring, orienting, or even training the employees. Merely issue them uniforms and send them off to clean rooms. Some employers may even be willing to relax their responsibilities regarding employment law such as immigration and naturalization requirements.

Management should never forget that once a contracted employee dons a company uniform, the guest believes (and has no reason not to) that person is an employee of the hotel. The guest also believes the hotel has made every reasonable effort to screen that person in the hiring process to ensure that he or she is of good moral character, who has the best interest of the guest at heart. Unfortunately, there have been several incidents in which the outsourced employees did not quite have the best interest of the guest in their hearts.

There have been more than a few cases in which outsourced workers were wanted felons who inflicted considerable bodily harm on guests during the performance of their duties. A number of these incidents have resulted in lawsuits, with awards against the hotel in the millions of dollars. This author does not recommend outsourcing in housekeeping, and cautions operators who ignore this advice to keep their guard up and continue to meet their legal and ethical responsibilities regarding employees and employment law.

Staffing for both hospital and hotel housekeeping operations involves the activities of selecting, interviewing, orienting, training, and developing personnel to carry out specific functions in the organization for which they are hired. Each activity should be performed with consistency, dispatch, and individual concern for each employee brought into the organization.

Whereas the major presentation of staffing in this text has been developed for the model hotel where a mass hiring has been performed, each and every aspect of selecting, orienting, and training new employees applies equally to situations in which replacement employees (perhaps only one) are brought into the organization. Job specifications are the documents that indicate qualifications, characteristics, and abilities inherently needed in applicants.

The Employee Requisition is the instrument by which specific numbers and types of candidates for employment are sought by the personnel department for each of the operating departments. The next step is interviewing, which should be done by people from various departments. Actual selection, however, should only be performed by the department manager for whom the employee will work. The employee acquisition phase is vital to the successful orientation of a new employee and should not be omitted.

Upon acquisition of the new employee, presentation of an Employee's Handbook is appropriate. This handbook should contain major company rules, procedures, and regulations, along with relevant facts for the employee. Orientation is the basis for allowing the new employee to become accustomed to new surroundings.

The quality of orientation will determine whether the new employee will feel secure in a new setting, and it will set the stage for the relationship that is to follow. As training begins, orientation continues but is now conducted by the specific department in which the new employee will work.

There are several methods of training, each of which should be used so as to gain the best effect for the least cost. Employee performance in training should be evaluated by methods similar to those used in evaluating operational performance that will follow.

After new employees receive approximately 24 hours of on-the-job training in the cleaning of rooms, they should become productive and be able to clean a reasonable number of rooms (about 60 per cent efficient). Continued application of skills will develop greater productivity as the new employee spends each day working at the new skills. As preliminary training ends, orientation should be completed by ensuring that an employee orientation meeting and a tour of the entire facility has taken place.

Failure to complete an orientation or to provide sufficient training can plant the seeds of employee unrest, discontent, and possible failure of the employee's relationship with the company that might well have been prevented. Whether conducting training or development, adequate records of employee progress should be maintained.

Records of training that have been successfully completed establish a base for future performance appraisal. Employees have a right to expect evaluations, and usually consider objectively prepared statements about their performance a mark of management's caring about employees.

BASIC SKILLS TRAINING OF HOUSEKEEPING EMPLOYEE

A sample list of skills in which a basic housekeeping employee must be trained follows:

1. Bed making: Specific techniques; company policy
2. Vacuuming: Techniques; use and care of equipment
3. Dusting: Techniques; use of products
4. Window and mirror cleaning: Techniques and products
5. Setup awareness: Room setups; what a properly serviced room should look like
6. Bathroom cleaning: Tub and toilet sanitation; appearance; methods of cleaning and results desired
7. Daily routine: An orderly procedure for the conduct of the day's work; daily communications
8. Caring for and using equipment: Housekeeper cart; loading
9. Industrial safety: Product use; guest safety; fire and other emergencies
   The best reference for the skills that require training is the job description for which the person is being trained.

EMPLOYEES NEED ATTITUDE GUIDANCE

Employees need guidance in their attitudes about the work that must be done.

They need to be guided in their thinking about rooms that may present a unique problem in cleaning. Attitudes among housekeepers need to be such that, occasionally, when rooms require extra effort to be brought back to standard, it is viewed as being a part of rendering service to the guest who paid to enjoy the room.

Carol Mondesir, director of housekeeping, Sheraton Centre, Toronto, states that: A hotel is meant to be enjoyed and, occasionally, the rooms are left quite messed up. However, as long as they're not vandalized, it's part of the territory.

The whole idea of being in the hospitality business is to make the guest's stay as pleasant as possible. The rooms are there to be enjoyed. Positive relationships with various agencies and people also need to be developed.

The following is a list of areas in which attitude guidance is important:

1. The guest/patient
2. The department manager and immediate supervisor
3. A guestroom that is in a state of great disarray
4. The hotel and company
5. The uniform
6. Appearance
7. Personal hygiene Staffing Housekeeping Positions.

The most important task of the trainer is to prepare new employees to meet standards. With this aim in mind, sequence of performance in cleaning a guestroom is most important in order that efficiency in accomplishing day-to-day tasks may be developed. In addition, the best method of accomplishing a task should be presented to the new trainee. Once the task has been learned, the next thing is to meet standards, which may not necessarily mean doing the job the way the person has been trained.

5

Maintenance Department

MAINTENANCE

A plan to do maintenance work in the future is usually of two types:

- Scheduled maintenance
- Preventive maintenance.

SCHEDULED MAINTENANCE

Scheduled maintenance is that type of work that requires longer durations to complete, planning of manpower and tools and materials required co-ordination with other trades and possibly outside contractors.

The timely replacement or maintenance on a major piece of equipment could involve shut downs of other departments or blocks of guest rooms. Projects such as building of walls or complete painting of areas could also come under scheduled maintenance. Indeed, any project requires scheduling and planning.

PREVENTIVE MAINTENANCE

Preventive Maintenance, as it's name implies is the intent to perform timed inspections, minor adjustments, lubrication based on manufacture's recommendations with the ultimate goal of preventing unscheduled breakdowns and prolonging the life and efficiency of the equipment. During the course of the inspection if it is determined that major work may be required, then work orders are generated to schedule the maintenance.

ROOM MAINTENANCE

Room Maintenance, both guest and meeting rooms again follows the above with inspections and generating work orders to schedule and correct deficiencies. The frequency of inspections should be determined to happen sometime before the area slow periods.

If guest room's occupancy is peak in summer then schedule the inspection just prior to the downturn as it will give time to order necessary materials and schedule the labour to accomplish the tasks. The importance of inspections cannot be over emphasized because you have yet to see room attendants or banquet staff adequately report deficiencies.

BREAKDOWN MAINTENANCE

Breakdown maintenance can be both negative and positive. Negative if it has an impact on guest comfort, safety, or is detrimental to the smooth flow of production that keeps other departments operational.

Breakdowns can be very expensive if it happens after hours and outside contractors are required, or if say the main chiller shuts down and all your guests walk out. Positive as you would not want to spend 100 a year on preventive maintenance on a blender worth 50. Also, in maintenance repairs don't waste 20 worth of time to repair something only worth 1000.

TYPES OF MAINTENANCE

EXPLANATION

Maintenance is something that never ends in a hotel and just when one thinks it is under control either something expensive breaks or it is time to remodel or upgrade!

PREVENTIVE AND BREAKDOWN MAINTENANCE

Maintenance management distinguishes between preventive maintenance and breakdown maintenance. While preventive maintenance can be planned, the breakdown maintenance is invariably unplanned.

As regards plant preventive maintenance, the experience with oil refineries, industrial blast furnace, dock facilities and thermal projects have all shown that a thorough planning and a scheduling of preventive maintenance can be immensely time-saving and cost-reducing. The same is applicable in case of tourism transport operations and hotels maintenance, vehicle breakdown or bad maintenance in hotels can adversely affect the business.

Transaction-processing systems have looked at the records of components, spare-parts, jugs, fixtures and tools as inputs, and consumption statements and maintenance accounts as outputs.

These inputs can still be valid for building up a corporate MIS with such additional data as equipment conditions, history of failures, direct cost of maintenance, inventory values and materials movement, man-hours spent, overtime paid, other resource usage, maintenance of employee's performance, reliability and maintainability of equipment, and maintenance contribution to the finances.

From such a comprehensive database, one can generate MIS reports for transport control, such as vehicle register (to provide vehicle specifications and project details), vehicle history (to provide maintenance particulars), major failure report, forecast on maintenance (providing probable failure time and period), office non-availability, reliability and maintainability, and maintenance schedules (providing maintenance activities to be done during a specific period).

One can also generate MIS reports on work control, such as, craft performance report (providing planned and actual performance of each craft), craftsman's performance report, maintenance planning efficiency report (providing an efficiency ratio on planned activities), overtime report, resource levelling report (providing analysis of resource required job-wise), delay cause report, etc. One can finally generate materials control reports and cost control reports providing management details of costs and material transactions involved in maintenance management.

CONTRACT MAINTENANCE

Contract maintenance is mandated in some instances such as for elevator service, kitchen hood exhaust cleaning and fire systems. The reasoning behind this is to ensure that the work is performed by qualified technicians, and may also require licenses and special knowledge. Local regulations and insurance companies usually require these contracts. It also serves the purpose of making sure the work gets done irregardless of budget restraints. Maintenance contracts or contracting out is almost always necessary to complement an engineering department that is undersized.

MAINTENANCE DECLINING EFFICIENCY

EFFICIENCY – STAFF PRODUCTIVITY

Basically, for the hotels engineering and maintenance staff, the day-to-day operation and maintenance of a large hotel is time-consuming.

Therefore, one of the striking advantages of Integrated Building Solutions (TBS) is the complete harmonization of the hotel's HVAC (heating, ventilation and air conditioning), fire, intrusion and CCTV (closed-circuit television) systems.

The integration of all of these disciplines means improved functionality for the hotel, and centralized display of all building information at the touch of a button. Furthermore, TBS also includes voice evacuation capabilities and controls for the hotel's phone system, guest services and background music. In total, the integrated TBS reduced significantly the workload of all involved maintenance staff.

At time when every penny counts, PMWorks, the preventive-maintenance solution from MTech, based here, is streamlining property efficiencies and protecting long-term capital investments for hotels. MTech is a leading provider of guest-response and preventive-maintenance solutions for the worldwide hotel industry. The hotel management company is one such client. "We welcome Hospitality to our PMWorks family," said Luis Segredo, MTech president. "Management companies looking to grow, particularly with a diverse portfolio, need tools to help them manage the growth and justify it.

With PMWorks, Winston Hospitality can show owners how they are protecting their properties and saving them costly repair dollars. As a subscription service that has been proven across many brands, PMWorks can meet Winston Hospitality's needs at the property level and provide the corporate office with operational and strategic reports.

"Co. continues to add management companies to its growing list of PMWorks users, even in this economic climate, because staffing cuts are requiring automation to help keep service and product levels high," he added. Michael president of Winston Hospitality, says that the proactive nature of PMWorks helps keep their hotels looking in great shape.

"We use PMWorks for everything from plumbing and paint touch-up to case goods and the HVAC system," Heeden said. "HVAC is really important because if it were to malfunction, it affects air quality and the noise is the number one complaint from guests."

Brand quality-assurance marks most often fall in the "outstanding" range for Hospitality properties.

Heeden anticipates property mechanical systems will see fewer repairs and have a longer shelf life if each hotel follows the planned preventive-maintenance programme and PMWorks schedule.

WORKING

The Accounts Manager and liaison officer, explained that PM Works enables management companies to better manage the scheduling processes.

"The system provides a work load balanced schedule that lets you focus on the work that needs to be done," Edson said. "Time is no longer wasted preparing a complex schedule that must include critical reminders for Life, Health and Safety. They are all there, in the system. It's a cost-effective solution for management companies that demand corporate-driven quality and consistency across a multi-branded portfolio."

STEPS TO IMPLEMENTING WORKS AT HOTEL

- Enroll the property by faxing or e-mailing a signed agreement.
- Complete the Web data collection wizard. This is a simple and fast "prompted" collection of data. The hotelier is asked what the equipment is called (Ice machine One) and where it's located. A list of guestroom numbers completes the set up. On average a 100-room property will take about two or three hours to set the entire programme up.

- Data is sent to a regional person, or back to the GM for a quick review to make sure the data is complete.
- The following Monday the hotel will receive its first work order packet VIA e-mail.

When the schedule is in place, hotels receive weekly service orders via e-mail. Each service includes step-by-step instructions on how to do the job right the first time.

As technicians complete tasks, they close orders from any touch-tone phone or Web browser. Every week new orders are sent to the property. Included are tasks not completed during previous weeks so nothing falls through the cracks? The management company receives an e-mail showing what properties are keeping up and which are falling behind.

"We receive status reports [green, yellow or red] to see which tasks are completed and which are not," Heeden said. "PMWorks customizes the process to fit the needs of each hotel.

It generates the work orders once a week and let's us know where we are in the process. We use PMWorks in all of our hotels, have it ready to go at our properties under construction, and plan to use it in all of our new hotels. "It takes a lot of the guess work out of the PM programme and keeps us on top of critical Life, Health and Safety PM's," he added. The Hospitality offers services including management, development, rehabilitation, repositioning, and hotel ownership. Its senior management team brings years of experience and a wealth of knowledge to each of these areas and is committed to ensuring the satisfaction of guests and its partners. Its current portfolio includes four hotels, and at press time it was due to open one more.

REPLACEMENT POLICY OF HOTEL EQUIPMENT

PURPOSE

To establish a (PC) equipment replacement and upgrade policy for the Youngstown Metropolitan Housing Authority {CO.}rder to utilize the benefits of next-generation office environments, simplify technical support issues, and increase CO.ility to deploy new solutions to business problems.

STATMENT

Guidelines and procedures are required to maintain a replacement cycle of personal Hotel equipment within the useful and expected lifetime of the equipment, while preventing a proliferation of aging, obsolete, out-of-warranty, unsupported, and incompatible systems.

CYCLE OF REPLACEMENT

It is Co. policy to cycle replaced computers through the major classifications of technology users PCs that have been replaced and are no longer appropriate for one classification of technology users should be used to upgrade and replace a PC with older technology within the agency.

In this manner, the PC with the oldest technology in the agency is phased out and the agency can continue to benefit from their investment in PCs.

REPLACEMENT RATIONALE

Hotel equipment, by their nature are relatively inexpensive Part and devices that have a limited life compared to other office equipment.

The rule of thumb for obsolescence of Hotel equipment *is 3-4 years.* However, changing business practices, new technology, and new software applications can impose increased demands on computing power that can force a more frequent replacement cycle for employees affected by the changing business practices or those using the new technology or software.

REPLACEMENT VERSUS UPGRADE

It is Co. policy to replace PCs with the latest technology rather than to apply major upgrades to existing PCs.

Current research indicates that:

- Upgrading is expensive because, more often than not, multiple system components must be upgraded in order to achieve the intended performance improvement.
- The purchase price of the various hardware components needed to accomplish an upgrade will exceed the purchase price of a new el equipment The cost of labour to install an upgrade to existing hardware will far exceed the cost of labour to install a new PC./ equipment
- Upgraded PCs have uncertain maintenance profiles and support costs.
- There is no increase in residual value of upgraded PCs.
- Upgrading PCs tend to increase the overall complexity in the installed hardware base.

CLASSIFICATIONS OF TECHNOLOGY USERS

There are three major classifications of technology users defined as:

LEADING EDGE TECHNOLOGY USERS

Those individuals within the agency who need to be at the forefront of technology.

Those individuals carry out but not limited to the following functions:

- Heavy usage of the CCS application (processing, programming, upgrading and maintenance)
- Heavy usage of database applications (Access)

- Heavy usage of the Internet (downloading virus fixes, programmes, HUD reports, uploading data to various HUD organizations, viewing HUD reports in PIC, research and analysis)

POWER USERS

Those individuals within the agency whose daily business operations require heavy utilization of information technology.

They have a standardized suite of applications on their desktops; customized applications beyond the standardized suite; may use servers for database and decision-support; and often have access to department-specific applications, e-mail, Intranets and the Internet.

Functions performed by these users are(but not limited to) the following:

- Moderate to heavy usage of the Microsoft Office suite (Excel, Word, Power Point, Publisher, Outlook, Access)
- Moderate to heavy usage of Adobe Acrobat and other applications used to complete grants, reports and forms for HUD
- Moderate to heavy usage of the Internet (uploading data to HUD, e-mailing, viewing HUD reports in PIC and other HUD areas, purchasing and reservations)
- Occasional to heavy usage of the CCS application

MAINSTREAM TECHNOLOGY USERS

Those individuals within the agency whose daily business operations require moderate utilization of technology for everyday office functions. They have a standardized suite of applications, access to file and print servers, and access to some host-based application using terminal emulation programmes. Functions performed by these users are(but not limited to) the following:

CONSERVATIVE TECHNOLOGY USERS

Those individuals within the agency whose daily business operations require the utilization of technology for everyday office functions only. They have a standardized suite of applications, access to file and print servers, and access to some host-based application using terminal emulation programmes.

Functions performed by these users (but are not limited to) are the following:

REPLACEMENT SCHEDULE

The following is a general guideline for replacing PCs. Departments should consult with "IS" for assistance in determining their specific replacement needs. Replacement schedules vary according to the four major classifications of technology users:

Leading Edge Technology Users

- Should maintain no more than two generations of technology.

- Should consider replacing PCs every second or third year, depending on applications in use.

Power Users

- Should maintain no more than two generations of technology
- Should consider replacing PCs every three to four years

Mainstream Technology Users

- Should maintain no more than two generations of technology.
- Should consider replacing PCs every four to five years.

Conservative Technology Users

- Should maintain no more than two generations of technology.
- Should consider replacing PCs every five years.
  - "IS" is not responsible for the installation and reconfiguration of "unsupported" software packages.
  - "IS" will NOT transfer the entire contents of a user's hard drive. Users who have not properly prepared their machine before their scheduled "upgrade installation date/time" will automatically be placed on the waiting list for future installations.
  - "IS" will NOT be responsible for the installation and reconfiguration of "unsupported" peripheral devices or devices that were installed by users. Equipment originally installed by users will be the user's responsibility to re-install on their new system.

REGULAR AND PROPER MAINTENANCE OF THE HOTEL BUILDING

To ensure regular and proper maintenance of the hotel building and its various machines installed in its premises and to ensure proper hotel functioning, an Engineering or Maintenance departments is there in every hotel. Qualified engineers along with necessary staff are appointed for this work. These staffs are in fields of electrical, mechanical and civil. The engineers look after the boilers, hot water supply, air-conditioning, plumbing etc. Electricians ensure that the electrical appliances and gadgets are perfectly in order.

Engineering is responsible for the maintenance and repair of the physical plant and all of its features, including:

- Day-to-day system operation and maintenance routines
- Preventive maintenance
- Minor and major repairs and improvements
- Support for other operating departments and guest activities

As the facility is our "product" and the means through which we deliver our valuable services, high performance in this function is critical to the overall, long-term success of the business.

The department plays a critical role in maintaining a safe environment for building occupants and compliance with various federal, state and local environmental, health, safety, operating and building codes, standards and regulations. This department head position carries out managerial processes including budgeting, forecasting, labour scheduling, personnel administration, work order tracking and various record-keeping duties.

The successful candidate is self-starting, proactive, a team player, able to grasp "the big picture" as well as being involved in the details, and is an effective trouble-shooter and problem-solver. The individual must be technically familiar with the many aspects and disciplines involved in constructing and operating a large, complex facility, while effectively performing as a member of the management team. Experience with developing and managing complex improvement projects is important. Successful Engineering department managers have often been promoted to positions of greater responsibility after initially hiring into the department at the craft level. By acquiring additional skills and demonstrating appropriate qualities, the craftsperson may be given the responsibility of a lead craftsperson or supervisor as an opportunity arises, then eventually managerial duties if further developmental progress is made.

Other managers transfer their proven skills and experience from facility-related positions in other industries or from the construction industry. Those who make the commitment are rewarded by a fast-paced, interesting and challenging technical career within an attractive business environment.

DEPARTMENT OF ORGANIZATION AND MAINTENANCE

ROOM DIVISION

Statistics conducted by the Lodging Industry in 1995, has shown that the majority of hotels revenues is generated from Rooms Division Department under the form of room sales. This very department provides the services guests expect during their stay in the Hotel.

Lastly, the Rooms Division Department is typically composed of five different departments:

- Front Office
- Reservation
- Housekeeping
- Uniformed Services
- Telephone

Beneath is a brief description of the different departments decomposing the Rooms Division Department, along with their related main responsibilities?

FRONT OFFICE

- Sell guestrooms; register guests and design guestrooms

- Coordinate guest services
- Provide information
- Maintain accurate room statistics, and room key inventories
- Maintain guest account statements and complete proper financial settlements

RESERVATION

- Receive and process reservation requests for future overnight accommodations.
- With technology development, the Reservation Department can, on real time, access the number and types of rooms available, various room rates, and furnishings, along with the various facilities existing in the hotel
- There should be close relation-ships with Sales and Marketing Division concerning Large Group Reservations

HOUSEKEEPING

- Inspects rooms before they are available for sale
- Cleans occupied and vacant rooms
- Communicates the status of guestrooms to the Front Office Department
- Cleans and presses the property's linens, towels, and guest clothing (if equipped to do so, free of charge or for a pre-determined fee)
- Maintains recycled and non-recycled inventory items

UNIFORMED SERVICES

- Bell Attendants: Ensure baggage service between the lobby area and guestrooms
- Door Attendants: Ensure baggage service and traffic control at hotel entrance(s)
- Valet Parking Attendants: Ensure parking services for guest's automobiles
- Transportation Personnel: Ensure transportation services for guests from and to the hotel
- Concierge: Assists guests by making restaurant reservations, arranging for transportation, and getting tickets for theater, sporting, or any other special events

TELEPHONE DEPARTMENT

- Answers and distributes calls to the appropriate extensions, whether guest, employee, or management extensions
- Places wake-up calls

- Monitors automated systems
- Coordinates emergency communications

FOOD AND BEVERAGE DEPARTMENT

According to Lodging statistics, F&B Department constitutes the second largest revenue generator of a typical hotel with an average of 23.1 for Food sales, and 8.6 per cent for Beverage sales.

In a five-star hotel, Food and Beverage outlets might have the following forms:

- Quick Service
- Table Service
- Specialty Restaurants
- Coffee Shops
- Bars
- Lounges
- Clubs
- Banquets
- Catering Functions Þ Wedding, Birthdays...

SALES AND MARKETING DIVISION

A typical hotel should usually have Sales and Marketing division. However, if the staff size, volume business, hotel size, expected group arrivals is low enough, the hotel might have marketing staff placed under the reservation department (*i.e.* No need for a Sales and Marketing Division).

A typical Sales and Marketing Division is composed of four different departments:

- Sales
- Convention Services
- Advertising
- Public Relations

ACCOUNTING DIVISION

The Accounting Division monitors the financial activities of the property.

Some of the activities that are undertaken in the Accounting Division are listed below:

- Pays outstanding invoices
- Distributes unpaid statements
- Collects amounts owed
- Processes payroll
- Accumulates operating data
- Compiles financial reports
- Makes bank deposits

- Secures cash loans
- Performs other control and processing functions

ENGINEERING AND MAINTENANCE DIVISION

This very department maintains the property's structure and grounds as well as electrical and mechanical equipment. Some hotels might have this very division under different names, such as maintenance division, property operation and maintenance department...

SECURITY DIVISION

Security division personnel are usually screened from in-house personnel, security officers or retired police officers, across certain physical skills, and prior experience.

Some of the functions of the security division are listed below:

- Patrols the property
- Monitors supervision equipment
- Ensures safety and security of guests, visitors, and employees

HUMAN RESOURCES DIVISION

Some of the duties of the human resources division are listed below:

- Responsible for external and internal recruitment
- Calculates employees' salaries, compensation, and tax withholding...
- Administrates employees' paperwork, monitors attendance...
- Maintains good relations with Labour Unions
- Ensures employees' safety and working conditions

OTHER DIVISIONS

All the above mentioned departments and/or divisions should exist in a typical five-star hotel, however there might be some revenue generators that are specific to certain hotels but not existing in others.

Below is a list of some possible extra or other divisions that might exist in a hotel:

- Retail Outlets (*i.e.*: Shops rented to outsiders or managed by the hotel)
- Recreation Facilities (ex: Fitness Centre, Tennis Courts, and Cinema Saloons...)
- Conference Centers
- Casinos

MISSION OF ORGANIZATION

- At the formation stage of a company, establishers shall come together to discuss the broad guidelines that the company will follow in the future. This is called preparing the mission statement.

- A Mission is the unique purpose that sets one hotel or motel company apart from others. Moreover, the mission statement gives meanings and directions to hotel policies. In fact, when faced with any problem, confusion, or strategic decision to be taken, managers shall, always, make sure that their decisions match the mission statement. In addition, the mission statement shall be general and broad. For, if mission were specific, and numerical, it would be impossible to apply it at any future circumstance. Lastly, the mission statement shall reflect the interests of the agents interacting in the hotel industry named:
  - *Guest:* Guest(s) constitute one of the most important agents in the hotel industry. For, no guests means no accommodation sector!
  - *Employee:* A hotel with no employees means simply that guests would not be welcomed, registered, assisted for whatsoever specific needs they have...That's why, employees are a primordial agent in the hotel industry
  - *Management and owners:* A hotel with no managers resembles to an army without generals. Moreover, to have a hotel, investors shall poor some amount of money to build it, refurnish it, and operate it.

Therefore, the mission statement should tell how it is going to satisfy all the above mentioned agents so that they continue acting in the hotel industry. An illustration of a mission statement is given below:

The mission of our hotel is to provide outstanding lodging facilities and services to our guests. Our hotel focuses on individual business and leisure travel, as well as travel associated with group meetings.

We emphasize high quality standards in our Rooms and Food and Beverage divisions.

We provide a fair return on investment for our owners and recognize that this can not be done without well-trained, motivated, and enthusiastic employees

GOALS

- After the preparation of the mission statement, at least prior to any financial year, managers shall, bearing in mind the company's mission statement, come up with company's global objectives, and then break them down to departmental goals and objectives.
- By definition, goals are those activities and standards an organization must successfully perform or achieve to effectively carry out its mission. Moreover, goals shall be:
- Specific and numerical

- Observable
- Measurable

If objectives were general and non-quantifiable, then, it would be impossible at the end of a certain period of time to see whether company actual results match with the planned objectives or not.

STRATEGIES

After determining departmental goals and objectives, department heads and/or managers shall design the best methods their respective departments or divisions shall use to achieve its goals.

These methods are refereed to as strategies:

- Later, department heads shall move one further step, as to break down each strategy to tactics (*i.e.* day to day methods to reach the strategies). An illustration, to one of the Front Office department goal (a registration-related goal), a strategy to reach it and a related tactic is given below:
  - *Goal:* Operate the front desk efficiently and courteously so that guests register within 2 minutes of arrival.
  - *Strategy*: Pre-register guests with reservation guarantees as room become available from the housekeeping.
  - *Tactic*: Pre-print registration cards for arriving guests and separate the cards of all gusts with a reservation guarantee
- It is of extreme importance that managers shall continuously control and evaluate their strategies and tactics, and hence revise them (if necessary) so that department goals and objectives are reached fully at the end of the planned period.

ORGANIZATION

GENERAL MANAGER

The General Manager oversees all aspects of the hotel operations including: guest relations, front desk, housekeeping, maintenance, finances, team building, and staff development. The General Manager must possess strong communication skills, both verbal and written, and demonstrate outstanding leadership. The manager must be able to delegate responsibilities, organize complex projects, and establish priorities consistent with hotel objectives.

ASSISTANT GENERAL MANAGER

The Assistant General Manager position will support the General Manager with all aspects of the hotel operations. The Assistant General Manager must also demonstrate strong communication skills and superior leadership abilities.

FRONT OFFICE MANAGER

The Front Office Manager is responsible for all duties of the front desk operation which includes: staff training, inter-department communications, and staff scheduling. The FOM usually works a regularly scheduled front desk shift and must be available to work any shift as needed. The Front Office Manager should possess strong communication skills and demonstrate leadership abilities.

CONCIERGE

The concierge is available to answer any guest enquires regarding the city, events, and attractions. This individual will provide exceptional customer service to all of our guests and will support other departments including Sales, Front Office, and Bellman/Van, as needed.

GUEST SERVICE AGENT

Guest Service Agents are responsible for greeting and registering the guest, providing outstanding guest service during their stay, and settling the guest's account upon completion of their stay. However, the realm of responsibilities will extend beyond that of a typical front desk agent. This allows the Guest Service Agent to expand their skill sets and work in a fast paced environment with new challenges daily.

Primary responsibilities include: registering guests, making and modifying reservations, hotel operator, and concierge duties.

Guest Service Agents must possess a positive and upbeat personality with a desire to deliver outstanding customer service to our guests. Guest Service Agents must have the ability to multi-task, be detail-oriented, and be able to problem solve in order to effectively deal with internal and external customers.

NIGHT AUDITOR

Night Auditors are responsible for the front desk operation during the overnight shift. Primary responsibilities include: registering guests, making reservations, preparing daily reports, balancing transactions, and conducting security walks.

Night Auditors must be able to work independently and with minimal supervision. They must also be able to problem solve and troubleshoot in order to resolve guest issues that may arise and respond to emergency situations.

SECURITY

The Security position will encompass aspects of both the Night Audit and Front Desk positions as well as overseeing the safety and security of the hotel and guests throughout the evening hours. Additional responsibilities include: conducting security walks throughout the hotel property and responding to guest requests and any noise complaints. Security agents must be able to problem solve and troubleshoot in order to resolve guest issues and respond appropriately to emergency situations.

VAN DRIVER/BELLMAN

Van Drivers are responsible for transporting guests to and from the hotel to local area attractions as well as assisting the guest with recommendations for restaurants and tourist activities.

The Van Driver is also expected to support with front desk operations. Primary responsibilities include: driving guests to designated locations, assisting guests with luggage, maintaining vehicle cleanliness, and concierge duties.

Van Drivers must have strong analytical and navigation skills with the ability to coordinate multiple pick-ups and drop-offs on a schedule under continuously changing circumstances. A valid driver's license and acceptable driving record is required.

DIRECTOR SALES

The Director of Sales is responsible for maximizing the occupancy and the average daily rate of the hotel, while upholding excellent guest service and accommodations to all guests. This position will work closely with the hotel's preferred accounts and group reservations. The Director of Sales manages the sales effort and supports the General Manager on operational issues. This position requires excellent communication skills, both written and verbal.

SALES MANAGER

The Sales Manager assists the Director of Sales to increase corporate client base through consistent solicitations while establishing trust and rapport with clients to generate and boost revenues for the hotel. The Sales Manager services new and existing accounts to ensure repeat business. This position requires excellent communication skills, both written and verbal.

SALES COORDINATOR

The Sales Coordinator assists the Director of Sales and Sales Manager in sales operations including: reserving meetings and conferences, coordinating wedding groups, general administrative functions, and arranging sales blitzes and giveaways. This position requires strong communication skills, both written and verbal.

SALES AND CATERING ASSISTANT

The Sales and Catering Assistant is responsible for assisting the Sales team by booking and servicing groups, meeting rooms, and conferences while providing exceptional customer service to guests and clients of the hotel. This position requires excellent guest service skills and the ability to understand the guests' needs and ideas.

EXECUTIVE HOUSEKEEPER

The Executive Housekeeper is responsible for all duties of the housekeeping operation and cleanliness levels in all areas of the property.

Responsibilities include: staff training, inter- department communications, and staff scheduling. The Executive Housekeeper will promote an atmosphere that insures the company mission statement, "Friendliness and Cleanliness". This position requires strong attention to detail, leadership skills, and the ability to effectively deal with department heads, guests, and team members.

ASSISTANT EXECUTIVE HOUSEKEEPER

The Assistant Executive Housekeeper supports the Executive Housekeeper in all duties of the housekeeping operation and cleanliness levels in all areas of the property.

Responsibilities include: staff training, inter-department communications, and staff scheduling. The Assistant Executive will promote an atmosphere that insures the company mission statement, "Friendliness and Cleanliness". This position requires strong attention to detail, leadership skills, and the ability to effectively deal with department heads, guests, and team members.

CONTINENTAL BREAKFAST ATTENDANT

The Continental Breakfast Attendant is responsible for setting up the daily complimentary continental breakfast, ensuring that the breakfast items are well stocked, and cleaning up after breakfast.

This position requires multi-tasking abilities and ability to effectively communicate with guests regarding breakfast offerings and basic hotel information. A valid Food Handler's permit is required.

HOUSEPERSON

The Houseperson is responsible for maintaining the cleanliness and appearance of the hotel and providing customers with quality service in a timely and friendly manner.

Responsibilities vary but may include: cleaning and maintaining the appearance of the public areas of the hotel, deep cleaning of assigned areas, setting-up and maintaining complimentary hotel lobby functions including the coffee service and nightly concierge events, cleaning and setting-up meeting room functions, restocking housekeeping stations, delivering service items to guest rooms upon requests from the front desk, and driving shuttle van when needed.

ROOM ATTENDANT

Room Attendants are responsible for the cleanliness of guest rooms, hallways, and public areas in the hotel. Responsibilities include: servicing guest rooms daily in accordance with hotel procedures, stocking cart with room supplies, and replacing bed linens and replenishing guest room supplies.

This position requires strong attention to detail, ability to communicate effectively with guests and team members verbally or in written form, and the ability to bend, lift, and be standing or walking all day.

OBSOLESCENCE MANAGEMENT PROCESS FLOW

The V-22 programme office's OMT is guided by an obsolescence management plan that establishes a proactive process for predicting, identifying, and controlling obsolescence impacts that affect the programme from conceptual design through retirement.

Processes defined within the plan provide the V-22 programme with a notice of obsolescence, the degree of impact of obsolescence, recommendations for mitigation, and an assessment of how soon the problem will impact the aircraft availability.

Those impacts are provided, in accordance with the V-22 change management process, as information to the IPTs charged with implementing a solution. All obsolescence notices are entered into a V-22 obsolescence verification and analysis system by means of case sheets. This allows tracking and status updates to be maintained and distributed. Case sheets are closed based on the resolution developed and approval by the appropriate IPTs. The information is then provided back to the maintenance plan to ensure currency of the data.

The first step in the V-22 obsolescence process is to assess and continuously monitor availability of the components used in the equipment for potential obsolescence risk. This is necessary so the programme can identify areas where it is vulnerable to potential obsolescence problems and plan for risk mitigation.

In addition to continuous monitoring and contractor input, the V-22 OMT uses discontinuance notices delivered through GIDEP and the shared data warehouse or other available sources to provide an easy-to-use interface for part number enquiry listings. These processes enable the V-22 programme to take a focused, total-look approach.

Once a component has been identified as obsolete, an obsolescence risk assessment is performed. This verifies the current availability of a part, forecasts its future availability, identifies its sourcing depth, and identifies possible solution options if it is already obsolete.

Once the initial assessment is complete, the team conveys the results to the appropriate points of contact for those systems, enabling them to take action.

The parts are then monitored for availability status changes, and timely notifications are sent to the appropriate points of contact as changes are identified.

An obsolescence verification and analysis case sheet is assigned and completed on each unique part in order to verify current availability, forecast future availability, indicate sourcing depth, and identify possible solution options for those parts already obsolete.

The case sheet provides the basis for insight on the obsolescence impact at the next higher assembly or system level.

The assessment results are intended as an aid to decision makers managing V-22 systems to help them improve afford-ability by minimizing costly redesigns. Information from the development, production, and/or sustainment IPTs on the solution development and the approved implementation plan/ funding is required for closure of the initial obsolescence notice entered into the reporting system.

Finally, after an obsolescence impact has been resolved, its solution is fed back into the process. It is important to maintain visibility of implemented solutions to ensure system changes are also managed for obsolescence.

Resolution feedback will indicate when new parts are introduced into a system to replace or redesign obsolete parts, allowing the parts to be obtained and assessed for obsolescence and then monitored.

Resolution feedback can provide insight into when a system or component may no longer require monitoring (for example, if a system is replaced through attrition and will not be maintained by the government).

MONITORING TOOLS

The OMT employs a variety of obsolescence monitoring/prediction tools. No one tool can perform all of the necessary functions required to properly monitor each component. Each tool serves as a check and balance system to the others and provides notices, health analysis, prediction, and projection of component life span.

The OMT uses, in comb-ination, AVCOM (Advanced Component Obsolescence Management); Total Parts Plus; QSTAR (Qinetic's Sustainment Technology Assessment Resource); TACTRAC (Transition Analysis of Component Tracking) andOMIS

RESULTS TO DATE

To date, the OMT has worked on over 400 obsolescence case sheets, resulting in the resolution and/or closure of over half in the past year. The OMT monitors over 50,000 components for the V-22.

From fiscal year 1998 through fiscal 2004, the estimated cost avoidance for obsolescence management totaled over 39 million. Through the OMT's continuous efforts to streamline processes and become more efficient, the team has achieved an estimated cost avoidance of over 27 million for fiscal 2008 alone.

BENEFITS

- Minimize the impact of obsolescence to maximize your return on investment.
- Avoid costly re-designs due to component obsolescence.
- Minimize your obsolescence management overhead costs using.

Spectrum's Obsolescence
Management Service:

- Reduce the effect that Moore's Law has on your product life cycle.
- Receive long-term professional Technical Support from Spectrum extending throughout the Obsolescence Management Plan period.

FEATURES

- Spectrum's Obsolescence Management Plans are based on the unique needs of each customer.
- Spectrum maintains a bonded inventory of customer-owned parts for future builds.
- Customers receive quarterly reports showing status of bonded inventory.
- Spectrum continuously monitors product billof- materials (BOMs) to identify additional component obsolescence that may require Obsolescence Management Plan updates.
- Technical Support service and repair facilities continue throughout the Obsolescence Management Plan period.

OBSOLESCENCE MANAGEMENT

Defence industry electronic equipment suppliers providing commercial off-the-shelf (COTS) solutions require Obsolescence Management to support the extended product life cycles typical of the industry. Moore's Law states that the transistor density on integrated circuits doubles every couple of years. This exponential growth and ever-shrinking transistor size results in increased performance and decreased cost. As a result, the direct impact for COTS vendors is near-term component obsolescence, leading to product end-of-life (EOL) or product re-design much earlier than desired in view of the product life cycle needs of the defence industry.

SERVICE OVERVIEW

Spectrum's Obsolescence Management Service is offered under our Product Life Cycle Management programme. It provides customer options beyond EOL notification and a single last time buy (LTB) opportunity for products going EOL. Upon product EOL, we work with our customer to prepare a unique Obsolescence Management

Plan that specifies the quantity of product required over a duration of time. LTB quantities of the component(s) going obsolete is placed into bonded inventory.

The components placed into bonded inventory is customer-owned material. Spectrum monitors the product bill-of-materials (BOM) for further component obsolescence. Upon such occurance, Spectrum notifies the customer of the additional component(s) EOL and works with the customer to update the Obsolescence Management Plan.

COMPONENT MANAGEMENT SYSTEM

Spectrum product BOMs are continuously monitored for component obsolescence and/or other component changes using a state-of-the-art component database monitoring facility.

Upon receiving component change/obsolescence notification, we work with our customers to update their existing Obsolescence Management Plans to effectively reset the EOL clock. Proactive BOM monitoring provides Spectrum and our customers the ability to react quickly to critical information maximizing product life cycle and associated revenue.

BONDED INVENTORY

Based on the needs of the customer specific Obsolescence Management Plan, a LTB for components going obsolete will be purchased as customer-owned inventory and bonded. Customers are given credit for the components used from the bonded inventory upon shipment of the product.

6

Financial Planning in Hotel Management

Accounting (methodology) is the measurement, disclosure or provision of assurance about financial information that helps managers, investors, tax authorities and other decision makers make resource allocation decisions. The names come from the use of financial accounts. Financial accounting is one branch of accounting and historically has involved processes by which financial information about a business is recorded, classified, summarized, interpreted, and communicated. Accounting is also widely referred to as the "language of business".

Auditing, a related but separate discipline, has two sub-disciplines: Internal and External auditing. External auditing is the process whereby an independent auditor examines an organization's financial statements and accounting records in order to express an opinion — that conveys reasonable but not absolute assurance — as to the truth and fairness of the statements and the accountant's adherence to Generally Accepted Accounting Principles (GAAP), in all material respects.

Internal auditing is an examination in which management, and not the external public, is the main beneficiary. It is carried out usually by auditors employed by the company, but sometimes by external service providers. The internal auditor's role is broader, and basically depends on what kind of assurance management wants. It usually certifies the efficiency and effectiveness of processes, departments, projects or internal controls. The Institute of Internal Auditors is generally accepted as the custodian of Internal Auditing best practice.

At the heart of accounting is the measurement of financial transactions which are transfers of legal property rights made under contractual relationships. Non-financial transactions are specifically excluded due to conservatism and materiality principles.

Practitioners of accountancy are known as accountants. There are many professional bodies for accountants throughout the world. Many allow their members to use titles indicating their membership. Examples are Chartered Certified Accountant (ACCA or FCCA), Chartered Accountant (FCA, CA or

ACA) and Certified Public Accountant (CPA). Accountancy attempts to create accurate financial reports that are useful to managers, regulators, and other stakeholders such as shareholders, creditors, or owners. The day-to-day record-keeping involved in this process is known as bookkeeping.

At the heart of modern financial accounting is the double-entry bookkeeping system. This system involves making at least two entries for every transaction: a debit in one account, and a corresponding credit in another account. The sum of all debits should always equal the sum of all credits. This provides an easy way to check for errors. This system was first used in medieval Europe, although claims have been made that the system dates back to Ancient Greece.

According to critics of standard accounting practices, it has changed little since. Accounting reform measures of some kind have been taken in each generation to attempt to keep bookkeeping relevant to capital assets or production capacity. However, these have not changed the basic principles, which are supposed to be independent of economics as such. In recent times, the divergence of accounting from economic principles has resulted in controversial reforms to make financial reports more indicative of economic reality.

Accountancy's infancy dates back to the earliest days of human agriculture and civilization (the Sumerians in Mesopotamia), when the need to maintain accurate records of the quantities and relative values of agricultural products first arose. Simple accounting is mentioned in the Christian Bible in the book of Matthew, in the Parable of the Talents (Matt. 25:19). Twelfth century writer Ibn Taymiyyah mentioned in his book Hisba (verification, calculation), detailed accounting systems used by the Muslims as early as in the mid-seventh century. The accounting practices were influenced by the Roman and the Persian civilizations that Muslims interacted with. The most detailed example of a complex governmental accounting system is the Divan of Umar, the second Caliph of Islam in which all revenues and disbursements were recorded. The Divan of Umar has been described in detail by various Islamic historians and was used by Muslim rulers with mofidications and enhancements until the fall of the Ottoman Empire.

MODERN ACCOUNTANCY

The first book on accounting was written by a Croatian merchant Benedetto Cotrugli, who is also known as Benedikt Kotruljeviæ, from the city of Dubrovnik. During his life in Italy he met many merchants and decided to write, Della Mercatvra et del Mercante Perfetto (On Trade and the Perfect Merchant) in which he elaborated on the principles of modern, double-entry book-keeping. He finished his lifework in 1458. However, his work was not published until 1573, as a result of which his contributions to the field have been overlooked by the general public.

For this reason, Luca Pacioli, also known as Friar Luca dal Borgo, is credited for the "birth" of accounting. His Summa de arithmetica, geometrica, proportioni et proportionalita (Venice 1494), a synthesis of the mathematical knowledge of his time, includes the first published description of the method of keeping accounts that Venetian merchants used at that time, known as the double-entry accounting system. Although Pacioli codified rather than invented this system, he is widely regarded as the "Father of Accounting". The system he published included most of the accounting cycle as we know it today. He described the use of journals and ledgers, and warned that a person should not go to sleep at night until the debits equalled the credits! His ledger had accounts for assets (including receivables and inventories), liabilities, capital, income, and expenses — the account categories that are reported on an organization's balance sheet and income statement, respectively. He demonstrated year-end closing entries and proposed that a trial balance be used to prove a balanced ledger. His treatise also touches on a wide range of related topics from accounting ethics to cost accounting.

The first known book in the English language on accounting was published in London by John Gouge (or Gough) in 1543. It is described as A Profitable Treatyce called the Instrument or Boke to learn to knowe the good order of the kepyng of the famouse reconynge, called in Latin, Dare and Habere, and, in English, Debitor and Creditor.

A short book of instructions was also published in 1588 by John Mellis of Southwark, in which he says, "I am but the renuer and reviver of an ancient old copie printed here in London the 14 of August 1543: collected, published, made, and set forth by one Hugh Oldcastle, Scholemaster, who, as appeareth by his treatise, then taught Arithmetics, and this booke in Saint Ollaves parish in Marko Lane." John Mellis refers to the fact that the principle of accounts he explains (which is a simple system of double entry) is "after the forme of Venice".

A book described as The Merchants Mirrour, or directions for the perfect ordering and keeping of his accounts formed by way of Debitor and Creditor, after the (so termed) Italian manner, by Richard Dafforne, accountant, published in 1635, contains many references to early books on the science of accountancy. In a chapter in this book, headed "Opinion of Book-keeping's Antiquity," the author states, on the authority of another writer, that the form of book-keeping referred to had then been in use in Italy about two hundred years, "but that the same, or one in many parts very like this, was used in the time of Julius Caesar, and in Rome long before."

An early Dutch writer appears to have suggested that double-entry book-keeping was even in existence among the Greeks, pointing to scientific accountancy having been invented in remote times.

There were several editions of Richard Dafforne's book - the second edition in 1636, the third in 1656, and another in 1684. The book is a very complete treatise on scientific accountancy, beautifully prepared and containing elaborate explanations. The numerous editions tend to prove that the science was highly appreciated in the 17th century. From this time on, there has been a continuous supply of literature on the subject, many of the authors styling themselves accountants and teachers of the art, and thus proving that the professional accountant was then known and employed.

The requirements for entry in the profession of accounting vary from country to country. Accountants may be licensed by a variety of organisations, such as the British qualified accountancy bodies including Association of Chartered Certified Accountants (ACCA) and Institute of Chartered Accountants, and are recognized by titles such as Chartered Certified Accountant (ACCA or FCCA) and Chartered Accountant (UK, Australia, New Zealand, Canada, India, Pakistan, South Africa), Certified Public Accountant (Ireland, Japan, US, Singapore, Hong Kong, the Philippines), Certified Management Accountant (Canada, U.S.), Certified General Accountant (Canada), or Certified Practising Accountant (Australia). Some Commonwealth countries (Australia and Canada) often recognise both the certified and chartered accounting bodies. The majority of "public" accountants in New Zealand and Canada are Chartered Accountants; however, Certified General Accountants are also authorized by legislation to practise public accounting and auditing in all Canadian provinces, except Ontario and Quebec, as of 2005. There is, however, no legal requirement for an accountant to be a paid-up member of one of the many Institutes and other bodies which are effectively a form of professional trade union. Unlike the Law Society, which can legally stop a solicitor from practising, accountancy institutes do not have such authority. However, auditors are regulated.

Before the Enron and other accounting scandals, there were five large firms and were called the Big Five. Since Arthur Andersen's assurance practice split (after the firm was found guilty in the Enron scandal), with a plurality joining KPMG in the US and Deloitte and Touche outside of the US, Arthur Andersen left from the group. Previous to this there were also groupings referred to as the "Big Six" (Arthur Andersen, plus Coopers and Lybrand before its merger with Price Waterhouse) and the "Big Eight" (Ernst and Young prior to their merger were Ernst and Whinney and Arthur Young and Deloitte and Touche was formed by the merger of Deloitte, Haskins and Sells with the firm Touche Ross).

Enron turned out to be only the first of a series of accounting scandals that enveloped the accounting industry in 2002.

This is likely to have far-reaching consequences for the U.S. accounting industry. Application of International Accounting Standards originating in International Accounting Standards Board headquartered in London and bearing more resemblance to UK than current US practices is often advocated by those who note the relative stability of the UK accounting system (which reformed itself after scandals in the late 1980s and early 1990s). Accounting reform of a far more comprehensive sort is advocated by those who see issues with capitalism or economics, and seek ecological or social accountability.

According to Accountancy Age's 2005 league table, fee income amongst the Top 50 accounting firms in the UK rose from £6.3bn to £7.0bn. This followed two successive years in which fee income had declined, largely a result of the sale by some of the larger firms of their consultancy arms. As detailed in the next section, fee income in most business areas - audit, tax, corporate finance and consultancy - rose in the 2005 survey, with insolvency and wealth management being the only segments where revenue fell.

PricewaterhouseCoopers remains the largest firm with fee income totalling £1,780m followed by Deloitte (£1,350m), KPMG (£1,066m) and Ernst and Young (£945m).

The combined revenue of the Big Four accounted for £5.0bn, 72 per cent of the fee income of the Top 50, down from 78-79 per cent in the years up to the 2002 survey and the third year in succession a decline in their share has occurred (Chart 1). Ernst and Young's fee income is the smallest of the largest four firms, but still over three times that of the next largest firm, Grant Thornton. The amount of fee income tapers off amongst the mid-tier firms so that in total there were only 25 firms that each generated more than £15m of revenue in the 2005 survey.

For more details regarding British qualified accountancy professionals, please refer to the page of British qualified accountants.

MANAGEMENT ACCOUNTING

Management accounting is concerned with the provisions and use of accounting information to managers within organizations, to provide them with the basis in making informed business decisions that would allow them to be better equipped in their management and control functions. Unlike financial accountancy information (which, for the most part, is public information), management accounting information is used within an organization (typically for decision-making) and is usually confidential and access to which is only available to a select few.

According to CIMA, The Chartered Institute of Management Accountants, Management Accounting is "the process of identification, measurement, accumulation, analysis, preparation, interpretation and communication of information used by management to plan, evaluate and control within an entity and to assure appropriate use of and accountability for its resources. Management accounting also comprises the preparation of financial reports for non- management groups such as shareholders, creditors, regulatory agencies and tax authorities" (CIMA Official Terminology)

AIMS

1. Formulating strategies;
2. Planning and constructing business activities;
3. Making decisions;
4. Well use of resources;
5. Supporting financial reports preparation; and
6. Safeguarding assets.

In the late 1980s, accounting practitioners and educators were heavily criticized on the grounds that management accounting practices (and, even more so, the curriculum taught to accounting students) had changed little over the preceding 60 years, despite radical changes in the business environment. Professional accounting institutes, perhaps fearing that management accountants would increasingly be seen as superfluous in business organizations, subsequently devoted considerable resources to the development of a more innovative skills set for management accountants.

The distinction between 'traditional' and 'innovative' management accounting practices can be illustrated by reference to cost control techniques. Traditionally, management accountants' principal technique was variance analysis, which is a systematic approach to the comparison of the actual and budgeted costs of the raw materials and labour used during a production period.

While some form of variance analysis is still used by most manufacturing firms, it nowadays tends to be used in conjunction with innovative techniques such as life cycle cost analysis and activity-based costing, which are designed with specific aspects of the modern business environment in mind. Lifecycle costing recognizes that managers' ability to influence the cost of manufacturing a product is at its greatest when the product is still at the design stage of its product lifecycle (*i.e.*, before the design has been finalised and production commenced), since small changes to the product design may lead to significant savings in the cost of manufacturing the product. Activity-based costing (ABC) recognizes that, in modern factories, most manufacturing costs are determined by the amount of 'activities' (*e.g.*, the number of production runs per month, and the amount of production equipment idle time) and that the key to effective cost control is therefore optimizing the efficiency of these activities. Activity-based accounting is also known as Cause and Effect accounting.

Both lifecycle costing and activity-based costing recognize that, in the typical modern factory, the avoidance of disruptive events (such as machine breakdowns and quality control failures) is of far greater importance than (for example) reducing the costs of raw materials. Activity-based costing also deemphasizes direct labour as a cost driver and concentrates instead on acitivities that drive costs, such as the provision of a service or the production of a product component.

The most significant recent direction in managerial accounting is throughput accounting, which recognizes the interdependencies of modern production processes and provide managers with a tool that will allow them to measure the contribution per unit of constrained resource for any given product, customer or supplier. (For a detailed description of Throughput Accounting.)

A seldom expressed alternative view of management accounting is that it is neither a neutral or benign influence in organizations, rather a mechanism for management control through surveillance. This view locates management accounting specifically in the context of management control theory.

There are several related professional qualifications in the field of accountancy including:

- Management Accountancy Qualifications
  - CIMA— CMA
  - Institute of Cost and Works Accountants of India
  - AAFM
- Other Professional Accountancy Qualifications
  - Chartered Certified Accountant, (ACCA)
  - Chartered Accountant, (CA)
  - Certified Public Accountant, (CPA)

Accounting Management (Business) is the practical application of management techniques to control and report on the financial health of the organization. This involves the analysis, planning, implementation, and control of programmes designed to provide financial data reporting for managerial decision making. This includes the maintenance of bank accounts, developing financial statements, cash flow and financial performance analysis. Accounting management is a mandatory knowledge module of any MBA programme.

Accounting is often referred to as billing management. The goal is to gather usage statistics for users.

Using the statistics the users can be billed and usage quota can be enforced.

Examples:

- Disk usage
- Link utilisation
- CPU time

For non-billed networks, 'Administration' replaces 'Accounting'. The goals of Administration is to administer the set of authorized users, by establishing users, passwords and permissions; and to administer the operations of the equipment such as by performing software backup and synchronization.

Activity-based Costing

Activity-based costing (ABC) is a method of allocating costs to products and services. It is generally used as a tool for planning and control. This is a necessary tool for doing value chain analysis.

The concepts of ABC were developed in the manufacturing sector of the U.S. during the 1970s and 80s. During this time, the Consortium for Advanced Manufacturing-International, now known simply as CAM-I, provided a formative role for studying and formalizing the principles that have become more formally known as Activity-Based Costing.

Robin Cooper and Robert Kaplan, proponent of the Balanced Scorecard, brought notice to these concepts in a number of articles published in Harvard Business Review beginning in 1988. Cooper and Kaplan described ABC as an approach to solve the problems of traditional cost management systems. These traditional costing systems are often unable to determine accurately the actual costs of production and of the costs of related services. Consequently managers were making decisions based on inaccurate data especially where there are multiple products.

Instead of using broad arbitrary percentages to allocate costs, ABC seeks to identify cause and effect relationships to objectively assign costs. Once costs of the activities have been identified, the cost of each activity is attributed to each product to the extent that the product uses the activity. In this way ABC often identifies areas of high overhead costs per unit and so directs attention to finding ways to reduce the costs or to charge more for costly products.

Activity-based costing was first clearly defined in 1987 by Robert S. Kaplan and W. Bruns as a chapter in their book Accounting and Management. They initially focused on manufacturing industry where increasing technology and productivity improvements have reduced the relative proportion of the direct costs of labour and materials, but have increased relative proportion of indirect costs. For example increased automation has reduced labour, which is a direct cost, but has increased depreciation, which is an indirect cost.

Traditionally cost accountants had arbitrarily added a broad percentage onto the direct costs to allow for the indirect costs. However as the percentages of overhead costs had risen, this technique became increasingly inaccurate because the indirect costs were not caused equally by all the products. For example one product might take more time in one expensive machine than another product, but since the amount of direct labour and materials might be the same, the additional cost for the use of the machine would not be recognised when the same broad 'on-cost' percentage is added to all products. Consequently, when multiple products share common costs, there is a danger of one product subsidising another.

Like manufacturing industries, financial institutions also have diverse products which can cause cross-product subsidies. Since personnel expenses represent the largest single component of non-interest expense in financial institutions, these costs must also be attributed more accurately to products and customers. Activity based costing, even though developed for manufacturing, can therefore be a useful tool for doing this. This extended use of ABC to financial institutions was presented in 1990 in an article appearing in the Journal of Bank Cost and Management Accounting (Volume 3, Number 2) by Richard Sapp, David Crawford and Steven Rebishcke.

Direct labour and materials are relatively easy to trace directly to products, but it is more difficult to directly allocate indirect costs to products. Where products use common resources differently, some sort of weighting is needed in the cost allocation process. The measure of the use of a shared activity by each of the products is known as the cost driver. For example, the cost of the activity of bank tellers can be ascribed to each product by measuring how long each product's transactions takes at the counter and then by measuring the number of each type of transaction.

Even in activity-based costing, some overhead costs are difficult to assign to products and customers, for example the chief executive's salary. These costs are termed 'business sustaining' and are not assigned to products and customers because there is no meaningful method. This lump of unallocated overhead costs must nevertheless be met by contributions from each of the products, but it is not as large as the overhead costs before ABC is employed.

Although some may argue that costs untraceable to activities should be "arbitrarily allocated" to products, it is important to realize that the only purpose of ABC is to provide information to management. Therefore, there is no reason to assign any cost in an arbitrary manner. Management accountants can be creative in finding other ways to represent these costs on internal reporting statements.

Budgeting

Budget generally refers to a list of all planned expenses and revenues. A budget is an important concept in microeconomics, which uses a budget line to illustrate the trade-offs between two or more goods.

A personal budget is among the most important concepts of personal finance. In a personal or family budget all sources of income (inflows) are identified and expenses (outflows) are planned with the intent of matching outflows to inflows (Making ends meet).

There are a wide variety of personal budgeting methods and tools that can be employed to help individuals and families with the budgeting process. Also the level of planned finance available to a person, corporation or government, as set by a certain person.

The budget of a government is a summary or plan of the intended revenues and expenditures of that government. In the United States, the federal budget is prepared by the Office of Management and Budget, and submitted to Congress for consideration. Invariably, Congress makes many and substantial changes.

Nearly all American states are required to have balanced budgets, but the federal government is allowed to run deficits. In the UK the budget is prepared by the Chancellor of the Exchequer, the second most important member of the government, and must be passed by Parliament. The Parliament seldom makes changes to the budget.

The budget of a company is compiled annually. A finished budget usually requires considerable effort and can be seen as a financial plan for the new financial year. While traditionally the Finance department compiles the company's budget, modern software allows hundreds or even thousands of people in the various departments (operations, human resources, IT etc) to contribute their expected revenues and expenses to the final budget.

If the actual numbers delivered through the financial year turn out to be close to the budget, this will demonstrate that the company understands their business and has been successfully driving it in the direction they had planned. On the other hand, if the actuals diverge wildly from the budget, this sends out an 'out of control' signal and the share

Cost-plus pricing is a pricing method commonly used by firms. It is used primarily because it is easy to calculate and requires little information. There are several varieties, but the common thread in all of them is that you first calculate the cost of the product, then include an additional amount to represent profit.

Cost-plus pricing is often used on government contracts, and has been criticized as promoting wasteful expenditures.

Calculating Price Using the Cost-plus Method

There are several ways of determining cost, and the profit can be added as either a percentage markup or an absolute amount. One example is:

P = (AVC + FC%) * (1 + MK%)

where:

- P = price
- AVC = average variable cost
- FC% = percentage allocation of fixed costs
- MK% = percentage markup

For example: If variable costs are 30 yen, the allocation to cover fixed costs is 10 yen, and you feel you need a 50 per cent markup then you would charge a price of 60 yen:

P = (30 + 10) · (1 + 0.50)

P = 40 · 1.5

P = 60

An alternative way of doing a similar calculation is:

P = (AVC + FC%)/ (1 " MK%)

To make things simpler, some firms, particularly retailers, ignore fixed costs and just use the purchase price paid to their suppliers as the cost term. They indirectly incorporate the fixed cost allocation into the markup percentage. To simplify things even further, sometimes a fixed amount is applied rather than a percentage. This fixed amount is usually determined by head-office to make it easy for franchisees and store managers. This is sometimes referred to as turnkey pricing.

Another variant of cost plus pricing is activity based pricing. This involves being more careful in determining costs. Instead of using arbitrary expense categories when allocating overhead, every activity is linked to the resources it uses.

Cost will need to be recalculated and the percentage markup will likely need to be adjusted as the product goes through its life cycle. This is sometimes referred to as product life cycle pricing, although it is seldom done deliberately or in a planned and organized manner. Price skimming and penetration pricing are also types of product life cycle pricing but they are demand based pricing methods rather cost based.

Advantages of Cost-plus Pricing

1. Easy to calculate
2. Minimal information requirements
3. Easy to administer
4. Tends to stabilize markets - insulated from demand variations and competitive factors
5. Insures seller against unpredictable, or unexpected later costs
6. Ethical advantages

Disadvantages

1. Tends to ignore the role of consumers
2. Tends to ignore the role of competitors
3. Use of historical accounting costs rather than replacement value
4. Use of "normal" or "standard" output level to allocate fixed costs
5. Inclusion of sunk costs rather than just using incremental costs
6. Ignores opportunity costs
7. Contractors may not focus on performance because the cost is always covered by the client

In microeconomics, Production is simply the conversion of inputs into outputs. It is an economic process that uses resources to create a commodity that is suitable for exchange.

This can include manufacturing, storing, shipping, and packaging. Some economists define production broadly as all economic activity other than consumption. They see every commercial activity other than the final purchase as some form of production. Production is a process, and as such it occurs through time and space. Because it is a flow concept, production is measured as a "rate of output per period of time". There are three aspects to production processes:

1. The quantity of the commodity produced,
2. The form of the good produced,
3. The temporal and spatial distribution of the commodity produced.

A production process can be defined as any activity that increases the similarity between the pattern of demand for goods, and the quantity, form, and distribution of these goods available to the market place.

A production process is efficient if a given quantity of outputs cannot be produced with any less inputs. It is said to be inefficient when there exists another feasible process that, for any given output, uses less inputs. Some economists (in particular Leibenstein) use the term X-efficiency to indicate that production processes tend to be inherently inefficient due to satisficing behaviour. The "rate of efficiency" is simply the amount of (or value of) outputs divided by the amount of (or value of) inputs. If a production process uses 50 units of input (or $5000 worth of inputs) to produce one unit of output it is more efficient than a process that uses 55 units of input (or $5500 worth of inputs) to produce the same level of output. It is said to be 10 per cent more efficient ({55-50}/50=1/10=10 per cent).

The inputs or resources used in the production process are called factors by economists. The myriad of possible inputs are usually grouped into four or five categories. These factors are:

- Raw materials (natural capital)
- Labour services (human capital)
- Capital goods
- Land

Sometimes a fifth category is added, entrepreneurial and management skills, a subcategory of labour services. Capital goods are those goods that have previously undergone a production process. They are previously produced means of production. Some textbooks use "technology" as a factor of production.

In the "long run" all of these factors of production can be adjusted by management. The "short run" however, is defined as a period in which at least one of the factors of production is fixed. A fixed factor of production is one whose quantity cannot readily be changed. Examples include major pieces of equipment, suitable factory space, and key managerial personnel. A variable factor of production is one whose usage rate can be changed easily. Examples include electrical power consumption, transportation services, and most raw material inputs. In the short run, a firm's "scale of operations" determines the maximum number of outputs that can be produced. In the long run, there are no scale limitations.

The total product (or total physical product) of a variable factor of production identifies what outputs are possible using various levels of the variable input. This can be displayed in either a chart that lists the output level corresponding to various levels of input, or a graph that summarizes the data into a "total product curve". The diagram shows a typical total product curve. In this example, output increases as more inputs are employed up until point A. The maximum output possible with this production process is Qm. If there are other inputs used in the process, they are assumed to be fixed.

The average physical product is the total product divided by the number of units of variable input employed. It is the output of each unit of input. If there are 10 employees working on a production process that manufactures 50 units per day, then the average product of variable labour input is 5 units per day.

The average product typically varies as more of the input is employed, so this relationship can also be expresses as a chart or as a graph. A typical average physical product curve is shown (APP). It can be obtained by drawing a vector from the origin to various points on the total product curve and plotting the slopes of these vectors.

The marginal physical product of a variable input is the change in total output due to a one unit change in the variable input (called the discrete marginal product) or alternatively the rate of change in total output due to an infinitesimally small change in the variable input (called the continuous marginal product). The discrete marginal product of capital is the additional output resulting from the use of an additional unit of capital (assuming all other factors are fixed). The continuous marginal product of a variable input can be calculated as the derivative of quantity produced with respect to variable input employed. The marginal physical product curve is shown (MPP). It can be obtained from the slope of the total product curve.

Because the marginal product drives changes in the average product, we know that when the average physical product is falling, the marginal physical product must be less than the average. Likewise, when the average physical product is rising, it must be due to a marginal physical product greater than the average. For this reason, the marginal physical product curve must intersect the maximum point on the average physical product curve.

MPP keeps increasing till it reaches its maximum. Up until this point every additional unit has been adding more value to the total product than the previous one. From this point onwards, every additional unit adds less to the total product compared to the previous one. But the average product is still increasing till MPP touches APP. At this point, an additional unit is adding the same value as the average product. From this point onwards, MPP starts to reduce and so does APP because every additional unit is adding less to APP than the average product. But the total product is still increasing because every additional unit is still contributing positively. Therefore, during this period, both, the average as well as marginal products, are decreasing, but the total product is still increasing. Finally we reach a point when MPP crosses the x-axis. At this point every additional unit starts to diminish the product of previous units, possibly by getting into their way. Therefore the total product starts to decrease at this point. This is point A on the total product curve.

Diminishing returns can be divided into three categories: 1. Diminishing Total returns, which implies reduction in total product with every additional unit of input. This occurs after point A in the graph. 2. Diminishing Average returns, which refers to the portion of the APP curve after its intersection with MPP curve. 3. Diminishing Marginal returns, refers to the point where the MPP curve starts to slope down and travels all the way down to the x-axis and beyond. Putting it in a chronological order, at first the marginal returns start to diminish, then the average returns, followed finally by the total returns.

These curves illustrate the principle of diminishing marginal returns to a variable input (not to be confused with diseconomies of scale which is a long term phenomenon in which all factors are allowed to change). This states that as you add more and more of a variable input, you will reach a point beyond which the resulting increase in output starts to diminish. This point is illustrated as the maximum point on the marginal physical product curve. It assumes that other factor inputs (if they are used in the process) are held constant. An example is the employment of labour in the use of trucks to transport goods. Assuming the number of available trucks (capital) is fixed, then the amount of the variable input labour could be varied and the resultant efficiency determined. At least one labourer (the driver) is necessary. Additional workers per vehicle could be productive in loading, unloading, navigation, or around the clock continuous driving. But at some point the returns to investment in labour will start to diminish and efficiency will decrease. The most efficient distribution of labour per piece of equipment will likely be one driver plus an additional worker for other tasks (2 workers per truck would be more efficient than 5 per truck).

Resource allocations and distributive efficiencies in the mix of capital and labour investment will vary per industry and according to available technology. Trains are able to transport much more in the way of goods with fewer "drivers" but at the cost of greater investment in infrastructure. With the advent of mass production of motorized vehicles, the economic niche occupied by trains (compared with transport trucks) has become more specialized and limited to long haul delivery.

There is an argument that if the theory is holding everything constant, the production method should not be changed, *i.e.*, division of labour should not be practiced. However, the rise in marginal product means that the workers use other means of production method, such as in loading, unloading, navigation, or around the clock continuous driving. For this reason, some economists think that the “keeping other things constant” should not be used in this theory. The total, average, and marginal physical product curves mentioned above are just one way of showing production relationships. They express the quantity of output relative to the amount of variable input employed while holding fixed inputs constant. Because they depict a short run relationship, they are sometimes called short run production functions. If all inputs are allowed to be varied, then the diagram would express outputs relative to total inputs, and the function would be a long run production function. If the mix of inputs is held constant, then output would be expressed relative to inputs of a fixed composition, and the function would indicate long run economies of scale.

Rather than comparing inputs to outputs, it is also possible to assess the mix of inputs employed in production. An isoquant relates the quantities of one input to the quantities of another input. It indicates all possible combinations of inputs that are capable of producing a given level of output.

Rather than looking at the inputs used in production, it is possible to look at the mix of outputs that are possible for any given production process. This is done with a production possibilities frontier. It indicates what combinations of outputs are possible given the available factor endowment and the prevailing production technology.

You can use a lot of labour with a minimal amount of capital, or you could invest heavily in capital equipment that requires a minimal amount of labour to operate, or any combination in between. For most goods, there are more than just two inputs. For example in agriculture, the amount of land, water, and fertilizer can all be varied to produce different amounts of a crop. An isoquant, in the two input case, is a curve that shows all the ways of combining two inputs so as to produce a given level of output. In the three input case it will be a surface. Iso is Latin for equal and quant is short for quantity. Movement along an isoquant depicts a constant rate of output, but a changing input ratio. A unique isoquant can be constructed for every level of output, and a family of isoquants can be created to represent various output levels. Isoquants further from the origin represent greater amounts of output. Isoquants are usually considered to be everywhere dense, meaning an infinite number of them could be plotted in any two input space.

A typical isoquant is illustrated in the diagram to the right. At point A in the diagram Ka units of capital are combined with La units of labour to produce 100 units of output. It is downward sloping, convex to the origin, and non-intersecting (additional isoquants, not shown, would be drawn parallel to this one). A complete isoquant is actually a closed curve, but only the “down sloping to the right” portion makes economic sense. The upward sloping parts of isoquants, for example, indicate that that level of output could be produced by less of both inputs so this section is of little interest to decision makers. The economic section of the isoquants is defined by a pair of lines called ridge lines.

The "downward to the right" slope of the economic region of an isoquant is due to the possibility of substituting one input for another in the production process while keeping the level of output constant.

Isoquants are typically convex to the origin reflecting the fact that the two factors are substitutable for each other at varying rates. This rate of substitutability is called the "marginal rate of technical substitution" (MRTS) or occasionally the "marginal rate of substitution in production".

It measures the reduction in one input per unit increase in the other input that is just sufficient to maintain a constant level of production. For example, the marginal rate of substitution of labour for capital gives the amount of capital that can be replaced by one unit of labour while keeping output unchanged.

To move from point A to point B in the diagram, the amount of capital is reduced from Ka to Kb while the amount of labour is increased only from La to Lb. To move from point C to point D, the amount of capital is reduced from Kc to Kd while the amount of labour is increased from La to Lb. The marginal rate of technical substitution of labour for capital is equivalent to the absolute slope of the isoquant at that point (change in capital divided by change in labour). It is equal to 0 where the isoquant becomes horizontal, and equal to infinity where it becomes vertical.

The opposite is true when going in the other direction. In this case we are looking at the marginal rate of technical substitution capital for labour (which is the reciprocal of the marginal rate of technical substitution labour for capital).

It can also be shown that the marginal rate of substitution labour for capital, is equal to the marginal physical product of labour divided by the marginal physical product of capital.

In the unusual case of two inputs that are perfect substitutes for each other in production, the isoquant would be linear (linear, a straight line, with a function $y = a - bx$). If, on the other hand, there is only one production process available, factor proportions would be fixed, and these zero-substitutability isoquants would be shown as horizontal or vertical lines.

Fixed assets management

Fixed assets management is an accounting process that seeks to track fixed assets for the purposes of financial accounting, preventive maintenance, and theft deterrence.

Many organizations face a significant challenge to track the location, quantity, condition, maintenance and depreciation status of their fixed assets. A popular approach to tracking fixed assets utilizes serial numbered Asset Tags, often with bar codes for easy and accurate reading. Periodically, the owner of the assets can take inventory with a mobile barcode reader and then produce a report.

Off-the-shelf software packages for fixed asset management are marketed to businesses small and large. Some Enterprise Resource Planning systems are available with fixed assets modules.

Free cash flow

Free cash flow measures a firm's net increase in

- Cash from operations (this includes the reduction for interest),
- Less the dividends paid to preferred shareholders, and
- Less expenditures necessary to maintain assets.

Increases in non-cash current assets may, or may not be deducted, depending on whether they are considered to be maintaining the status quo, or to be investments for growth.

Problems with CapX

1. The expenditures for maintenance of assets is only part of the capx reported on the Statement of Cash Flows. It must be separated from the expenditures for growth purposes. This split is not a requirement under GAAP, and is not audited. Management is free to disclose maintenance capx or not. Therefore this input to the calculation of free cash flow is easy to manipulate. Since it is a very large number, maintenance capx's questionable validity is the basis for some people's dismissal of 'free cash flow'.
2. A second problem with the maintenance capx measurement is its intrinsic 'lumpyness'. By their nature, expenditures for capital assets that will last decades are infrequent, but costly when they occur. 'Free cash flow', in turn, will be very different from year to year. No particular year will be a 'norm' that can be expected to be repeated.

Uses of the Metric

1. Free cash flow measures the ease with which businesses can grow and pay dividends to shareholders. Even profitable businesses may have negative cash flows. Their requirement for increased financing will result in increased financing costs reducing future income. It is easier to grow with organic cash flows than with additional financing.
2. According to the discounted cash flow valuation model, the intrinsic value of a company is the present value of all future free cash flows, plus the cash proceeds from its eventual sale. The presumption is that the cash flows are used to pay dividends to the shareholders. Bear in mind the lumpyness discussed above.
3. Some investors prefer using free cash flow instead of net income to measure a company's financial performance, because free cash flow

is more difficult to manipulate than net income. The problems with this presumption are itemized at cash flow and return of capital.

4. The payout ratio is a metric used to evaluate the sustainability of distributions from REITs, Oil and Gas Royalty Trusts, and Income Trust. The distributions are divided by the free cash flow. Distributions may include any of income, flowed-through capital gains or return of capital.

This metric is used only by shareholders. Debt holders are not concerned with maintaining the operating capital assets, or with growing the business. Nor are they concerned with taxes paid since their payments come first. The appropriate metric for debt holders is EBITDA.

7

Hospitality Maintenance and Engineering

ESTABLISHING THE COLLECTIVE MODEL

Interest in employment, now the preserve of many individuals, but not all, in western economies, derives from the fact that'Work dominates the lives of men and women ... the management of employees both individually and collectively remains a central feature of organisational life'. Before beginning an examination of employment relations in the HI, it is useful to outline the historical development of employment relations and their relevance as a field of study, thereby introducing the reader to some of the key terms used throughout the book.

Hyman academic interest in employment relations was prompted when the potential stability of social order was put under threat by militant behaviour among a growing number of unionized industrial manual workers, who were no longer prepared to tolerate very bad terms and conditions of employment. This challenge to social order, which began in the late nineteenth century, was met by two responses. First, the social welfare reformers, in keeping with their predecessors who had successfully campaigned for health and safety legislation earlier in the nineteenth century, urged legal intervention to improve the conditions under which work was performed and the terms under which it was undertaken.

They achieved limited success, notably the introduction of minimum wages in four manufacturing industries in 1906. The second and main response, which was to characterize public policy on employment relations until 1979, was that voluntary collective bargaining provided the best means to secure order within employer-employee relations. Collective bargaining is a process whereby employers and trade unions negotiate the substantive terms and conditions of employment, such as pay and hours of work, and procedural agreements that facilitate the resolution of disputes between the parties.

Industrial relations, the term in usage at the time, focused on the institutions of collective bargaining in fixing these'rules' of employment, largely within male-dominated manufacturing environments. Collective agreements were not legally enforceable. While public services such as the health service, the railways and the coal mines came to assume importance in industrial relations following the mass nationalization programme after the Second World War, private services remained the'Cinderella' of British industrial relations. Even though the growth of private services such as retailing and hospitality opened up more employment opportunities for women, whose main work opportunities had been in domestic service in the earlier part of the century, unregulated, female service work was deemed not to be part of industrial relations.

Even so, the lack of collective bargaining arrangements prompted the Labour government to extend the scope of minimum wage legislation to embrace these sectors. Thus in 1945 the newly named wages councils, a form of'state-sponsored' collective bargaining, were able to fix remuneration and paid holidays for many'unprotected' workers in private services.

COLLECTIVE CONSENSUS AND A MORE ACTIVE STATE

Greater state intervention in employment matters was a response by both Conservative and Labour governments to the mounting economic difficulties of the 1960s, *e.g.* statutory and voluntary incomes policies. State intervention also constituted a response to the perceived failure of voluntary collective bargaining to provide an effective regulatory mechanism for social order and social welfare, notably to protect the interests of the low-paid, many of whom were women. This perceived breakdown prompted the government to appoint a Royal Commission in 1965, the Donovan Commission, to investigate the state of employer-worker relations, in order to recommend how the'system' could be reformed.

The Donovan prescription sought to maintain voluntarism, and placed the onus on employers to improve the rules of employment, and to introduce more formal procedures for the resolution of disputes. Donovan's prescription was not universal, because it could not be applied to large parts of private services comprising small, informally managed, non-union workplaces, where female and part-time employment was concentrated. A different approach based on legal intervention in employment relations began to develop, based on employment protection for individual employees. Early employment protection rights of the 1960s included the right to a written statement of terms and conditions of employment, statutory redundancy pay and equal pay. Workers lacking the protection of a trade union and with no recourse to formal workplace procedures could resolve an employment dispute, which is those in scope of the law, by going to an industrial tribunal.

The 1970s represented a significant turning point for legal intervention in employment relations. Britain joined the European Economic Community in

1972. This heralded the start of a wide-ranging programme designed to establish a floor of new rights relating to matters including unfair dismissal, maternity leave, sex and race discrimination and health and safety at work. The main beneficiaries were to be those working in private services. Events of the 1980s and early 1990s effectively killed the model of voluntary collective bargaining. In pursuit of an overriding objective to deregulate the labour market and employment, successive Conservative governments systematically dismantled institutions deemed to interfere with the free working of the labour market, notably the trade unions and wages councils.

Paradoxically, in spite of the government's antipathy to the EU's social action programme and subsequent opt out of the social chapter, the EU continued to influence British employment relations in a significant way. Rulings from the European Court of Justice obliged Britain to introduce new legislation, *e.g.* the transfer of undertakings or the amendment of existing legislation relating to equal pay and sex discrimination.

The floor of employment rights was both strengthened and extended. Managers reasserted the right to manage increasingly flexible and non-standard workers under the banner of'managerialism', in workplaces that might be labelled'bleak houses'. An alternative version of management thinking stressed the benefits of'commitment' over'control'. Both approaches came to signify the two variants of HRM.'Soft' HRM emphasized fostering commitment, improving quality and developing the human resource, whereas'hard' HRM was contingent and calculating in its utilization of the human resource.

If organizations were to survive the effects of adverse economic conditions, globalization and increasing competition, the imperative was to integrate HRM within business strategy. The impact of HRM on industrial relations was widely debated. Other key issues in the wider academic debate included the extent of continuity and change in industrial relations, the sharp decline in trade union membership, the impact of deregulation and whether employment relations could be re-regulated.

NEW LABOUR: NEW HOPE?

By the mid-1990s individual relationships were catapulted firmly to the forefront of analysis of the employment relationship. Recognition of this change had been apparent from WIRS in 1990, perhaps most notably within the HI. HI managers are free to exercise a high degree of managerial prerogative in the absence of unorganized labour, termed'unbridled individualism'.

The election of a Labour government for the first time in nearly 20 years in 1997 raised expectations that there would be a new agenda for employment relations, although Heery's assessment was that'it is extremely doubtful whether New Labour will issue in a new industrial relations'. New Labour's stakeholder economy is based on fairness and partnership. Fairness at work is to be achieved in two ways. The government signed up to the EU social chapter and set about introducing a new floor of minimum employment standards, including a National Minimum Wage, and family-friendly measures. Social partnership between employers and workers is designed to foster a more consensual and cooperative relationship between employers and employees.

The Low Pay Commission whose first task was to recommend the initial rate of the NMW, provides an early manifestation of social partnership comprising employer, worker and independent representatives. Although many of the Conservatives' trade union reforms remain in place, the introduction of statutory trade union recognition procedures might help reverse the steep decline in trade union membership.

By the time of WERS in 1998 the system of collective representation had crumbled'to such an extent that it no longer represented the dominant model'. In reality employment relations could conform to different and diverse patterns. Private service establishments employing 25 or more employees were numerically more important than private sector manufacturing and the public sector put together.

Their share of employment increased from 26 per cent in 1980 to 44 per cent in 1998, reinforcing the point that alternative ways to view and reform employment relations were long overdue, particularly in circumstances of'bleak house' or'black hole' employment. Although we find these terms wanting in respect of the HI, they highlight the relevance of the industry as a unit of analysis. Consequently we shall show how these types of workplaces throw up major problems for employment relations reform.

Agenda for the Twenty-first Century

In calling for a new industrial relations paradigm, Ackers now argues that the new problem of social order focuses on links between employment and society, and that such a link provides an explicit ethical framework for policies like social partnership. He rejects the traditional industrial relations notion of workers as unattached individuals in their out-of-work lives, and argues that industrial relations can no longer ignore issues of work-life balance and corporate social responsibility. Indeed social concerns underpin'Fairness at Work' and the'Welfare to Work' programme, and family-friendly issues are a new addition to WERS.

Hence a new definition of industrial relations as neo-pluralism: Employment relations are the study of the social institutions involved in the normative regulation of the employment relationship and business's interaction with other stakeholders in society. Thus Ackers rejects as inappropriate Kelly's industrial relations paradigm for the twenty-first century, which derives from a redefinition of Marxism based on socialism, workers' mobilization, economic militancy and strikes, and organized labour. Edwards identifies three pressing issues in contemporary employment relations:'high commitment' or'high involvement' work systems, the international context and economic performance.

The first, although interesting, is very rarely found anywhere in Britain. Its alternative of'low skills' and'low wages' strikes right at the heart of much hospitality employment. This links to economic performance, where the absence of collective bargaining is likely to have contributed to income inequality and the perpetuation of low pay in the HI, although pay may be subsidized by the state through social security and taxation. The further subsidy of low pay through tips as a defensible employment practice is a matter of conjecture. We shall also explore if particular employment relations practices can be linked to successful performance outcomes.

The international context and its implications for employment relations in the HI are considered below and in subsequent chapters. A fourth pressing issue can be added. Employment relations discourse needs to recognize that prejudice and bias have been built into much of the theoretical and practical analysis, thus distorting its perspective. Gender is not the only example, but may be the most obvious.

In spite of an increasing interest in what may be described as'women's issues', such as (un)equal pay and employment opportunities, family-friendly policies and sexual harassment, one major barrier to understanding employment relations is an assumption that they are gender neutral. The argument is that adding women's issues to the agenda is simply not good enough. Management, trade unions and the state are not gender neutral, and therefore we need to recognize the gendered characteristics of the employment relationship and work and integrate this into our understanding of the field of employment relations. Other'omissions' include age, ethnicity and the role of customers.

We shall explore these issues throughout the book where it is possible or relevant to do so. All these issues were placed under review in The Future of Work Programme launched by the ESRC in 1998. The Programme has supported 27 projects designed to rectify gaps in our understanding and improve the quality of information available to the policy-makers in the UK. Topics under investigation have included the future of unskilled work, business re-engineering and performance, the changing position of ethnic minorities and women in the labour market, the future for trade unions and the changing nature of the employment relationship.

EMPLOYMENT RELATIONS IN THE HOSPITALITY INDUSTRY

Three terms denote the relations between managers and workers in the employment relationship-industrial relations, employee relations and employment relations. These terms are often used interchangeably, but can also convey subtle differences of meaning. They may coincide with other fields of academic enquiry and practical activity concerned with'people management', namely personnel management and HRM. Edwards provides an insightful analysis of the employment relationship, taking as his starting point the distinction made by Fox and Flanders between market relations and managerial relations. At the root is an economic exchange between capital and labour, in which the price of labour is set as a contract of employment. In this economic exchange between the buyer and seller of labour, the parties do not share equal power resources.

In common law the employer has the right to command and the employee has a duty to obey. The commodity at the heart of the bargain is the worker's labour power. The employer will seek to maximize control over that'labour process' in order to generate a surplus as profit. The employment relationship, as an exchange and in recognition of its broader context, has also been termed the effort-reward bargain:'an economic, social and political relationship, for which employees provide manual and mental labour in return for rewards allotted by employers'. Labour only becomes useful if it can be persuaded by management to work, but this is only the beginning. Workers must demonstrate commitment, continue working to the required standards, and not deviate from those standards.

In other words workers must follow'rules', otherwise management may need to deploy corrective or punitive measures via the disciplinary procedure. Bonamy and May argue that a weakening of employment relationships since the 1970s has given rise to the emergence of employment as a service relationship.

This relationship demands increased recognition of the professional qualities of the'autonomous' worker, which poses problems of incompatibility with an employment contract built upon subordination. Pay is determined by time worked, whilst idle time due to poor organization and absenteeism is reduced.

This is manifested in new forms of employment contract, externalization of employment to agencies and the sub-contracting of activities. Edwards notes that, if we were starting from scratch, 'employment relations' might be the best label.

Employment relations do not rule out all variants within the employment relationship including:

- Trade unions and formal collective bargaining;
- Individually based management/workforce relations conducted informally;
- Managerialism;
- More democratic and highly participative non-union relations;
- Men, women and disadvantaged groups;
- Employees and workers, including atypical workers and the self-employed.

Further:

- Employment relations is the main term used in the WERS sourcebook;
- Industrial tribunals have been renamed employment tribunals;
- The cornerstone of New Labour's industrial relations policy is the Employment Relations Act 1999.

A necessary departure for this book, as noted earlier, is to relocate the nexus of the employment relationship to include a relatively ignored third actor in the employment relationship-the customer. The notion of the customer in the employment relationship has been increasingly incorporated into the sociology of work, but less so in employment relations. Front-line workers, such as receptionists and servers in bars and restaurants, have to serve two'masters': their superior manager and the customer. Individual workers can have a simultaneous and coterminous employment relationship with the organization and the customer.

Organizations in services are best seen as inverted pyramids, with most workers in direct customer contact. Direct service workers engage directly with customers in an exchange that carries both economic and social connotations. Their ability to deliver successfully hinges upon a social relationship with indirect service workers, whose actions are also instrumental to the provision of good customer service, *e.g.* an enjoyable meal or clean bedrooms. Indirect service workers are not in regular customer contact, so customer influence may be more economic than social. Hence, customers cannot be excluded from an analysis of the employment relationship.

An earlier definition has been revised:

- Employee relations in hotels and catering are about the management of employment and work relationships between managers and workers and, sometimes, customers; it also covers contemporary employment and work practices.
- Before exploring the facets of the employment relationship, we need to outline why our attitude towards things influences the way in which we see any given situation, and how it.
- Triplets watch a local football match from adjoining seats, getting an almost identical view of the game. The result is United 5 City 1. One triplet is deliriously happy, the second feels very low, while the third is able to provide a balanced analysis of events, conceding that the result was a fair one, although two of United's goals were the result of dubious refereeing and City deserved more than a single goal.
- Why did their particular attitude affect their view of the game?

Fox proposed two frames of reference as a means by which'the problems of industrial relations can be seen realistically and laid more open to solution'. The unitary perspective is a'management ideology' built on the belief that everyone in the organization shares the same goals, and that'conflict' is pathological and derives from deviance. Trade unions are seen as an intrusion, competing with management for worker loyalty.

Fox's main argument was that the unitary perspective was a naive and unrealistic frame of reference that might'distort reality and thereby prejudice solutions'. Yet in reality many managers do perceive their organizations in unitary terms, regarding themselves as the sole source of authority. Unitarism has underpinned the'human relations school' of management, including Mayo, Likert, McGregor, Schein and Herzberg, and reasserted itself in'managerialism' and HRM. Fox suggested that the more realistic approach to managing people was to recognize that organizations are pluralistic, comprising various groups, each with their own basis of authority and sets of interests.

The'rules' of employment are not just the preserve of management. A new pay rate set by management will not necessarily be seen as fair by workers, creating an issue of potential dispute. Therefore conflict or differences between individuals and groups are inevitable.

Management should recognize this inevitability, and find the ways and means to regulate such differences. An institutional approach-collective bargaining between employers and trade unions, and the development of formal procedures to deal with disputes about pay, grievances and discipline-was considered to be the most appropriate solution. However, this is flawed to the extent that it implies both parties to the bargain have equal power resources at their disposal.

Later Fox revised his thinking and added a third perspective of radicalism, prompted by a wave of'shop floor' discontent and'wildcat' strikes at workplace level. Such worker behaviour was perceived as a reaction against exploitative and oppressive employers whose sole aim was to maximize profit. Conflict was caused by the economic disparity of society as a whole, with the principal disparity between capital and labour-employers who own and manage the means of production and workers who have their capital to sell.

This view underpins the labour process approach. This approach stresses the contradiction of managerial goals, with regulation and control having to be balanced by the need to gain workers' consent. Even today Edwards argues that unitarism cannot be written off as naive and outdated any more than radicalism because of the apparent disappearance of discontent. Ackers' neo-pluralism refocuses the employment relationship beyond the workplace by connecting the old pluralist and voluntary frames of reference with new questions raised by contemporary society.

The health of society is put first, encouraging industrial relations policy initiatives that are driven by social concerns, not just a business agenda. Further he argues that the employment relationship bears hidden ethical considerations of trust and responsibility in relation to human beings.

As we shall show, both managers and workers in a variety of work and employment situations in the HI do see their workplaces in unitary terms, but this does not necessarily infer the absence of conflict. Areas of potential dispute, conflict and difference do exist between managers and workers, between managers and other managers, and between workers and customers, demonstrating that workplaces are pluralistic. In cases where workers'fiddle' or'pilfer' from their employer, the nature of their behaviour is more in keeping with a radical perspective.

Thus it is possible to observe facets of unitarism, pluralism and radicalism in the same employment relationship in which management, for the most part, remains the more powerful. Even so, areas of common interest self-evidently exist otherwise all these relationships would break down. Consent provides the basis for resolving conflict and achieving cooperation. Cooperation is built on trust between individuals engendered at workplace level rather than through elaborate organizational mechanisms. Yet securing workers' consent is neither a straightforward nor certain process. Therefore, a mix of overt and covert conflict and cooperation underpins all employment relationships and, as we shall argue, workplace harmony owes more to pragmatic acceptance and accommodation among the parties in the employment relationship than to ideological belief.

THE RULES OF EMPLOYMENT AND POWER RELATIONS

We have already noted that the employment relationship is underpinned by rules, hence the continuing validity of Clegg's definition of industrial relations as'The study of the rules governing employment' which Edwards explains in more detail: This does not limit the subject to the collective relations between managements and trade unions, for a rule can derive from other sources, and there are rules governing non-union groups; nor does it restrict analysis to one sector, for it covers all paid forms of employment. A rule is a social institution involving two or more parties which may have its basis in law, a written collective agreement, an unwritten agreement, a unilateral decree or merely an understanding that has the force of custom. In non-union settings, as much as union ones, rules determine rates of pay, hours of work, job descriptions and many other aspects of employment. The subject is about the ways in which the employment relationship is regulated. To regulate means to control, to adapt or adjust continuously or to adjust by rule.

MANAGERIAL ISSUES

While rules may be the substantive rules of employment, *e.g.* pay and conditions of employment, implicit in the notion of rules affecting people is the concept of behaviour. Management's job is to control and direct workers' behaviour to perform work to the desired standards, and thereby ensure that the rules of employment are adhered to.

Four key issues arise:

1. Rules are not always absolute and may be gendered.
2. Managerial control of workers' behaviour is underpinned by a power relationship.
3. This power relationship is unequal and may be gendered.
4. Managers have a choice of means to maximize control.

The first point is that one should caution against perceiving rules in too absolute a sense. At one end of the spectrum rules embodied in the law of the land provide a good example of formal rules. Any breach may incur very severe penalties, *e.g.* health and safety. In a workplace setting rules in practice may derive from informal understandings that can in one set of circumstances be interpreted by the worker as a permissive concession or in a different set of circumstances as something to be observed at all costs. Strawberries as a worker's perquisite during the Wimbledon lawn tennis championship are a good example. Experienced workers know that taking home unwanted strawberries is'permitted' during busy periods. When fewer staff are needed, increased managerial surveillance will be deployed to dismiss staff caught in possession of company property.

Rule-learning is part of what Polanyi refers to as'tacit skills'. As argued elsewhere:

Tacit skills, such as learning to deal with customers, are learnt in and through the very act of doing, often involving trial and error and not from following a body of procedurally-designed rules. They are seen as an interpretive achievement of the user as to how the'rules' fit the task in hand. By mastery of the rules comes the power to extend them.

This example embracing the customer provides a developmental point to Edwards' observation that rule-making is difficult, and that rules have to be interpreted in action for them to have any real meaning. Specifically in the labour contract this is because the worker's ability to work is only realised as useful labour in the course of carrying out that work, hence'a rule is a complex social institution'.

In service work physical appearance and'personality', or'aesthetic labour', are an implicit part of the employment contract. Only female flight attendants, not their male colleagues, are subjected to regular weigh-ins to ensure they comply to specified weight: height ratios. This demonstrates clearly how a rule may be gendered.

The second point to note is that the very essence of management seeking to control workers' behaviour is underpinned by a power relationship. Power is the capacity to pursue one's own interests individually and collectively, involving the capacity to oppose the actions of others and to pursue one's own objectives, and is embedded in continuing relationships. This does not mean power has to be exercised by either party in an overt sense. The threat of power may be sufficient to maintain broadly consensual employment relationships, such that any disputes or differences are resolved amicably without recourse to either party seeking to deploy sanctions against the other. The third point assumes a power inequality in the employment relationship. Self-evidently an employer is more powerful than an individual worker. The employer's ability to terminate a worker's services is likely to be more detrimental to the worker than to the employer, in spite of employment protection legislation.

Yet the individual behaviours of workers, such as high labour turnover, may be detrimental to an employer, even though they are not concerted. When workers combine collectively, with or without the backing of a trade union, there is some tilt in the balance of power, because collective sanctions may be imposed against the employer. Ultimately the outcome of the process by which each side seeks to gain concessions will depend on the relative power of the parties. For example, a plentiful supply of suitable workers in the labour market makes existing workers more readily dispensable and replaceable on the employer's terms. The opposite would be true for workers with scarce skills who can command high wages.

As Wajcman argues, gender relations are power-based and women's subordination in the workforce and workplace owes as much to trade unions as it does to managers. Spradley and Mann provide a graphic account of how the subordination of one group of female workers was brought about by another group of male workers who were the custodians of the male proprietor's trust. The male bartenders controlled the orders, and sought to make the cocktail waitresses' job difficult by giving orders in an inconsistent and confusing way. Any mistakes became the waitresses' responsibility, even if they had been caused by the bartenders.

Such was the power of the bartenders that pleasing them became more important than pleasing the customers. The fourth point is that managers have a choice of means to maximize control over workers. Friedman's'direct control' is a variant of Taylorism. Management is responsible for planning, designing and organizing the labour process, while cheap, unskilled workers perform standardized, simple repetitive tasks. Fast food is a good case in point, and also epitomizes McDonaldization, a social critique of how contemporary society and culture are being shaped by rationalist scientific management. While Taylorism sought to control the organization of work, McDonaldization is based on rationalization, replication, standardization of products and service, and quantification. In this low trust strategy worker behaviour is controlled through the use of standardized scripts in the service encounter.

In Friedman's alternative of'responsible autonomy', a high trust approach, managers delegate control to relatively privileged skilled workers who may already have elements of job control and discretion. The objective is to get workers to identify with the competitive aims of the organization so they will behave responsibly with minimum supervision. An obvious example of where such an approach might be used is in a luxury hotel, but it is also associated with empowerment and much customer-service work. As we shall argue and implied in the example of cocktail waitresses, these and other similar approaches including'hard' and'soft' HRM provide a useful framework for analysis, but are not necessarily alternatives.

The history of hotel internationalization has been characterized by American chains that secure control and integration through highly standardized procedures and manuals of operational procedures. Yet a'soft' focus on the service encounter as the driver of competitive advantage necessitates developing a culture of customised service. Mass customization illustrated by Burger King's have it your way' slogan as a challenge to McDonald's hold on the market is proposed as an alternative paradigm to McDonaldization.

WORKERS AND CUSTOMERS

Other tensions within the employment relationship impinge upon the rules of employment and power relationships. If management is about the achievement of organizational goals through people it can be argued that managers will be successful to the extent that these goals coincide with the aims and aspirations of those people, be they workers or customers. This'matching' of broadly reciprocal needs between employers and workers may be referred to as a'psychological contract', or set of contracts. It suggests managers and workers can share goals, but this is not at all straightforward. There is not a necessarily clearcut distinction between boss and worker, or a'them and us' scenario. Further we must also account for a psychological contract with customers.

Two key points are noteworthy:

1. Organizations comprise people and are, therefore, social organizations.
2. People, as social animals, may behave in unpredictable ways.

Workers

Human beings do not necessarily behave consistently or predictably, even in the same sets of circumstances. People are citizens and customers as well as employees, and these multiple identities bring different and sometimes conflicting expectations of the organization.

This makes the management of the employment relationship an uncertain process within which there is a blend of contradictory principles around the need to control and to gain the consent of workers. Workers may seek to regain control individually or collectively when they perceive that management has operated outside the rules.

At that point workers' consent has been withdrawn and management will need to find ways to restore order and regain consent. In Lucas workers' individual response to organizational rules is seen in three main ways-to conform or be deviant in employment, or to terminate their employment. These responses are similar to Marchington's'getting on','getting by' and'getting back'. These are behaviours deployed in circumstances where customer care and service quality are dependent on workers' use of their tacit skills, which contain both technical and attitudinal elements. Limiting the definition of tacit skills to employer-employee relations is too narrow. Marchington overlooked how workers exhibit their tacit skills in ways other than in respect of their relationship with the employer, notably the customer. The point that'getting back','getting by' and'getting on' are as much resistance strategies in the labour process as coping mechanisms is developed.

At workplace level personal relationships are likely to be closely connected to morale and success. Managers often'muck in' when required. In small workplaces the existence of a single leader, often the owner, may serve to inspire loyalty from the workforce, but it is not a one-way process, as workers' respect has to be earned. Is it realistic to suggest that Mina, Jo and Sadie, who wait on table in the restaurant, share all the same goals as their boss? The hotel may not be doing very well, so there may be mutual concern for the survival of the business. Yet these ladies' main goal may be to serve their customers cheerfully and effectively, while at the same time enjoying some social banter among themselves and with their customers in the process of earning a reasonable wage.

Customers

Within the triadic employment relationship a simultaneous and coterminous relationship with the organization and the customer directly impinges on how workers carry out their work, and such interactions may be rewarding or stressful. The consequent effect on workers' performance may have positive or negative implications for the rules of employment: what they can earn, their prospects of promotion or actually keeping their job.

Unequivocally the worker-customer relationship affects the rules governing employment and workplace behaviour. But so do employer-customer relationships, hence the employment relationship embodies a triadic set of power relations. This relationship embodies a socio-economic exchange, and is not simply an economic exchange around the price of labour. Fox provides a useful starting point, since he noted that organizations are social organizations and how people behave is a crucial issue in the employment relationship.

Even Edwards' point that'a rule is a complex social institution' does not adequately encapsulate our position. The main justification for widening the scope of this relationship derives from the fact that the service encounter is the interaction of the producer and consumer of services, and is a more complex phenomenon where financial considerations are interwoven with social ones.

In hospitality the social function of service work derives from the provision of a'home away from home'.

The service encounter entails'emotion work'-the assumption of a social-self, which effectively masks the individual's own personal dispositions to act, including the need to smile and be pleasant in an uninvolved way. We have already noted that'aesthetic' and sexual labour may also be inherent in service work.

It is the'normalizing' social role of service labour that distinguishes it from other wage labour. Service work cannot be understood in terms of economic rationality alone.

Examination must be based on the supposition that service work is the intended outcome of a necessarily social process in which some social interaction occurs between one or more producers and one or more consumers. The relations between three groups of people-managers, workers and customers-embody the potential for contradiction between, on the one hand, uncertainty, unpredictability, conflict and difference and, on the other hand, consent, team effort and concerted performance. The practical benefit this book seeks to convey accrues from an understanding of the nature and scope of the rules of employment in this triadic employment relationship, and how it is regulated, primarily at workplace level.

THE EMPLOYMENT RELATIONSHIP IN A WIDER CONTEXT

This chapter concludes by considering some key external contextual influences on workplace employment relationships at two levels-internationally and, in more detail, nationally in Britain.

The International Context

The national context of British employment relations increasingly needs to be understood within a much wider international context.

Three international dimensions have particular resonance for this book:

- International competition has created more open economies that have attracted investment from foreign-owned businesses. For example the French-owned groups Accor and Envergure have respectively opened hotels within their Novotel and Campanile brands in the United Kingdom.
- On a larger scale American multinational corporations have created world brands. McDonald's, Burger King, KFC and Marriott are among those that are now household names in many countries across the world.
- Spin-offs from European integration, especially on employment law in Britain, have provided an important underpinning to the employment relationship in the HI.

Foreign investment and MNCs are clearly important factors underpinning the expansion of hospitality and tourism not only in Britain but also in developing countries. Examples of'better' employment practices, in so far as they may exist in the British HI, have been associated with foreign-owned businesses.

Aspects of the American model of employment relations, that is non-union and market-driven, may seem to reflect some aspects of observed employment relations practice in the British HI, but the similarity has been overstated.

The United States has substantially more legal regulation than Britain, which has benefited American HI workers, while the trade unions are not entirely powerless-issues we highlight in later chapters. The European model based on social partnership designed to forge a common agenda between capital and labour is considerably more diverse and different across the member states than is often acknowledged. While we cannot expect it to reflect current developments in HI employment relations in most British workplaces, it has not necessarily produced wholesale benefits for HI workers across the EU either.

The British experience is not necessarily mirrored in other countries across the world. Differences in other countries' institutional arrangements and cultural considerations are among the factors that will affect their employment relations systems. Detailed comparison with other countries is beyond the scope of this book, but key instances of international employment relations within hospitality and tourism are cited throughout the remaining chapters.

THE BRITISH CONTEXT

Workplace employment relationships cannot be immune from wider economic, social, legal and political contextual influences. Contemporary examples, which may be influential in Britain today. The distinctions between these sets of influences are not always clear-cut as they can be interrelated.

The State

Although we have already touched upon some aspects of the state's interest in employment relations, we need to examine its role in a little more detail. The state is not a single or cohesive body, and comprises a number of institutions that have an interest in the employment relationship, whose objectives do not necessarily coincide. Parliament is the legislature, government ministers form the executive, the judiciary enforces the law, and civil servants are the administrators.

The state sponsors specialist agencies in the field of employment, and has done so since the end of the nineteenth century. Three government departments impinge on employment relations within a much wider brief. The most important is the DTI, which has overall responsibility for employment relations, small firms and competitiveness. The Employment Relations directorate is responsible for developing policy and legislation affecting individual workers and trade unions, EU legislation, promoting partnership and best practice, regulation of employment tribunals and the dates of public holidays. The DTI publishes consultation documents, research papers, practical guidance on how to implement employment legislation and regulations, and codes of practice on matters such as picketing.

The Department for Education and Skills is responsible for developing the skills of young people and adults. he Department for Work and Pensions delivers support and advice in areas of work and work-related benefits, including New Deal, sickness and accidents at work, and retirement. Although publicly funded, other state agencies and bodies are independent of government because they are controlled and managed by their own executive. The main institutions discussed later in the book are ACAS, the Central Arbitration Committee and employment tribunals.

The Equal Opportunities Commission, Commission for Racial Equality and Disability Rights Commission each have overall responsibility for specific types of anti-discrimination or equal opportunities legislation.

The Health and Safety Commission and Health and Safety Executive have responsibility for health, safety and welfare legislation. Their roles include the publication of codes of practice. Other bodies assist with the enforcement of minimum employment standards. The Inland Revenue's powers include obtaining information from employers, issuing enforcement notices requiring employers to pay the NMW and imposing penalties on employers not observing the NMW.

Environmental Health Officers are responsible for the enforcement of health and safety standards. Many other institutions, some of which may have a political bias, offer a mixture of fact and opinion on employment relations. National bodies, which take either an employer or management view, include the Confederation of British Industry, the Institute of Directors, and the Chartered Institute of Personnel and Development.

The British Hospitality Association, Restaurant Association, the British Beer and Pub Association the Hotel, Catering and International Management Association and the British Institute of Innkeeping are specific to the HI. The HtF, formerly the HI's National Training Organisation is recognized by government as the employer-led voice on all issues relating to hospitality training, education and qualifications.

The HtF also carries out research, and produces useful statistical information about the labour market. The Trades Union Congress Institute of Employment Rights and the Low Pay Network serve to defend workers' interests.

The HCIMA can also be regarded as having a worker perspective since, as the professional body of hospitality managers; it serves to defend their interests as well as disseminating good management practice. Three large unions have special sections for hospitality workers: the General, Municipal and Boilermakers' Union, the Transport and General Workers Union and the Union of Shop, Distributive and Allied Workers. The National Association of Licensed House Managers was self-standing for many years, but has recently become part of the TGWU.

8

Service Quality in Hospitality

SATISFACTION AND BEHAVIOURAL INTENTIONS

A primary goal of park and recreation agencies is to provide opportunities from which users may derive satisfaction. This goal stems from a belief that users who are highly satisfied with their experience are likely to be repeat visitors, to be loyal users, to disseminate positive word-of-mouth communications to others, and to be supporters of the providing agency. The centrality of satisfied users to an agency accomplishing its mission and securing its future well-being, accounts for the substantial literature on satisfaction research in the leisure field which dates back at least to the 1960s. Delivering quality service will be one of the major challenges facing hospitality managers in the opening years of the next millennium.

It will be an essential condition for success in the emerging, keenly competitive, global hospitality markets. While the future importance of delivering quality hospitality service is easy to discern and to agree on, doing so presents some difficult and intriguing management issues. Since the delivery of hospitality service always involves people, these issues centre on the management of people, and in particular on the interactions between guests and staff, interactions that are called service encounters. In the eyes of our guests, our hospitality businesses will succeed or fail depending on the cumulative impact of the service encounters in which they have participated. It is easy to check the importance of managing these service encounters. Think back to the last time you visited a hotel or restaurant. How did you feel about the quality of the experience? Was it one that you would recommend to others? What were the specific interactions that made a difference? If you can't remember, is this something that should matter to the hospitality business concerned? Surely something should have gone especially well? Service encounters are the building blocks of quality hospitality service.

How can hospitality businesses manage them more effectively? We suggest a two step process in the evaluation of a service chain. First, hospitality managers should identify each encounter in the chain that they wish to take apart, and then single out those that are of operational or strategic significance-in effect, focusing in on the few encounters that really make a difference to guest experience and thus to the bottom line. Second, apply what we have called the 6 S's to improving these critical encounters through effective redesign. While the first step may seem obvious, it is important to identify a service chain and then to break it down into the component encounters.

Just how much detail is needed? Too much detail takes time and resources, and may confuse rather than clarify. Too little and we may miss important problems. The process is iterative, with more detail needed in some areas and less in others, and with an overriding consideration that the chain is assessed not just from the point of view of a manager but also from that of a guest. Which are the encounters that really matter? Those that add significant value to the guest, those that cost in time or money, those that help to differentiate the business from its competitors, and those where significant innovation is possible or occurring. Hospitality service encounters run the gamut from those that are very trivial to those that are highly critical.

They vary greatly in their nature and may be simple or complex, standard or custom, low tech or high tech, remote or friendly, low or high skill, frequent or occasional, and so on. They can be instrumental dealing with the performance of necessary utilitarian activities or can involve emotion-laden hospitality events. An initial management task is to understand a service encounter by discerning and dealing with those attributes that are most important to guests. In doing so, pertinent questions must be raised about the specific service encounter under consideration.

With respect to a particular service encounter, hospitality managers might raise many questions like the following:

- Exactly what happened?
- What were the guest reactions?
- Should it be done differently?
- What resources would assure optimal performance?
- What changes should be made?
- How can such changes best be put into effect?

The specific encounter under consideration will, of course, indicate the kinds of questions that should be pursued. It is important to obtain adequate information to understand the situation thoroughly. Determining the context of a situation relating to a hospitality encounter that has gone wrong establishes parameters for improvement. All this is part of the second step. With the information at hand hospitality managers can organize, and analyse the data and it is here that the 6S approach can help.

These are:

1. Space
2. Specification

3. Staff
4. Style
5. Support
6. System

Specification means clearly detailing information about the what, when, where, and how, of service encounters. It requires giving careful thought to the linkages between particular service encounters and others in the service chain.

The starting point for hospitality service encounter analysis is specifying clearly the overall service strategy and what it is designed to achieve. Is the purpose cost or service quality leadership? Is it to provide unique service values, customised or standardized, complex or simple, frequent or occasional? Is it to provide service at any reasonable cost? Is service limited to a luxury package, or does it include budget travellers? Which staff members are involved in providing the service? What skills do they need? What training has been provided?

How committed are they to service goals? Is team cooperation or individual empowerment required? What attitudes are appropriate--friendly, open, helpful, warm service, or efficient, unobtrusive, uninvolving, unthreatening service? What staff members deal with guests? How close are the'backroom' staff to guests? Are staff presentations and appearances appropriate? To what extent are guests involved in the provision of service? What skill, knowledge, information, or experience do guests need to fulfill their roles? What are likely guest expectations?

What communication occurred between guest and service provider? Did the dynamics of the exchange proceed smoothly? Do any language and cultural barriers exist? Where will the service encounter occur? Is the space appropriately designed to facilitate the service encounter? Is there adequate space to handle each of the activities such as waiting, completing forms, storing or handling luggage, assembling tours? Is signage appropriate? Is the decor attractive to guests and supportive of activities that have to be carried out? Are the necessary systems to support the encounter in place? Is the information necessary to respond effectively to guests' needs readily available?

Is the appropriate technology being fully used? Are the interfaces between different functions such as housekeeping and front office, sales and front office, fully operational? What measurements of quality, or performance, are in use? Are they the most helpful for both service providers and managers? Are the criteria for success clearly defined? Is everyone involved aware of guest needs and concerns? Are the service providers given the facilities and financial and human support needed to do the job? Is the technology appropriate? Have employees been given the training needed? Are incentive and reward systems geared to the tasks to be performed? Is supervision supportive? Does organization structure help or hinder performance?Are the suggested procedures appropriate? How should the service encounter be conducted, given the enterprise culture? Is the management style, and marketing orientation, appropriate for the tasks?

Do service providers have the appropriate attitudes? Is the right emphasis being placed on service quality? When hospitality managers have carried out this two step process they will be in an excellent position to make decisions that will both improve the quality of hospitality services provided and guest perceptions of them. Zeroing in on hospitality service quality in this manner will help hospitality businesses meet the service challenges of the millennium, enhance their market positions, and reap the associated profit rewards. More recently a related stream of research in the leisure field has emerged in the area of service quality. This research stream stems from the pioneering work of Parasuraman, Berry and Zeithaml in the marketing field.

They were the first to conceptualize and operationalize the concept of service quality in 1985 and have remained prominent contributors to the service quality literature as it has grown exponentially in the last decade. The dominant theory used in the conceptualization of both service quality and satisfaction has been the expectancy-disconfirmation paradigm. This paradigm is derived from two processes: the development of expectations of outcomes, and the disconfirmation judgement that results from comparison of the perceived outcomes against these expectations. Confirmation results when the actual performance matches initial expectations.

When performance exceeds or falls short of expectations, positive or negative disconfirmation results. Positive disconfirmation leads to satisfaction or perceptions of high service quality, while negative disconfirmation leads to dissatisfaction or perceptions of low service quality. This common theoretical basis has resulted in considerable confusion in differentiating the satisfaction and service quality constructs. The literature is replete with reports that use the two terms interchangeably as synonyms and do not recognize them as distinctively different constructs. For example, Howat el al. evaluated visitor satisfaction by using indicators based on Parasuraman *et al.*'s five dimensions of service quality. Despite this confusion there is a consensus that satisfaction and service quality are different constructs. The purpose of this study was to empirically explore the relationship between the two constructs and their impact on behavioural intentions.

CONCEPTUAL FRAMEWORK AND HYPOTHESES

The conceptual framework which guided development of the study's hypotheses. The framework examines service quality and satisfaction at two levels: the transaction level and the global level. At the global level, the model depicts overall service quality and overall visitor satisfaction as two different constructs which influence behavioural intentions. At the transaction level, the concepts of quality of performance and quality of experience are conceptualized as direct antecedents of overall service quality and overall satisfaction. Quality of performance refers to visitors' perceptions of the attributes of a facility that are controlled by management.

Quality of experience is defined as the psychological outcomes which visitors derive from visiting a facility. It reflects visitors' perceived benefits they obtain from the experience. Oliver notes that visitors are likely to use more dimensions to form quality of experience judgements than quality of performance judgements. He maintains that the dimensions underlying quality judgements are rather specific, whether they are cues or attributes. Satisfaction judgements, however, can result from any dimension, quality-related or not. Quality of performance is only one dimension that influences quality of experience, which is influenced by a broader array of inputs. The two constructs are likely to be positively correlated, but the relationship is unlikely to be linear. It has been pointed out that a high quality experience may result even when quality of performance is perceived to be low because, for example, social group interactions are sufficiently positive to offset the low quality service. The opposite can also occur when a low quality of experience results, even though perceived quality of performance is high. For example, visitors ma y recently have had a bad experience while traveling to the site, such as receiving a speeding ticket, so they are not in a receptive mood to enjoy the experience. Thus, there are likely to be occasions when the quality of experience has relatively little to do with the quality of an agency's performance in delivering the service.

The production of a recreational experience involves both visitors and resources. Management can only provide opportunities such as services and facilities. How visitors avail themselves of those opportunities determines the quality of experience they receive. Since visitors' participation is involved in delivering the service it means that a recreation experience can be influenced, both by the services provided by suppliers and the emotional states brought to the site by visitors. The quality of performance provided by recreation suppliers can be controlled by management, while factors brought to the site by visitors are outside a supplier's control. Visitors' perceptions of performance quality on each attribute strongly influence their overall perceptions of service quality while quality of experience which is comprised of a set of specific psychological benefits leads to overall visitor satisfaction.

Like quality of experience and overall satisfaction, quality of performance and overall service quality are two distinct constructs. Quality of experience refers to the specific benefits people obtain, while overall satisfaction is visitors' levels of satisfaction towards their total experience with the recreation service, *i.e.*, it is the summation of the specific benefits. Quality of performance relates to evaluation of specific service attributes, while overall service quality is the evaluation of the quality of the service in general, rather than that of particular attributes. Perceptions of individual attributes and specific benefits are conceptualized as being compensatory. The compensatory nature of attributes was tested by Lue, Crompton and Stewart in the context of multi-destination travel behaviour. Lue *et al.* reported that destinations could offset negative attributes, if they were perceived to provide other attributes that visitors preferred. Thus, the authors concluded that service attributes were compensatory and cumulative.

Visitors can have perceptions of high overall quality or high levels of overall satisfaction, even though they perceive specific service attributes to have low quality or they are not satisfied with particular benefit dimensions of the experience. Over time, the summation of visitors' evaluative beliefs about individual service attributes will contribute to their overall evaluation of service quality of the recreation service.

Likewise, visitors' overall satisfaction is a summation state of the psychological outcomes they have experienced over time. As Bitner and Hubbert pointed out, multiple positive/negative experiences, which occur within a visit, are likely to lead to a high/low level of overall satisfaction. Perceptions of the quality of performance of individual attributes influence perceptions of overall service quality. Perceptions of the quality of experience relating to individual benefits influence overall satisfaction.

The model postulates that quality of performance has impact not only on overall service quality, but also on overall visitor satisfaction. Likewise, visitors' quality of experience influences their perceptions of overall service quality. When visitors perceive a leisure service's attributes to be high quality, they are likely to experience higher levels of overall satisfaction with the service. At the same time, the stronger the psychological benefits that visitors obtain from their visits, the more positive attitude they are likely to have towards overall service quality.

Quality of experience positively impacts visitors' perceptions of overall service quality. Quality of performance positively impacts visitors' levels of overall satisfaction. Visitors' levels of overall satisfaction contribute to their attitudes towards overall service quality. This follows the conceptualization of the relationship between service quality and satisfaction suggested by Parasuraman, Berry and Zeithami and Teas. It suggests that high levels of overall satisfaction lead to perceptions of high overall service quality, while low levels of overall satisfaction result in perceptions of low overall service quality. The direction of this flow derives from the recognition that overall satisfaction is experience specific while overall service quality is not.

Since overall service quality is visitors' perceptions of overall performance, visitors can have a general impression towards the quality of a recreation site even if they have never been there. This can occur when visitors have acquired knowledge of the site from external sources such as word-of-mouth communication, television programmes, or newspaper or magazine articles. For example, based on their knowledge of Yellowstone National Park, potential visitors may have a general impression of the quality of the park, even though they have never visited it. However, they cannot express their levels of overall satisfaction with it because this impression can only be formed after visiting and experiencing the benefits the park offered at least once. Levels of overall satisfaction can only be derived from firsthand experience.

Overall satisfaction positively influences overall service quality. Once visitors form an overall evaluation towards service quality and towards overall satisfaction, the model indicates that these judgements are likely to influence visitors' future behavioural intentions. Thus, when a visitor perceives an attraction to have high overall service quality, the individual is likely to say positive things about the attraction and to come back and visit it again in the future.

Likewise, if a visitor's level of overall satisfaction is high with the attraction, the individual is likely to disseminate positive word-of-mouth about the attraction and to visit it again in the future. Overall service quality is positively associated with visitors' behavioural intentions. Overall satisfaction is positively associated with visitors' behavioural intentions. To test the hypotheses in the study, data were collected from visitors to Aransas National Wildlife Refuge in Texas. During a two-weekend period, one adult member from each of the 355 visitor groups entering the interpretive centre in this time period was given a questionnaire, a pre-paid envelope and a cover letter explaining the purpose and the importance of the study. Participants were requested to complete and return the questionnaire in the enclosed pre-paid envelope. A drawing for a $500 US savings bond was used as an incentive to encourage response.

A modified Dillman approach was used to collect the data. It involved one postcard reminder and two other follow-ups, which included replacement questionnaires, to those who did not respond. These procedures resulted in the return of 282 completed instruments. There was almost an equal proportion of male (50.3 per cent) and female (49.7 per cent) respondents, and 62.5 per cent of the sample were aged between 40 and 69. Over 83 per cent had at least one college degree and 34 per cent were retired. Almost half of the respondents (47 per cent) had an income in the $30,000 to $60,000 range, while 18.4 per cent reported incomes over $90,000. First time visitors to the refuge constituted 51.6 per cent of the sample while 53.1 per cent resided within the state of Texas. Five constructs were included in the hypotheses that were tested.

They were: quality of performance, quality of experience, overall service quality, overall visitor satisfaction, and visitors' future behavioural intentions. Quality of performance was operationalized by a list of attributes of the wildlife refuge selected from a pool developed from previous literature and from extended discussions with refuge managers. They were categorized into six domains and an expert panel, which included the researchers and refuge managers, was used to select five items from those assigned to each domain to represent the dimensions of that domain. The six domains were Education and Conservation, Staff/Volunteers, Comfort Amenities, Cleanliness, Information, and Wildlife. A pretest using a sample of university students was conducted to examine the validity and reliability of these scales. Responses to the items were measured on 7-point Likert-type scales anchored by "very poor" and "excellent". A factor analysis on the pretest sample resulted in the number of items being reduced from a total of 30 to 25, and in some reassignment of items and re-tiding of the domains. To evaluate the factor structure in the scales for the construct of quality of performance, data from the study's respondents were subjected to a principal components factor analysis of the six scales to see if the six scales were unifactorial.

The analysis confirmed that they were, but a low communality estimate and low reliability resulted in one factor, Wildlife, being dropped. The scales used to measure the quality of performance construct, with their factor loadings and reliabilities. The benefit items used to operationalize quality of experience were adapted from the Recreation Experience Preference scales that have been used in past benefits research. Manfredo *et al.* demonstrated the reliability and validity of 19 REP scales using a meta-analysis of 36 studies. The expert panel used in the current study judged that 15 of the 19 REP scales potentially could be relevant to a refuge visitation experience.

Items were measured on 7-point Likert-type scales anchored by "strongly disagree" and "strongly agree". After a pretest with the university student sample, the 51 items drawn from the 15 domains were reduced to 39 items, which were assigned to 8 domains. The eight domains were: Nature Appreciation/Learning, Achievement, Introspection/Nostalgia, Escape, Similar People, Physical Fitness, Family Togetherness and New People.

A factor analysis using principal component factor analysis was also conducted on the sample data to examine th e factor structure of the scales measuring the construct. The factor analysis resulted in 2 factors. As shows, six of the eight scales loaded on Factor 1 while Similar people and Family Togetherness loaded on Factor 2. As a result, a decision had to be made regarding whether to treat the second factor as a separate variable distinctively different from the latent quality of experience variable, or just to delete the second factor.

Since the objective of the present study was to test the proposed theoretical model rather than to explore an additional latent construct, and there was no theoretical rationale for adding a second dimension into the structural model, it was decided to delete the two scales Similar People and Family Togetherness from the study. Overall service quality was measured on a 10-point scale with a single item that asked respondents their perceptions of overall quality of the refuge's attributes. The anchors on the scale were, extremely low quality and extremely high quality.

Responses ranged from 4 to 10, but 89 per cent were in the 7 to 10 range and the mean was 8.2. This manifest variable is labeled V19 in the measurement model. Overall satisfaction was measured with a 4-item, 7-point modified semantic differential scale. This scale was originally adapted by Childress and Crompton from Crosby and Stephens. Since there were no pre-determined domains among the items measuring overall satisfaction, a factor analysis was conducted on the four individual items. As expected, the principal component method extracted only one factor, meaning that the scale was unifactorial.

The Cronbach's alpha reliability score for the scale was.97. The final construct, behavioural intentions, was measured with a seven-item, 7-point scale derived from Zeithaml, Berry and Parasuraman. Respondents were requested to indicate how likely they were to take each of the seven actions. The seven items were not unifactorial because two factors were extracted from the principal component factor analysis on the 7 items. The loadings of the items are listed. One item was deleted because it did not have a salient loading above. 40 on either factor. The two items loaded on Factor 2 were also deleted for the same reason as the two items in quality of experience were deleted. One of the items from Factor 1 was also deleted to improve the reliability measure of behavioural intentions.

THE MEASUREMENT MODEL

The naming of its components follows Bender's convention. Since overall service quality was measured by a single item scale, it was a manifest variable, labeled with the letter "V" for variable. Quality of performance, quality of experience, overall satisfaction and behavioural intentions are latent variables prefaced by the letter "F" for factor. The quality of performance construct was measured by the five manifest variables Vi through V5. The quality of experience construct was measured by manifest variables V6 through Vii. The overall satisfaction construct was measured by manifest variables V12 to V15.

The behavioural intention construct was measured by manifest variables V16 through V18 which are keyed. V1 through V5 represent the five scales that measured the quality of performance construct. Each of these variables was calculated as the grand mean score of respondents' ratings of each item in the individual scale. For example, in the first scale "Education and Conservation" there were five items. V1 is the average score of respondents' ratings on these five items. The same method was applied to V6 through Vii. However, V12 through V19 were the respondents' actual responses to each individual item.

The measurement model posits no unidirectional paths between latent variables. Instead, a covariance is estimated to connect each latent variable with every other latent variable. This is indicated by the curved, two-headed arrow connecting each F variable and V19 to every other F variable. Letter "L" represents the coefficients of the "V" variables to "F" factors. Letter "E" represents measurement errors for each manifest variable. Letter "C" represents covariance between latent factors and the manifest variable V19. The measurement model was estimated using the maximum likelihood method, and the goodness of fit indices.

It has been recommended that the model chi-square test be used as a goodness of fit index, with a smaller chi-square value indicating a better model fit. The chi-square value for the initial measurement model was statistically significant. However, the chi-square test usually is not considered as the absolute standard by which the goodness of fit of the model is judged because it is sensitive to sample size. Other tests, such as goodness of fit index, adjusted goodness of fit index, Bender's comparative fit index and Bender and Bonett's non-normed fit index, should also be used to judge the goodness of fit of the model. Values over.9 on these indices indicate an acceptable fit. It was thus concluded that there was a problem with the model's fit. To identify the problem, the patterns of normalized residuals, parameter significance tests, and LaGrange multiplier tests were examined.

All coefficients were significant, indicating the indicators were good measures of the underlying latent factors. However, of the ten largest standardized residuals, nine of them were related to V6, which is the variable "Nature Appreciation/Learning" measuring quality of experience. Nine of the ten largest LaGrange multipliers tests were also related to V6. The researchers' interpretation of this problem was that nature appreciation and learning about nature is so pervasive in a visit to a wildlife refuge that it permeates into all aspects of the experience. Given the premise that to experience nature was such a dominant pervasive theme in the process of visiting the refuge, it would be represented in the model even if it was excluded as an explicit variable. Thus, V6 was eliminated from the measurement model, and the model was re-calibrated.

Goodness of fit indices for the re-specified measurement model are also presented. The t values for the coefficients of the standard factor loadings were still all significant. Moreover, NNFI now exceeded.9, and the GFI improved to.86. The results indicated that the revised measurement model had a reasonable fit to the data. Therefore, this measurement model was tentatively accepted as the study's "final" measurement model. Reliability and validity of the constructs and their indicators were assessed. The reliability of an indicator variable is the square of the correlation between a latent factor and that indicator. In this case, the R-square values are indicator reliabilities which indicate the per cent of variance in the indicator that is explained by the common factor that it is supposed to measure. Overall satisfaction indicators had very high reliabilities, while reliabilities for quality of performance indicators, quality of experience indicators and behavioural intention indicators were relatively low. A composite reliability index for each latent factor was calculated to measure the internal consistency of the indicators measuring a given factor. This procedure is similar to the use of Cronbach's alpha for measuring the scale reliability of multiple items in a scale. The composite reliability for latent factor overall satisfaction was.96.

Although indicator reliabilities for quality of performance, quality of experience and behavioural intentions were relatively low, the composite reliabilities for these factors were.79.83 and.81, respectively, which all exceeded the minimally acceptable level of.70 reliability for scale instruments? The relatively high composite reliabilities suggested that the individual scales, when taking as a group, performed fairly well in the model. Convergent validity and discriminant validity of the constructs were assessed to see if the indicators were measuring what they were intended to measure. Convergent validity is demonstrated when different scales are used to measure the same construct, and scores from these different scales are strongly correlated. In the confirmatory analysis, convergent validity was examined by reviewing the t tests for the factor loadings.

Hatcher states: "if all factor loadings for the indicators measuring the same construct are statistically significant this is viewed as evidence supporting the convergent validity of those indicators". In the present model testing, all t tests were significant providing evidence to support the convergent validity of the indicators. Discriminant validity is demonstrated when different scales are used to measure different constructs and the correlations between the measures are relatively weak. Discriminant validity for the latent factors was assessed by performing confidence interval tests. The confidence interval was calculated by adding or subtracting two standard errors around the correlation between two factors. If this confidence interval includes the value of 1.0, then it is very likely that, for the actual population, the two factors are perfectly correlated. In the present model testing, none of the confidence intervals approached 1.0, demonstrating the discriminant validity of all measures used in the study. It differs from the model that depicts the causal relationship among exogenous and endogenous variables.

An exogenous variable is an independent variable whose causes lie outside the model. In this case, quality of performance is the only exogenous variable in the structural model. In contrast to exogenous variables, the postulated causes of endogenous variables are included in the model. In the current model, quality of experience, overall service quality, overall satisfaction and behavioural intentions are all endogenous variables. The standard errors for the factor loadings and path coefficients in the initial structural model were not near zero, and none of them appeared to be unacceptably small. All factor loadings that were tested had t values greater than 1.96. All of the path coefficients were significant except for the path from F2 to V19.

The goodness of fit indices for the structural model indicated the model has a relatively good fit to the data. However, these indices represent the overall fit of the measurement model and the structural model combined. The current theoretical model consists of a relatively small number of latent variables and a relatively large number of indicator variables. This suggests that indices of overall model fit may be more influenced by the fit of the measurement model than by the fit of the structural model. However, the present study is more concerned with the fit of the structural model than the fit of the measurement model.

Therefore, the relative normed-fit index was calculated to evaluate the fit of only the structural model when free from the influence of the fit of the measurement model. The RNFI for the structural model was.94, indicating a reasonably good fit of the theoretical model without considering how well the latent variables were measured by their indicators. Since both the measurement model and the structural model had relatively good fit to the data, it was necessary to perform a chi-square difference test to determine whether there was a significant difference between the fit provided by the structural model and that provided by the measurement model. This test provides evidence for the nomological validity of the structural model.

The difference chi-square value between the structural and the measurement model was 20.07, which was greater than the critical value of 13.82 with df = 2. Thus, there was a significant difference between the fit provided by the measurement model and the fit provided by the structural model. In other words, the fit of the structural model was significantly poorer than the fit of the measurement model. This result suggested that the structural model contained some misspecifications that needed to be modified. To identify sources of the misspecifications in the model, the modification indices were reviewed. The multivariate Wald tests suggested the path from F2 to V19 should be deleted. This was consistent with the factor loadings' significance tests because the t-test for the coefficient of the path from F2 to V19 was found to be non-significant.

It indicated that the relationship between quality of experience and overall service quality was not significant. Thus, this path was eliminated from the model. They were relatively similar to the initial structural model, but it was marginally more parsimonious. The chi-square difference test was conducted on the measurement model and the revised structural model to see if the structural model had a reasonable fit with the data, like the measurement model did. The test was highly significant, revealing that there were still misspecifications in the revised model 1. Wald tests conducted on the initial structural model did not reveal any additional causal paths between latent constructs that could be deleted without affecting the model's fit. Thus, results of LaGrange multiplier tests were reviewed to identify new causal paths that should be added to the model. The results showed that paths should be added from two variables to F4, together with a path from F2 to F4. Since V8 and V9 are indicators of F2, a path from F2 to F4 should be added to the model. There was previous empirical evidence to support the direct influence of quality of experience on visitors' future behavioural intentions.

This evidence is discussed later in the paper. A path from quality of experience to behavioural intentions was then added and the new model, revised model 2, was then estimated. The fit indices for revised model 2 were all higher than those of revised model 1 and the parsimonious NF1 did not decrease, meaning that revised model 2 was as parsimonious as revised model 1. The RNFI for revised model 2 was 0.99 indicating that revised model 2 was a much better fit than revised model 1, independent of the measurement model. All of the coefficient estimates of the standard loadings were significant and in the predicted direction. The distribution of normalized residuals for revised model 2 was symmetrical and centreed on zero.

Only three of the normalized residuals were greater than the absolute value of 2.0, and the largest of the three was 2.7. The chi-square difference test between the measurement model and the revised structural model 2 resulted in a value of 1.23, which was much smaller than the critical value of 13.82. Thus, the chi-square test was not significant, indicating that the fit of revised model 2 was not significantly different from the fit of the measurement model in which the F variables were free to covary. In other words, the causal relationships described in the revised model 2 successfully explained the observed relationships between the latent constructs.

The addition of the causal path from quality of experience to behavioural intentions resulted in revised model 2 being superior to revised model 1, and this addition did not decrease the model's parsimony. Thus, this model was the final model for the study. All parameter estimates in the final model were significant at [alpha] =.05. Standardized instead of unstandardized coefficients were then used to evaluate the strength of path coefficients estimated, because the variables involved were not measured on the same scale.

EFFECTS OF EXOGENOUS AND ENDOGENOUS VARIABLES

The standardized coefficients for each path in the model. They represented the strength of the direct effect of an exogenous variable on an endogenous variable, and that of one endogenous variable on another. The direct effect refers to the influence of one variable on another that is not mediated by any other variables in the model. Bollen noted that the direct and indirect effects can help to answer important questions regarding the influence of one variable on another, but "it is the total effect that is more relevant". He explained that the direct effect could be misleading when the indirect effect has an opposite sign, for in such cases the total effect may not be as strong as the direct effect shows. The direct, indirect and total effects of all endogenous and exogenous variables in the final model.

Direct effects, just as to Bollen, "are the influences of one variable on another that are not mediated by any other variable... Indirect effects are ones that are mediated by at least one other variable, and the total effects are the sum of direct and indirect effects". While direct effects as the values of direct path coefficients, indirect effects are calculated by multiplying all the path coefficients for each route of indirect influence.

If an independent variable has more than one route of indirect influence on a dependent variable, then the indirect effects for each route are summed to calculate the overall indirect effects of the independent variable on the dependent variable. Quality of performance had a positive direct effect on quality of experience.

Quality of performance had a stronger direct effect on overall satisfaction, than did quality of experience. In addition, quality of performance also indirectly influenced overall satisfaction through quality of experience. Thus, the total effects of quality of performance on overall satisfaction were stronger than those of quality of experience. Overall service quality is directly and/or indirectly influenced by quality of performance, quality of experience and overall satisfaction. Quality of performance not only directly contributed to overall service quality, but it also indirectly influenced overall service quality through two routes. One route was through quality of experience [right arrow] overall satisfaction right arrow overall service quality, while the second route was through overall satisfaction right arrow overall service quality.

Thus, quality of experience had total effects of.73 on overall service quality, with a direct influence of.60 and an indirect influence of.13. The direct influence of overall satisfaction on overall service quality was.30. Since the direct path from quality of experience to overall service quality was not supported by the data, quality of experience only had an indirect influence of.07 (.07 =.23 X.30) on overall service quality through overall satisfaction. Thus, of the three independent variables that impact overall service quality, quality of performance had the highest degree of influence on overall service quality. Visitors' future behavioural intentions were either directly or indirectly influenced by quality of performance, quality of experience, overall service quality and overall satisfaction.

Quality of performance had the strongest total effect on behavioural intentions even though it did not have any direct effect on this variable. While overall satisfaction had the second strongest total effects on behavioural intentions, its direct effect was the highest. Quality of experience both directly influenced behavioural intentions, and indirectly influenced it through overall satisfaction and overall service quality. Overall service quality had the lowest total effect on behavioural intentions among all variables.

Hypothesis 1 stated that quality of performance has a positive direct influence on quality of experience because perception of service attributes can contribute to the benefits visitors receive from their visiting experience. This hypothesis is shown as the path from F1 to F2. The standardized coefficient of this path was.48.

The t value was 7.29, which was significant at [alpha] =.001. The significant coefficient provided evidence of support for hypothesis 1. Hypothesis 2 explored the relationship between visitors' perceptions of individual attributes' performance and their perceptions of overall service quality and is shown as the path from F1 to V19. Hypothesis 2 was supported since the t-test for the path coefficient was significant, indicating that visitors' perceptions of quality of performance positively influenced their perceptions of the overall service quality of the refuge. The specific benefits visitors received that constituted their quality of experience were expected to relate positively to their overall satisfaction level.

The greater the perceived psychological benefits visitors obtained from the visit, the higher it was anticipated would be their levels of overall satisfaction with the refuge in general. This relationship, indicated by the path from F2 to F3, was found to be significant at an alpha level of.05 with a t value of 2.82, so Hypothesis 3 was supported. It was hypothesized that quality of experience would influence overall service quality. In the initial structural model, the path coefficient from F2 to V19 was found to be non-significant, and thus was eliminated from the model, so Hypothesis 4 was not supported. Hypothesis 5 stated that perceptions of quality of performance of the refuge's individual attributes positively influenced overall satisfaction.

The higher the perceived quality of individual service attributes, the higher it was anticipated would be the levels of overall satisfaction. The significant coefficient from path F1 to F3 enabled Hypothesis 5 to be supported. It was postulated that the higher visitors' overall satisfaction was with the refuge, the higher would be their perceptions of overall service quality. The path from F3 to V19 was significant so Hypothesis 6 was supported. Visitors' future behavioural intentions were expected to be influenced positively by both overall service quality and overall satisfaction.

When visitors have high perceptions of overall service quality and high levels of overall satisfaction with the refuge, they are more likely to visit the refuge again in the future or to encourage their friends to do so. The path coefficients from V19 to F4 and from F3 to F4 were both found to be significant, so hypotheses 7 and 8 were both supported. The results provided empirical support for the conceptualization of service quality and satisfaction. However, it was found that the particular psychological benefits visitors obtained from the visit did not contribute to their perceptions of service quality in a major way.

They only contributed to overall service quality indirectly through overall visitor satisfaction. This finding of the study contradicts those who insist transaction-specific satisfaction influences overall service quality. One explanation for this contradiction lies in the different conceptualizations of satisfaction at the transaction level.

The present study views satisfaction at the transaction level as the specific benefits received from a visit, while others have considered it to be evaluation of individual service attributes, or as overall satisfaction with the service. While the study found that both visitors' evaluations of individual service attributes and their levels of overall satisfaction directly influenced their perceptions of overall service quality, when satisfaction was conceptualized as psychological benefits visitors receive at the transaction level, it did not contribute to overall service quality directly.

This provides evidence supporting the distinction between quality of performance and quality of experience, and it also reinforces the notion that satisfaction should be specified at both the transaction level and the global level. Thus, when studying the relationship between satisfaction and service quality in general, the inter-relationship among transaction-level concepts and global-level concepts should be considered. Hypothesis 6 supported the proposition that visitors who were satisfied with their overall experience at the refuge tended to have high evaluations of its overall quality.

Although there is evidence that overall service quality and visitor satisfaction are independent of each other, "the main issue to be resolved is whether customers distinguish between customer satisfaction and service quality in their own minds". The present study did find discriminant validity between overall service quality and overall satisfaction. In addition, the results showed that the total effects of overall satisfaction on overall service quality were relatively low. This implies that although they are correlated, overall service quality and overall satisfaction are not the same construct. Support for hypotheses 7 and 8 suggests that high levels of visitor satisfaction, and/or perceptions of high service quality are likely to reinforce visitors' intentions of using the service again in the future and to engage in positive word-of-mouth communication with their family and friends.

However, the influence of overall service quality on behavioural intentions was found to be much weaker than that of overall satisfaction. Indeed, the results showed that overall service quality contributed least to behavioural intentions among all four constructs examined. In addition to the direct influences of overall service quality and overall satisfaction on behavioural intentions, this study also found that quality of experience directly contributed to behavioural intentions. This relationship was not hypothesized in the proposed model. The decision to add the path in the revised structural model was made because previous studies have provided empirical evidence for the influence of transaction-specific satisfaction on behavioural intentions.

For example, Westbrook studied the relationship of consumption-based psychological responses and post-purchase processes. He reported that both negative and positive dimensions of psychological responses were directly related to satisfaction judgements, complaint behaviour and word-of-mouth communication.

These results suggest that when visitors' psychological responses to particular benefits are strong enough, they can impact their future behavioural intentions. If visitors are not satisfied with specific benefits derived from the current visit, they may not return even if overall quality of the service is considered to be good. The issue of understanding the relationship between service quality and visitor satisfaction from a manager's perspective starts with a fundamental question: should management focus on visitor satisfaction or on perceived service quality?

Thus, Dabholkar has noted that practitioners "are not interested in the difference between these concepts *per se*, but are interested in both concepts mainly as predictors of customer behaviour". Thus, two aspects of the study are likely to be of especial interest to managers. First, it confirmed that improved service quality and visitor satisfaction can result in repeat visitation and positive word-of-mouth. Second, it clarified the relationship between service quality and satisfaction, and found that both constructs had an independent effect on visitors' future behavioural intentions. Service quality and satisfaction at the global level are overall evaluations.

However, the study suggests that change in overall evaluations starts with changes in perceptions of quality of performance and quality of experience. Hence, the priority of managers is at the transaction level of service quality and satisfaction. From management's perspective, quality of performance should be viewed as the most important aspect of a service, for as Berry and Parasuraman noted: "Service quality is the foundation of services marketing". While the refuge's attributes are under the control of the managers, benefits visitors obtain during the trip are not. Although quality of visitors' experience is partially a response to management's performance, in part it is also a reaction to factors that are brought to the refuge by visitors themselves. Further, the subjectivity of the psychological outcome of a refuge visit experience determines that tourism managers cannot control the psychological benefits visitors obtain from each visit.

Thus, at the transaction level, service quality is most important for managers. To influence visitors' future decisions, managers can improve the attributes of a refuge. Crompton and Lamb pointed out "Citizens don't buy programmes or service; they buy the expectation of benefits. Programmes themselves are not marketable. Only their benefits have a value to client groups.

A service programme is simply a vehicle for the user benefits that it conveys". Results of the study confirmed that quality of performance is only one factor that influences visitors' benefits obtained. However, it is the most accessible means available to management to achieve the ultimate goal-realization of benefits sought by visitors. Although structural equation modeling procedures deal with causal models, they do not establish causal relationships. Bollen asserts that "At best they show whether the causal assumptions embedded in a model match a sample of data".

Thus, results of the study only verify that the proposed relationships among constructs in the conceptual model for the most part were supported by the sample data collected for this study.

An important next step is to fit the proposed model to other samples of data so that its validity can be examined. Findings of the study supported the influence of overall satisfaction on overall service quality which suggests that overall service quality is a higher level construct. However, this is not conclusive because structural equation modeling shows only whether the relationship conceptualized in the model has support from the sample data. Although the impact of overall satisfaction on overall service quality was conceptualized based on previous studies, there is also evidence in the literature that there may be a reciprocal effect between overall service quality and satisfaction.

Future research could usefully examine this possible effect in order to determine which construct is superordinate at the global level. A related topic that awaits further research is examination of the interrelationships among dimensions of latent constructs in the model. The purpose of the present study was to test the structural model and, thus, it did not focus on examining the dimensions of the constructs. Future studies could investigate what service attributes contribute most to visitors' quality of experience, and what benefits should be promoted to current and potential visitors. In addition, the Nature Appreciation/Learning dimension was eliminated in this study because of its overwhelming influence on the model. This may be an important issue for future studies to address, because it seems likely that one or two powerful variables may consistently overwhelm similar models in leisure contexts where respondents are highly involved users.

9

Laundry

Whether you wash your clothes at home or send them to a laundry, you expect them to come out clean and crisp, looking and feeling as they did when they were new. The dirt, oils, perspiration, and stains should all have vanished, leaving the fabrics and their colours completely intact. Moreover, the clothes should retain their shapes, sizes, structures, and surface textures. With so many expectations, it's no wonder that the word "miracle" appears so frequently in advertisements for laundry detergents.

Achieving these many goals is something of a balancing act. The chemicals that contaminate clothes aren't always so different from those that give them their structures and colours. Trying to remove one chemical while leaving the other isn't easy and washday in the nineteenth century was hardly a treat for the garments being cleaned. However, in recent years laundering has developed from a simple art to an advanced technology. The miracles promised by the detergent commercials are almost reality. In this section, we'll examine physical and chemical mechanisms that make those miracles possible.

Questions to Think About: How do soaps and detergents help to clean clothes? What is the difference between a soap and a detergent? What is hard water and how do you "soften" it? Why does soap form soap scum in hard water? How do detergents keep soil from redepositing on the clothes? Is dry cleaning really "dry"? Why do some clothes wrinkle and shrink when you wash them in water but not when you dry clean them? How does bleach remove stains? Why do fabric softeners increase the volume and fluffiness of towels? Why do fabric softeners reduce static cling? How do "brighteners" make clothes appear whiter than white?

Experiments to Do: You don't have to do laundry to know that soaps and detergents help to remove oil and grease from just about anything. Spread a little oil on a rag or your hand and try to wash it off with water. You'll find that the oil is difficult to remove with water because it doesn't dissolve in water—oil and water don't mix. But if you add a little soap or detergent to the water and try washing again, you'll find that the oil is carried away in the water. The soap or detergent molecules surround tiny droplets of oil and allow the water to remove them. Soaps and detergents are remarkable materials. They are "at home" in both water and oil and they assist water in handling oil. That simple fact is the basis for laundering and the central issue in this section.

SOAP

One of the most difficult problems in laundering clothes is how to remove all of the different soils in a single operation. Some soils consist of polar molecules, those that have electric charges or electrically charged regions, while others consist of non-polar molecules, those that are effectively neutral throughout. These two types of soils are so different from one another that a liquid that dissolves one is unlikely to dissolve the other. To make things worse, there are also soils that don't dissolve well in anything, or at least not in anything that you could imagine putting on your clothes. Getting all of these soils out of the clothes without harming the clothes is what laundry is all about.

Polar soil molecules include salts from perspiration and ground dirt. These salts generally dissolve in water, where they become ions that are carried away in shells of water molecules. Because they are basically at home in water, these polar soils are described as hydrophilic (water loving). Because carbohydrates such as sugar have electrically charged regions and form hydrogen bonds with water, they dissolve easily in water and are thus also hydrophilic.

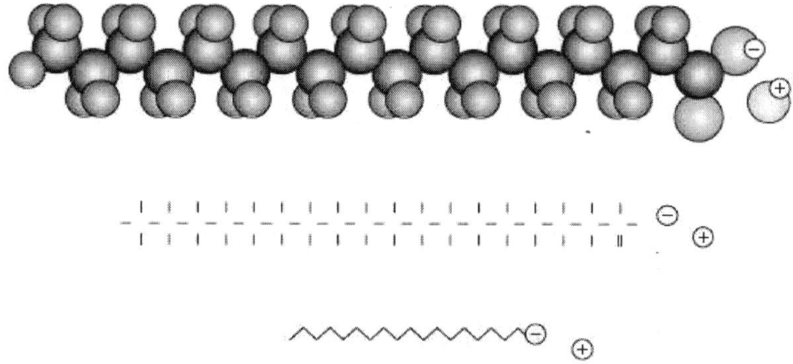

Fig. Soap is a peculiar salt. Its negative ion consists of a long hydrophobic (water avoiding) hydrocarbon chain attached to a hydrophilic (water loving) carboxylate group. A nearby positive ion, usually sodium (Na), balances the negative charge of the carboxylate group. A soap molecule can be represented as (*a*) balls, (*b*) letters, or (*c*) a zigzag hydrocarbon chain with charges attached to it.

Non-polar soil molecules include oils, fats, and waxes from skin, foods, and plants.

These oily molecules tend to dissolve in non-polar solvents such as gasoline or kerosene. Because they can't form hydrogen bond with water molecules, they don't bind well with water and are essentially insoluble in it. These non-polar soils are described as hydrophobic (water avoiding).

You could launder your clothes by first washing them in water to dissolve and remove hydrophilic soils and then laundering them in gasoline to dissolve and remove hydrophobic soils. But this would take a long time and would be very hard on the fabric. After the process was over, your clothes would have aged considerably, yet some of the soils would still remain. Cleaning clothes requires something more than water and gasoline. That's why we use soaps, detergents, bleaches, and brighteners in our laundry.

Soap is a peculiar type of salt. Like all salts, soap contains a mixture of positively and negatively charged ions. There is nothing special about the positive ions, which are usually just sodium or potassium atoms that are missing an electron. What makes soap so unusual and so effective at cleaning is its negative ions. The negative ions in soap have the negative charge located at one end of a very long molecule. The other end of the molecule is an uncharged hydrocarbon chain such as those encountered in oil molecules.

The negative soap ion is so long that its two ends operate independently. Its charged end is polar and hydrophilic. Water molecules cling to this end's electric charge and try to carry it into solution. But the soap ion's hydrocarbon end is non-polar and hydrophobic. This end of the soap molecule is expelled from water but binds nicely to oil molecules.

The one half of a soap ion is at home in water and the other half is at home in oil. The hydrophilic end is attracted to water while the hydrophobic oil end is attracted to oil.

This split affinity causes soap ions to accumulate at interfaces between water and oil. The negative ions spontaneously orient themselves at such an interface with their electrically charged ends in the water and their hydrocarbon ends in the oil. The positive ions hover around in the water near the interface to keep everything electrically neutral.

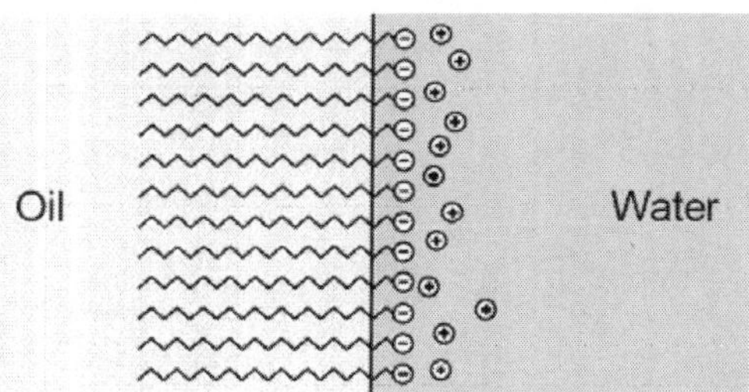

Fig. Soap negative ions move spontaneously to interfaces between water and oil. Their hydrophobic ends project into the oil and their hydrophilic ends project into the water.

This tendency for soap ions to order themselves at interfaces is an example of *self-organizing behaviour*. While mixtures of table salt and water are random and homogeneous, mixtures of soap and water are not. Even when there's no oil present, soap ions migrate to water's surface because individual soap ions don't mix freely with the water. Since water molecules don't bond well to the non-polar hydrocarbon chains, the water molecules push the soap ions to the water's surface.

A tiny amount of soap added to a bowl of water soon creates an ultra-thin layer of soap ions on the surface of the water—a layer that's only a single molecule thick. The soap ions arrange themselves with their polar ends in the water and their non-polar ends in the air. The uppermost water molecules in the bowl are then able to hydrogen bond to the soap ions above them and don't pull together as strongly as they would if they had only air above them. Thus the water molecules contribute little to the liquid's surface tension.

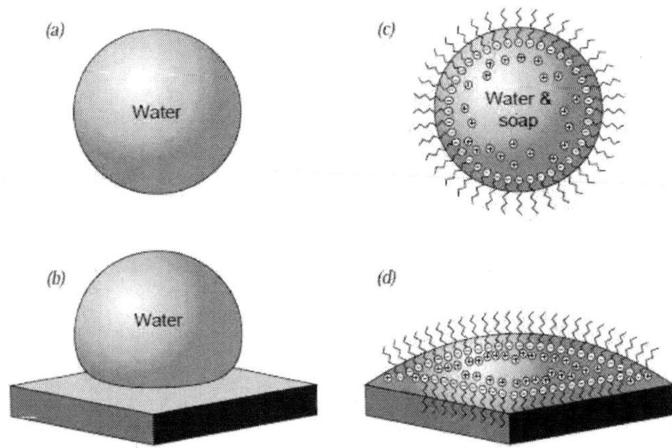

Fig. (*a*) Surface tension in pure water causes its droplets to be spherical. (*b*) These water droplets remain almost spherical on many surfaces. (*c*) Soap ions coat the outside of a water droplet and dramatically reduce the surface tension. (*d*) The soapy droplet is able to spread out more easily and wets many surfaces completely.

The hydrocarbon chains of the soap ions now form the uppermost layer in the liquid. With nothing above them to stick to, these chains pull together and create surface tension. However they attract one another with van der Waals forces, not hydrogen bonds, and create a surface tension only about 30 per cent that of water molecules. The soap's presence in the water significantly reduces its surface tension.

This reduced surface tension is soap's first contribution to the laundering process. Pure water keeps to itself, beading up on any surface that doesn't bind strongly to water molecules. Surface tension makes falling water droplets spherical and they remain almost spherical on oily, hydrophobic surfaces. But adding just a tiny bit of soap to the water reduces each droplet's surface tension and allows it to wet the surface. A soapy droplet spreads outward because van der Waals forces attracting the droplet to the surface are strong enough to stretch it out into a flat puddle.

In effect, soapy water is "wetter" than pure water. Soapy water doesn't bead up on fabrics; it soaks right in. When you are cleaning clothes and want the water to wet every fibre in the fabric, you add soap to the water. Because soap helps water to wet surfaces, it's a wetting agent. It's also a surfactant or *surfaceactive agent* because of its tendency to modify the properties of surfaces or interfaces. There are other kinds of surfactants, but soaps and soap-like materials are the most important group.

However, not all soap molecules make it to the water's surface. If you put lots of soap in the water, or the surface is far away, the soap ions assemble themselves into spherical structures called micelles and remain inside the water. In these micelles, all of the soap ions are oriented with their charged, polar ends pointing outward and their uncharged, non-polar ends pointing inward. The water molecules stick to the micelles' polar outsides and carry the micelles about. As usual, the positive soap ions hover about nearby to keep everything electrically neutral.

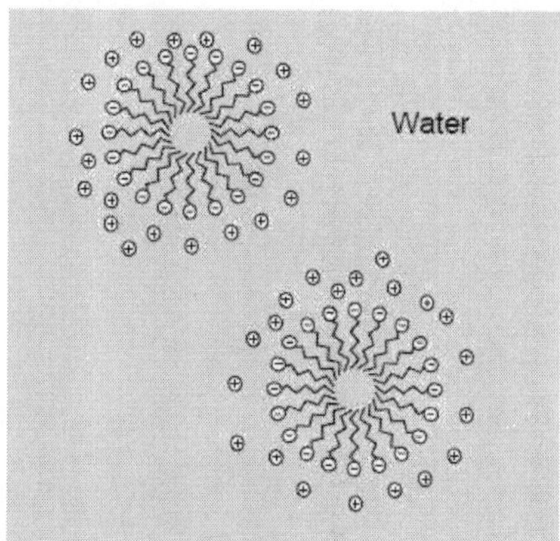

Fig. In water, negative soap ions form spherical micelles. The hydrophobic chains form the centers of these micelles and tend to accumulate oily soil molecules.

These micelles are soap's second contribution to the laundering process. They tend to trap and collect oily soil molecules. The inside of a micelle is a non-polar environment and ideal for oil molecules. When an oil molecule bumps into a micelle, the water pushes it into the center of the micelle and there it remains.

The micelles in soapy water move randomly, collecting any oil molecules they encounter in their travels. With a little thermal or mechanical agitation, micelles can even pluck oil molecules from the surfaces of fabrics. Naturally, this is helpful when you are doing laundry. Little by little, the oily soils in the clothes become trapped in micelles in the water.

Soap also helps to remove insoluble debris from clothes. Micelles form around dust particles and help the water to carry these particles away. Since most dust particles don't dissolve in any liquids, soap micelles are essential to their removal from clothing.

Since soap micelles are composed of negatively charged soap ions, they are negatively charged objects and tend to repel one another in the water. They remain separate and mobile and are easily washed down the drain along with their contents. In fact, most fabrics also become negatively charged in water. Their fibres include weakly attached hydrogen atoms that are carried away as positive ions by the water. The fibres are left with negative charges and they tend to repel the negatively charged soap micelles. This repulsion prevents soils from redepositing on the clothes.

(a)

```
 H   H   H   H
 |   |   |   |
-C - C - C - C - C - O - H
 |   |   |   |   ||
 H   H   H   H   O
```

Fatty acid

(b)

```
 H   H   H   H
 |   |   |   |
-C - C - C - C - C - O(-)
 |   |   |   |   ||
 H   H   H   H   O        H(+)
```

Fatty acid in water

Fig. (a) A fatty acid is a long hydrocarbon chain ending in a carboxylate group. (b) In water, the carboxylate group's hydrogen atom is carried away by water molecules as positive ion, leaving the rest of the molecule negatively charged.

This arrangement, soap micelles in water, is a stable emulsion. Unlike a simple mixture of oil and water, it doesn't separate when you let it sit. A surfactant that helps to form and stabilize emulsions is called an emulsifier. Emulsifiers are particularly important in food preparation, where egg yolks, lecithin, and various gums are used to make mayonnaise, chocolate, and other foods smooth and creamy.

Soap is clearly useful in laundering clothes, but where does it come from and what is its structure? Soap is made from naturally occurring oils and fats. Each molecule of oil or fat consists of three fatty acid molecules bound to a glycerin molecule. A fatty acid molecule resembles a paraffin or olefin molecule, with its long chain of carbon atoms surrounded by hydrogen atoms. But the fatty acid molecule has a special arrangement of carbon, oxygen, and hydrogen atoms, a *carboxylate group*, at one end that makes it an organic acid.

An acid is a molecule that can easily lose a positively charged hydrogen ion when it is mixed with water. One of the hydrogen atoms at the special end of the fatty acid falls off easily because the adjacent oxygen atom has largely removed its electron. Oxygen and hydrogen form a covalent bond, with a pair of electrons between them, but the oxygen atom attracts the pair of electrons more strongly than the hydrogen atom does. As a result, the hydrogen atom's nucleus is relatively exposed and is easily carried away by passing water molecules. This loss leaves a negatively charged fatty acid ion.

In an oil or fat, these three fatty acid molecules are not ionized. Instead, they have reacted with a glycerin molecule like three large ships docking at a small port. The glycerin molecule has a chain of three carbon atoms and each of these carbon atoms plays host to one of the fatty acids. The resulting structure is called a triglyceride. Assembled in this manner, the triglyceride is non-polar and virtually insoluble in water. It looks and feels like petroleum oil because both have the same long hydrocarbon chains. However triglycerides are digestible while petroleum oils are not.

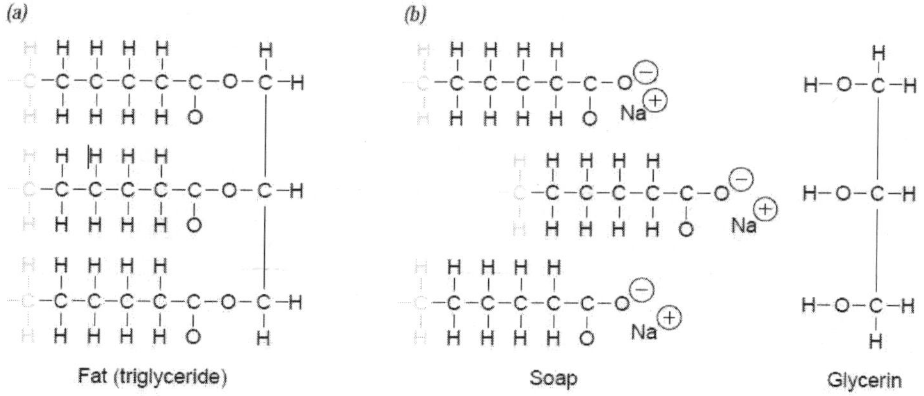

(a) Fat (triglyceride)

(b) Soap Glycerin

Fig. (*a*) A fat molecule or triglyceride consists of three fatty acids bonded to a glycerin molecule. When the triglyceride reacts with sodium hydroxide (lye), the fatty acids break free of the glycerin and produce a mixture of soap and glycerin (*b*).

Triglycerides composed entirely of paraffin-like fatty acids are called saturated fats because they have only single covalent bonds and as many hydrogen atoms as possible. Such molecules experiences strong van der Waals forces, forming fats that remain solid at relatively high temperatures. These fats are found in animals and tropical plants such as palms and coconuts.

Triglycerides containing olefin-like fatty acids are called unsaturated fats because they have double bonds that reduce their hydrogen atoms count. Double bonds stiffen the hydrocarbon chains and prevent them from bonding as strongly to one another. Oils contain these molecules melt at relatively low temperatures and are found in fish and temperate plants such as soybeans and corn. Unfortunately, people find the less healthy saturated fats more tasty and satisfying than the unsaturated fats. Converting unsaturated fats to saturated fats, a process called hydrogenation, is commonly used to stiffen oils for use in foods such as margarine and candy

Soap enters into this picture when triglycerides react with sodium hydroxide (lye). Sodium hydroxide is a salt consisting of positive sodium ions and negative hydroxyl ions (a hydrogen and an oxygen atom together) and it rapidly dissolves into independent ions when you put it in water. When you mix fat, water, and lye together, the hydroxyl ions from the lye attack the fat molecules and remove the fatty acids from the glycerin as negative ions. Soon the water is filled with glycerin molecules, negative fatty acid ions, and positive sodium ions. When the reaction is complete and most of the water is removed, the result is soap. The glycerin may or may not be removed.

The hardness of the soap depends on the fats from which it was made. Saturated fats produce hard bar soaps while unsaturated fats produce soft liquid soaps. Soft hand soaps often include the glycerin. While most modern soaps are made with lye and are thus sodium salts, earlier soaps where made with potassium hydroxide obtained from wood ash and lime and were potassium salts.

WATER SOFTENING

Unfortunately, laundering clothes isn't quite this easy. While soap is wonderful at removing oils and fats from fabric, it has problems in hard water. Hard water is any water with more than about 120 milligrams of positively charged calcium and magnesium ions per litre. These two metal ions, and a few others, bind with the negative soap ions and form insoluble soap scums that deposit themselves on sinks, showers, bathtubs, washing machines, and clothing. If you try to launder clothes with soap in hard water, you are in for a messy surprise.

The problem occurs because calcium and magnesium ions behave differently from the ions of sodium and potassium normally found in soap. Sodium and potassium atoms each have one more electron than they need to complete an electronic shell—a quantum physical structure that is particularly stable. That extra electron is relatively easily removed, creating a positively charged ion that is easily drawn into solution in water. Water is so strongly attracted to sodium ions that almost every sodium salt in existence dissolves in water. Sodium's fantastic solubility explains why there is so much sodium in seawater. Potassium ions are almost as soluble as sodium ions. Salts consisting of sodium or potassium positive ions and soap negative ions are extremely soluble in water.

But calcium and magnesium atoms have two more electrons than they need to complete an electronic shell. They give up those two electrons somewhat reluctantly to form positively charged ions and aren't particularly soluble in water. While some calcium and magnesium salts are modestly soluble in water, calcium and magnesium soap salts are not.

When you put soap in hard water, the positive calcium and magnesium ions in the water combine with the negative soap ions and quickly form insoluble salts. These salts are pasty solids that cling to everything. If you want to do laundry in a place where the water contains substantial amounts of dissolved minerals, you must either remove the calcium and magnesium ions from the water or replace the soap with something else. Actually, you often do both.

Removing the calcium and magnesium ions is the first option. This step is called *water softening* and is done routinely in most industrial laundries long before the water enters the washing equipment. There are several different ways to soften water, but the most interesting scheme and the one used most often in houses is called ion exchange. The water passes through an ion exchange material that replaces the calcium and magnesium ions with sodium ions.

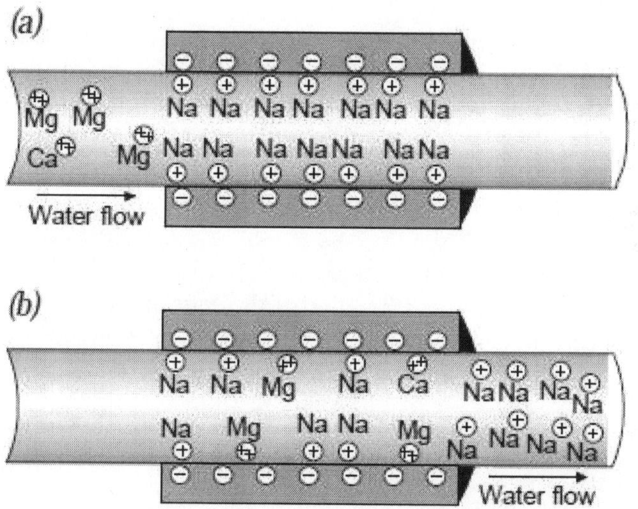

Fig. (a) A fresh ion exchange water softener contains sodium ions, located near negatively charged sites in a resin or zeolite ceramic. (b) As water containing magnesium (Mg) and calcium (Ca) ions passes through the softener, the sodium ions are released and the magnesium and calcium ions remain behind.

The ion exchange material is a special ceramic (zeolite) or plastic resin with many negatively charged regions in its porous structure. To keep the material electrically neutral, a positive ion is located near each negative region. The negative regions are part of the material, so they can't go anywhere, but the positive ions are mobile.

When the ion exchange material is fresh, nearly all of the positive ions inside it are sodium ions. As hard water flows through the material, the sodium ions are gradually replaced by calcium and magnesium ions. Since the sodium ions are more soluble in water than the calcium and magnesium ions, the sodium ions tend to enter the water and the calcium and magnesium ions tend to leave it. Each calcium or magnesium ion that sticks to the ion exchange material releases two sodium ions, which leave the water softener in the water itself.

While the water leaving an ion exchange water softener still contains dissolved ions, they are sodium ions rather than calcium or magnesium ions.

The sodium ions cause no trouble when laundering clothes or washing your skin, but people who are on low sodium diets should avoid softened water. Moreover, you shouldn't use softened water in a steam iron.

When all of the sodium ions in the ion exchange material have been replaced by calcium or magnesium ions, the water softener stops softening the water. To regenerate the ion exchange material, you must flush it with very concentrated salt water. The many sodium ions in the salt water dislodge most of the calcium and magnesium ions and return the ion exchange material to its original condition—it is once more full of sodium ions and ready to soften water.

Because many homes don't have water softeners, most laundry soaps soften the water themselves. They contain chemicals called builders that bind to the calcium and magnesium ions and keeping them away from the soap ions. The most effective of these builders is sodium tripolyphosphate and, at one time, most household detergents contained large amounts of it. However, phosphates encourage the growth of algae, threatening the ecologies of rivers, lakes, and bays, and have been banned from detergents in many regions. Builders such as sodium carbonate, citric acid, and sodium citrate are now often used instead.

Another building technique used in some products is to incorporate small zeolite ceramic particles directly in the detergent. These builder particles exchange sodium ions for calcium and magnesium ions and soften the water directly in the washer. They fall to the bottom of the washer and are rinsed away.

Detergents

But water softening is only half the solution. Because it's hard to eliminate all of the calcium and magnesium from water, the manufacturers also eliminate the soap from the laundry powder. That's right—most laundry detergents aren't soap at all. Instead, they are synthetic detergents that are structurally related to natural soap but aren't quite the same.

Actually, soap is a type of detergent. Detergents are a broad class of molecules that stabilize mixtures of oil and water. There are many other kinds of molecules that can perform this task and thus many types of detergents.

The most common laundry detergents are the linear alkylbenzenesulfonates. These petroleum products are sodium salts, just like most soaps, but the structures of the negative ions are different. Recall that a negative soap ion is a long hydrocarbon chain attached to a negatively charged carboxylate group. The detergent ion is also a long hydrocarbon chain, attached to an aromatic or benzene ring, attached to a negatively charged sulfonate group. The sulfonate group involves one sulfur atom and three oxygen atoms.

The two important parts of the detergent molecule are the charged head and the long non-polar tail. The charged end is a *sulfonate group* in which a sulfur atom attaches to four other atoms: a carbon atom and three oxygen atoms.

This arrangement is roughly tetrahedral in shape. But sulfur normally attaches to only two atoms, so how is this arrangement possible?

First, the sulfur atom forms normal covalent bonds with the carbon atom and with one of the oxygen atoms. That oxygen atom has an extra electron, making it a negatively charged ion that can only form a single covalent bond.

Second, the sulfur atom allows each of the two other oxygen atoms to share a pair of its electrons. Because these shared electrons can travel between both atoms, their wavelengths increase and their kinetic energies decrease. In this manner, the oxygen atoms become attached to the sulfur atom. The overall result is a negatively charged structure that's easily carried about by water molecules.

The detergent molecule's long non-polar tail is essentially an unbranched paraffin chain, also referred to as a *linear alkyl group*. This chain provides the oily tail of the detergent molecule. While early alkylbenzenesulfonate detergents included branched paraffin chains, these proved to be less biodegradable than the linear versions. Bacteria can metabolize long linear chains because those chains are common in animals and plants, but branched chains are rare in nature and bacteria are unprepared for them. To keep detergent foam out of streams and lakes, manufacturers have learned to produce purely linear detergent molecules.

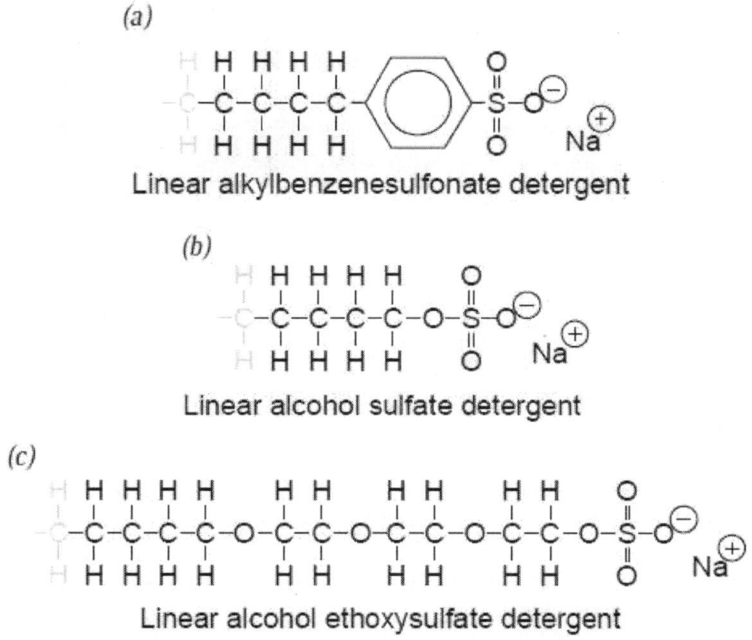

(a)

Linear alkylbenzenesulfonate detergent

(b)

Linear alcohol sulfate detergent

(c)

Linear alcohol ethoxysulfate detergent

Fig. (a) The most common laundry detergent has an aromatic or benzene ring connecting a long hydrophobic hydrocarbon chain to a hydrophilic sulfonate group. Common shampoo detergents connect the chain to the sulfonate with either (b) an oxygen atom or (c) a string of oxygen and carbon atoms.

The last piece of the detergent molecule is the aromatic or benzene ring. This ring is a vestige of the manufacturing process. It's much easier to attached the linear alkyl tail and the sulfonate head separately to an aromatic ring than it is to attach them directly to one another. Unfortunately, the ring actually reduces the biodegradability of the molecule somewhat. There are other detergents, such as linear alcohol sulfates and linear alcohol ethoxysulfates, in which the aromatic ring is replaced by an oxygen atom or a string of oxygen and carbon atoms. The most common linear alcohol sulfate is sodium lauryl sulfate, with 14 carbon atoms in its hydrophobic chain. Sodium laureth sulfate is a common linear alcohol ethoxysulfate, also with 14 carbon atoms in its chain. These detergents are derived from tropical oils and often used in shampoos and dishwashing liquids.

Since calcium and magnesium ions don't cause these sulfonate or sulfate detergents to form insoluble detergent scums, why do laundry detergents still worry about softening the water? Unfortunately, calcium and magnesium ions interfere with the micelles, making it difficult for them to extract soil from fabric and keep it suspended in water. Because each calcium or magnesium ion has twice the positive charge of a sodium or potassium ion, these highly charged ions approach the micelles closely and partially neutralize their surfaces. Since these neutralized micelles don't repel one another or the fabric well, they do a poor job of cleaning clothes. That's why laundries and laundry detergent still work to remove the calcium and magnesium ions.

Before leaving detergents, it's worth noting that not all detergents are negative ions (anions). It's also possible to construct detergent molecules that are positive ions (cations) and even ones that aren't ions at all. However, cationic detergents and surfactants aren't used in laundry detergents because they tend to stick to fabric—we'll discuss their use as fabric softeners later on. But non-ionic detergents are often used to launder clothes.

The only requirement for a detergent is that its molecules stabilize a mixture of oil and water. Non-ionic surfactant molecules don't have an electric charge, but they do have a hydrophilic end and a hydrophobic end. Like most detergents, the hydrophobic end is just a long hydrocarbon chain. But the hydrophilic end is also a long chain, consisting of oxygen and carbon molecules attached one after the next and decorated with hydrogen atoms. The oxygen atoms in this special chain form hydrogen bonds with water molecules, giving that end of the molecule its hydrophilic character. These non-ionic molecules form micelles and are very effective at removing grease.

Non-ionic surfactants are unaffected by hard water and are actually better than anionic detergents at removing some soils—they are particularly good at removing skin oils from synthetic fabrics. However, they aren't salts and exist either as liquids or waxy solids. As a result, non-ionic surfactants are difficult to formulate into powdered detergents but are common in liquid detergents.

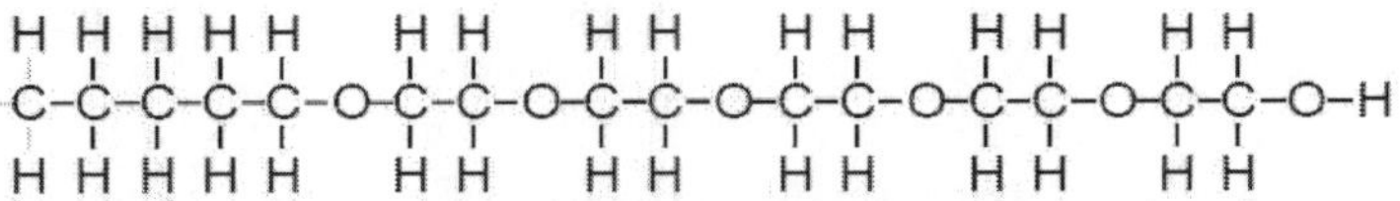

```
H H H H H   H H   H H   H H   H H   H H
| | | | |   | |   | |   | |   | |   | |
C-C-C-C-C-O-C-C-O-C-C-O-C-C-O-C-C-O-C-C-O-H
| | | | |   | |   | |   | |   | |   | |
H H H H H   H H   H H   H H   H H   H H
```

Nonionic surfactant

Fig. Non-ionic surfactants have a hydrophobic hydrocarbon chain (on the left) attached to a hydrophilic chain containing oxygen atoms (on the right).

Bleaches and Enzymes

Not all soils can be removed from fabrics with detergent and water. Molecules that form covalent bonds with the fabric create stains that can only be eliminated with bleaches or enzymes. Bleaches act to destroy the coloration of stain molecules or to cut them free from the fabric. Enzymes act to dice up large stain molecules into smaller fragments that can be washed away. With a little luck, these steps can be taken without destroying the fabric or its colour.

Unlike soaps and detergents, bleaches react chemically with the soil molecules. They are particularly aggressive at converting double bonds to single bonds by attaching oxygen and chlorine molecules to the two atoms involved. Double bonds often give organic molecules their colours so this sort of rearrangement tends to make them colourless.

Just as atoms absorb and emit photons of light that are characteristic of their electronic states, so molecules absorb and emit photons that are characteristic of their electronic states. Each electron in a molecule is sensitive to passing electromagnetic radiation and responds to photons that can transfer it to some unoccupied state with more energy. If the electron finds such a photon, it may undergo a radiative transition to the excited electronic state and absorb the photon.

The electron will eventually return to its original state, converting the extra energy into thermal energy, but the photon will be gone forever. If a particular molecule contains electrons that can absorb photons of visible light in this manner, it will appear coloured.

In most single covalent bonds, the two electrons are bound so tightly between the two nuclei that any transition to a new electronic state requires more energy than a photon of visible light can provide. Only ultraviolet light can cause radiative transitions in these electrons. Molecules based entirely on single covalent bonds are normally unaffected by visible light and are thus colourless.

However, the outer electrons in a double covalent bond aren't so tightly bound and can be transferred to other electronic states relatively easily—a photon of visible light may well be able to cause the transfer. A double bond that absorbs blue photons from passing light appears yellow. One that absorbs red photons appears cyan. The usual rules of subtractive colour apply.

Just how much energy it takes to cause this transfer depends on the chemical nature and environment of the double bond. Most important are the two atoms joined by the double bond. In addition to double bonds involving a pair of carbon atoms, there are also carbon-oxygen, carbon-nitrogen, nitrogen-oxygen, and nitrogen-nitrogen double bonds. These double bonds are often coloured, particularly the latter two. Groups of atoms that give rise to colour in molecules are called chromophores.

However the exact colour of a double bond is determined by the detailed structure of the molecule around it. Since all of the electrons in that molecule affect one another through electrostatic forces and the Pauli exclusion principle, the whole molecular structure contributes to the colour of the electrons in the double bond itself. A subtle change in a molecule's structure may change its colour from red to orange. That's how organic dye manufacturers construct rich pallets of colours from a small number of different chromophores.

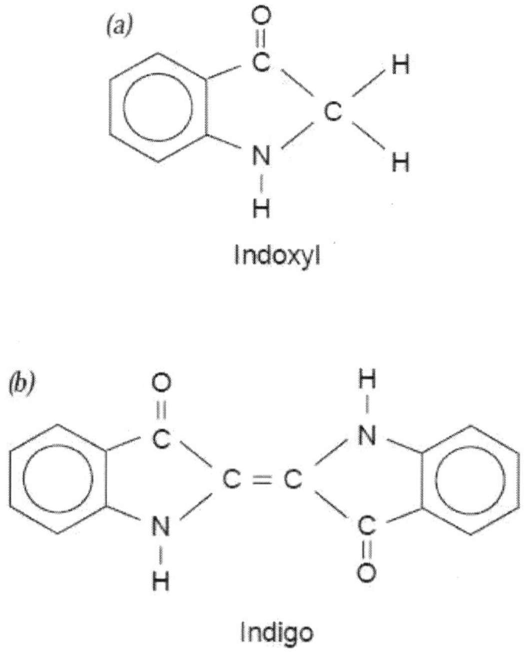

(a)

Indoxyl

(b)

Indigo

Fig. (*a*) Indoxyl is a colourless, water-soluble chemical obtained from a fermented plant extract. When indoxyl is exposed to oxygen in the air, it reacts pairwise to form water-insoluble indigo (*b*), the blue dye used in blue jeans. The double bonded carbon atoms at the center of this molecule are the chromophore and the rest of the molecule determines the precise colour of the dye. Bleaches and ultraviolet light can destroy the double bond, giving blue jeans a faded look.

Coloured molecules are wonderful if you are an artist, but you don't want extraneous ones attached to your clothes. That's where bleach comes in. Bleach attacks double bonds, destroying the chromophores in the stain molecules. The molecules may remain on the fabric but they no longer absorb visible light. The two major classes of bleaches are chlorine bleaches and oxygen bleaches. The chlorine bleaches tend to put chlorine and oxygen atoms on the two atoms involved in a double bond. The double bond vanishes as one of its atom binds to a chlorine atom and its other atom binds to the oxygen atom of a hydroxyl group (OH).

Unfortunately, chlorine bleaches are so effective at attacking chemicals that they damage the clothes, too. Sometimes they destroy the chromophores in dye molecules, turning coloured fabric white. Other times they modify the dye molecules and change the fabric's colour.

But chlorine bleaches also damage natural fibres themselves, breaking up their molecules and weakening the fabric. While chlorine bleach may succeed in cutting stain molecules free from your clothing, it may also cut holes in the clothing itself.

Oxygen bleaches used hydrogen peroxide to attack double bonds. A hydrogen peroxide molecule is a water molecule with an extra oxygen atom inserted between the oxygen atom and one of the hydrogen atoms. This molecule decomposes in water and its fragments, either ions or free radicals, attack double bonds. Once again, they destroy chromophores and decolorize stains.

Hydrogen peroxide is less reactive than chlorine bleach and causes less fabric damage. It's also less damaging to commercial dye molecules than chlorine bleach. However, since hydrogen peroxide is often used to bleach hair, oxygen bleaches can obviously destroy the colours in some natural fibres.

Hydrogen peroxide itself is rather unstable and is often generated right in the washer by the decomposition of another molecule, sodium perborate. This decomposition occurs only above about 50 °C, so bleaching must be done in hot water. Some laundry detergents contain activators that help sodium perborate decompose in cooler water but it still works best in hot water.

Enzymes are biological catalysts. Your body uses a great many different enzymes to catalyze various chemical reactions that would otherwise rarely occur at body temperature or that might proceed along the wrong paths without help. Enzymes help to construct molecules, to take them apart, or to rearrange their components.

The enzymes used most often in detergents are those that degrade proteins. Protein molecules cling tightly to fabrics, are insoluble in water, and prevent detergents from penetrating to the fibres. They act as binders for other molecules, creating stains that are hard to remove. Familiar proteinaceous stains include blood, milk, eggs, and gravy.

The most effective way to remove these stains is by taking the protein molecules apart. This decomposition is done by *proteolytic enzymes*—enzymes that catalyze reactions between water and protein. In these reactions, protein molecules are broken up and water molecule fragments cap the severed ends. In time, proteolytic enzymes can dice up long protein molecules into their constituent parts: *amino acids* and short sequences of amino acids called *peptides*. The stain falls apart and is carried away by the water and detergents. Meat tenderizers operate in a similar fashion, using papain—a proteolytic enzyme extracted from unripe papaya—to degrade protein in meat before cooking.

However, proteolytic enzymes may have an effect on the people who use them. You certainly don't want the protein in your body decomposed while you do laundry or while you wear freshly laundered clothes. Although studies seem to indicate that the enzymes in household detergents pose no serious health threat, they're used sparingly in detergents to avoid any possible adverse effects.

Brighteners and Fabric Softeners

Not all laundry chemicals disappear down the drain when the wash is done. Brighteners and fabric softeners do their jobs by remaining on the clothes long after they leave the drier. Brighteners affect the appearances of the clothes while fabric softeners affect their feels.

With age, white fabrics such as cotton tend to absorb more and more blue light and begin to look yellow. Cleaning and bleaching do little to reduce this effect.

In fact, bleached fabric molecules tend to appear slightly yellow themselves. The old fashioned solution to the yellowing problems was to adding *bluing* to the wash. This blue dye absorbed red and green light, balancing the blue absorption of the fabric itself so that the fabric appeared colourless. To mask the yellowing of age, bluing darkened the whole fabric to a light gray—the amount of light reflected by the fabric was noticeably less than that striking it.

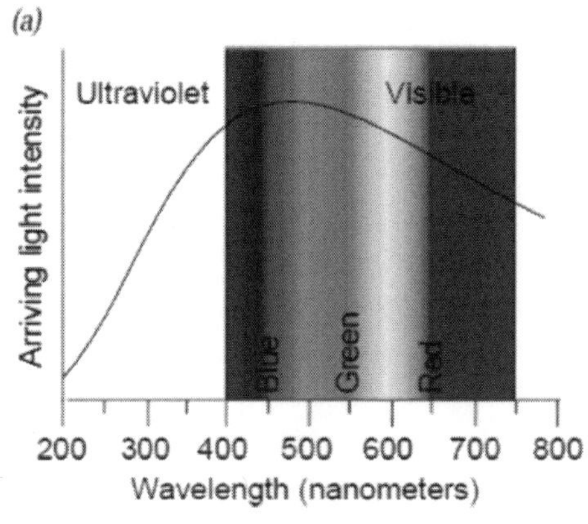

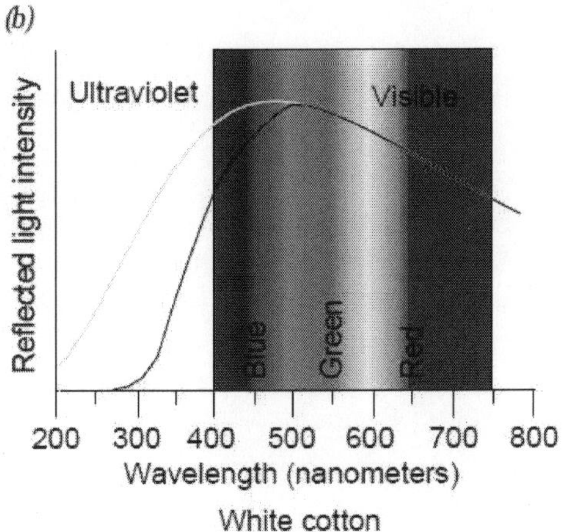

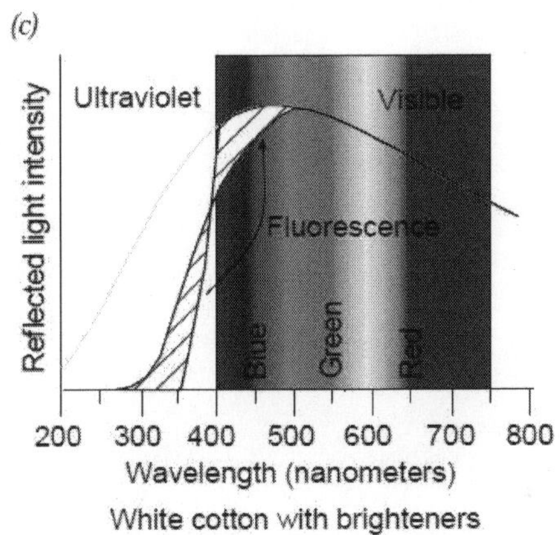

Fig. When white cotton cloth is exposed to sunlight (*a*), it reflects a little less blue light than it should (*b*) and appears slightly yellow. This yellowness increases with age. But when fluorescent brighteners are added to the cotton (*c*), they convert ultraviolet light into blue light and make the cloth appear dazzlingly white.

Instead of using bluing, virtually all modern laundry detergents add chemicals that optically brighten the fabric. These brighteners are actually fluorescent dyes, designed to absorb ultraviolet light and emit bluish-white visible light. Instead of absorbing red and green light to balance the white appearance of a fabric, the brighteners reintroduce the missing blue light. They work best in sunlight, which is rich in ultraviolet light. A brightener molecule absorbs a photon of ultraviolet light and reemits it as a photon of blue light. The energy not reemerging from the molecule in the second photon is converted through vibrations into internal energy in the clothes.

When clothes are washed in these fluorescent dyes, the dye molecules stick to the fabric to create brightened fabric. We can't see the ultraviolet light that the brightened fabric absorbs but we can see the bluish light that it emits. With the missing blue light restored by this fluorescence processes, the brightened fabric appears dazzlingly white. In fact, it may emit more blue light than it is exposed to, making it effectively "whiter than white." In a room illuminated only by ultraviolet light, the brighteners give clothes an eerie violet glow.

Fabric softeners are also chemicals that remain on fabrics after laundering. They are primarily cationic surfactants called *quaternary ammonium compounds*. These compounds are based on the positive ammonium ion, which is itself based on a positive nitrogen ion. A normal nitrogen atom has five valence electrons and must share three of these to reach the four pairs needed to complete an electronic shell. If it shares those electrons with three hydrogen atoms, it forms an ammonia molecule. But if it's missing an electron, the nitrogen atom must share four electrons to complete its shell and can actually bind to four hydrogen atoms. In that case, it forms a positive ammonium ion.

In quaternary ammonium compounds, a positive nitrogen ion forms covalent bonds with four other atoms. However, these atoms aren't necessarily hydrogen atoms. In fabric softeners, the central nitrogen ion binds to four hydrocarbon chains. Two of these chains are short, only one carbon atom long, while the other two chains may contain as many as 18 carbon atoms. These long chains are hydrophobic and have the same oily character as most lubricants.

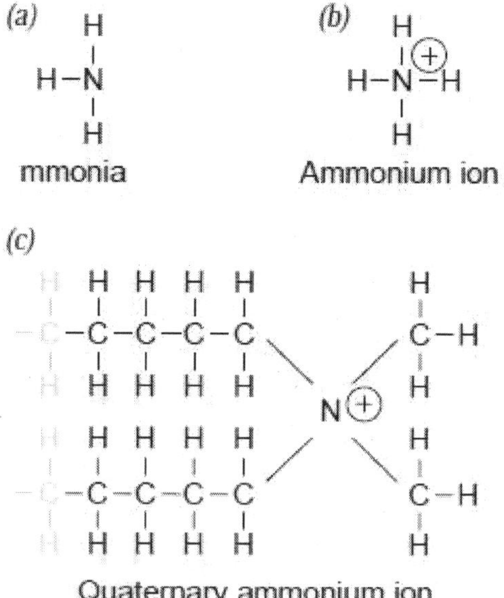

Fig. (a) An ammonia molecule is three hydrogen atoms bound to a nitrogen atom. (b) An ammonium ion is four hydrogen atoms bound to a positively charged nitrogen ion. (c) The quaternary ammonium ion used in fabric softeners is formed by replacing the four hydrogen atoms with hydrocarbon chains.

This oily character is what gives these compounds their fabric softening ability. When you apply the softener to wet fabric, its positively charged surfactant ions are drawn towards the negatively charged fibres and stick to them strongly. While anionic surfactants are repelled by wet fabric and help to clean it, cationic surfactants are attracted to wet fabric and help to soften it.

The surfactant molecules stick to the fabric with their long hydrophobic chains pointing outward. These molecules decorate every fibre in every thread of the clothing, giving them all an oily coating. The hydrocarbon chains lubricate the fabric so that each fibre slides easily within a thread and each thread slides easily within the fabric. This lubrication enhances the flexibility of the fabric and makes it feel softer and more flexible.

Fabric softeners also make fabric surfaces slightly hydrophobic, so that they dry more easily in the spin dry cycle of a washing machine. In this cycle, the clothes travel rapidly around in a circle, always accelerating towards the center of the circle and experiencing huge inward forces from the washer's metal drum. Water's inertia causes it to lag behind the accelerating clothes and it leaves the drum through perforations. By making the fabric slightly hydrophobic, the fabric softener helps the clothes to shed water as they spin, so that they don't have to spend as much time in a hot drier later on.

Fabric softeners also raise the nap on cotton terry towels. Cotton fibres are normally hydrophilic and cling tightly to water droplets. As water droplets dry up, they shrink and pull the cotton fibres towards one another. By the time an untreated towel is dry, its fibres have been crushed together by these forces and it has little nap.

But a towel that has been coated by quaternary ammonium compounds is hydrophobic enough that the water droplets can't pull its fibres together as they dry. The nap remains loose and thick, giving the towel a fluffy appearance and feel. Unfortunately, this same hydrophobic coating slightly reduces the towel's absorbency—a real problem for cotton diapers. To keep it under control, don't use too much fabric softener.

Despite their hydrophobic chains, quaternary ammonium compounds actually attract a few water molecules to the surface of the fabric. They are hygroscopic, meaning that they attract water molecules directly out of the air. Since water conducts electricity very weakly, fabric that has been treated with fabric softeners is very slightly conducting. This conductivity reduces the accumulation of static electricity on the fabric and eliminates static cling.

In a drier, untreated clothes rub against one another and sliding friction transfers electric charge from one region of fabric to another. Large charge imbalances are created and the clothes leave the dry clinging to one another with electrostatic forces. However, treated clothes are lubricated in the drier and experience weaker frictional forces. They transfer less electric charge as they tumble and the small charge imbalances that are created quickly dissipate through the moisture attracted by the fabric softener.

Quaternary ammonium compounds are also used in conditioners and shampoos to soften hair and reduce static electricity problems—they will coat and lubricate just about anything. They are actually bactericidal because they coat bacteria and smother them. These compounds also deactivate some of the enzymes in bacteria and upset their metabolisms. Some antiseptic throat lozenges and mouth washes use quaternary ammonium compounds to kill germs.

Unfortunately, the positive charges of cationic quaternary ammonium compounds make them relatively incompatible with the negative charges of anionic detergents. When they're present together in the water, these two types of ions attract one another and may clump together. This clumping is avoided by keeping the two types of surfactants separate, which is why softeners are usually added during the rinse cycle, in the drier, or in a separate conditioner when washing your hair. However, some detergent and shampoo formulators have successfully combined cationic softeners and anionic detergents.

Detergent Additives

Formulated detergents contain a number of important components that work together to clean clothes. We've already examined the anionic and non-ionic detergents (surfactants), the builders (water softeners), the bleaches, and the brighteners. But there are also foam stabilizers, corrosion inhibitors, soil redeposition inhibitors, and processing agents.

Foam stabilizers are there to control bubble formation. These chemicals can either enhance or suppress foaming. Believe it or not, foam is unrelated to a detergent's ability to clean clothes. The same goes for shampoos and dishwashing detergents. However, the amount of foam a detergent produces may influence its use. If the detergent foams excessively, you may think the detergent is more powerful than it is and cut back on the amount you use. As a result, you may not use enough to clean your clothes properly. If the detergent doesn't foam much, you may think that it isn't working and buy another brand. So the detergent and shampoo manufactures carefully control the foaminess of their products.

Air bubbles don't last long in pure water because water's surface tension causes them to tear. The final layers of water molecules on the bubble's outer and inner surfaces pull together so strongly that any tiny defect immediately initiates a rip that lets the air out of the bubble. By reducing water's surface tension, soaps and detergents remove its tendency to rip and stabilize air bubbles.

But how long each air bubble lasts depends on many features of the mixture and not on its ability to clean things. Some surfactant molecules make particularly stable and long lasting bubbles while other molecules deliberately introduce defects that pop the bubbles. Methyl silicone polymers ("methicones") are particularly effective at weakening bubbles so that they tear and collapse. These polymers are common in antifoam additives and are even included in some antiacid tablets.

Foam boosters are common in detergents and shampoos that are used by hand, where foam is regarded as a sign of effectiveness. Antifoaming agents are often used in washing and dishwashing machine detergents where you don't see the foam anyway and foam interferes with the machine's operation.

Corrosion inhibitors are important in detergent because the ions in detergent would otherwise quickly rust the steel in a washing machine. Rusting is an electrochemical reaction of the type explored in the supplement on batteries. In normal rusting, the iron in steel is attacked by negatively charged hydroxyl ions. However other negatively charged ions, including detergent ions, can also attack iron and rust it. So detergents include corrosion inhibitors. These compounds are usually sodium silicates—water soluble glasses that are discussed in Section 17.2. They form thin glassy coatings on the washer parts and inhibit rusting.

Soil redeposition inhibitors enhance the negative charge of wet fabric fibres. Some fabrics, particularly synthetic ones, don't acquire a strong negative charge in water. They need this electrostatic charge to keep the negatively charged detergent micelles from redepositing their soils on the fabric. So detergents include carboxymethyl cellulose, which attaches itself to the fibres and adds to their negative charge.

Finally, processing agents simply give the detergents the right structures in their boxes or bottles. Sodium sulfate helps to bulk up powdered detergent and make it pour easily. Sodium xylene sulfonate helps to keep all of the components of very concentrated liquid detergents in solution.

Dry Cleaning

Washing clothes in water isn't always a good idea. Fibres such as cotton, wool, silk, and rayon, are very hydrophilic and soak up water molecules like sponges. These fibres form hydrogen bonds with water molecules at various sites on their molecules and accumulate large quantities of water. This water takes up space and causes the fibres to swell. Cotton, wool, and silk fibres increase by about 1 per cent in length and about 15 per cent in thickness. Rayon expands even more, by 3 per cent in length and about 25 per cent in thickness. This swelling distorts the fabric and changes its structure. When the fabric eventually dries, it may have shrunk or wrinkled.

To avoid damage caused by this cycle of expansion and contraction, you can send your clothes to be dry-cleaned. Dry cleaning takes place in a non-polar solvent. Since this solvent doesn't form hydrogen bonds, it's only weakly attracted to the fibres by van der Waals forces and doesn't cause them to swell. The clothes don't lose their shapes.

The solvents used in dry cleaning have evolved over the years since petroleum oils were first found to remove stains. Early dry cleaning was done with gasoline, resulting in many dramatic fires. In 1928, a less flammable solvent became available. The Stoddard solvent, named for the president of the National Institute of Dry cleaning, W. J. Stoddard, is less volatile than gasoline because it contains larger hydrocarbon molecules. It's obtained by distilling crude oil and its vapor will not ignite in air at temperatures below 38 °C.

Nonetheless, Stoddard solvent is still dangerous during hot air drying so non-flammable non-polar solvents have largely replaced it. The most common solvent in dry cleaning is now perchloroethylene. Its molecule consists of a pair of carbon molecules connected by a double bond and each attached to two chlorine atoms. The chlorine atoms bind so strongly to the carbon atoms that the molecule doesn't react with oxygen and forms a non-flammable liquid.

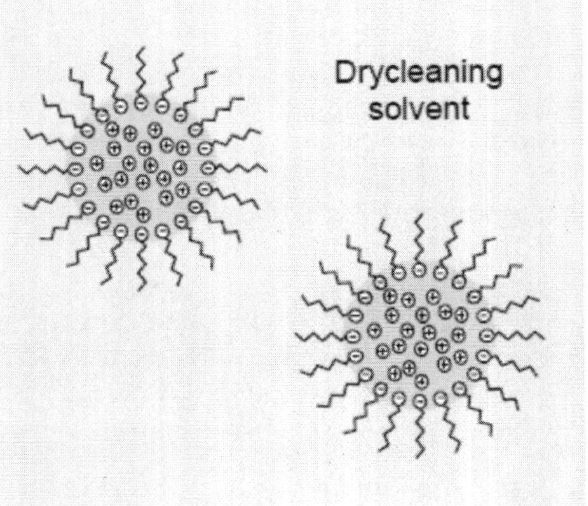

Fig. Detergents form inside-out micelles in dry cleaning solvent. The polar hydrophilic ends of the molecules project inward, towards a tiny drop of water. The non-polar hydrophobic ends project outward into the solvent.

When you put clothes in either Stoddard solvent or perchloroethylene, the oily soils dissolve. These non-polar solvents attract the oily molecules with van der Waals forces and carry them away. Chlorinated solvents clean better than hydrocarbons because they bind more strongly to oily soils. Chlorine atoms are more polarizable than hydrogen atoms and produce stronger van der Waals forces, which is why perchloroethylene doesn't boil until it is heated to 121 °C.

However, these non-polar solvents are unable to dissolve salts and other polar soils. They are also poor at removing insoluble soils such as dust. To help in removing these other soils, dry cleaning solvents include detergents and a little water. The detergents form inside-out micelles in the non-polar solvents, arranged with their non-polar ends on the outside and their polar ends on the inside. Each micelle surrounds a tiny droplet of water. Just as in water cleaning, detergents help to carry away substances that aren't soluble in the principal cleaning liquid.

The water in the dry cleaning mixture is carefully adjusted so that the clothes neither gain nor lose moisture during the cleaning process. In air, water molecules are continually leaving and returning to the clothing and an equilibrium is reached. At this equilibrium, the water molecules still move back and forth but the moisture in the clothing doesn't change significantly. The actual moisture level in the fabric then depends only on the relative humidity of the air, which is typically about 70 per cent in a dry cleaning shop.

The same leaving and returning process takes place in the dry cleaning solvent. Water molecules move back and forth between the fabric and the solvent and establish an equilibrium. Like air, the dry cleaning solvent has a relative humidity and a dry cleaner tries to maintain this relative humidity at the same value as the air in the shop. That way, the fabrics don't accumulate too many water molecules and swell, nor do they lose too many water molecules and dry out. But the polar soils leave the fabrics, become trapped in the detergent micelles, and never return.

With the help of detergents, non-polar dry cleaning solvents carry away non-polar, polar, and insoluble soils from clothes without affecting the structure of the cloth. The dry cleaner then removes the solvent from the clothes by spinning them and drying them in hot air. Because solvents are expensive and environmentally damaging, dry cleaners collect the solvents for reused. They do this by filtering and distilling the liquid solvents and by condensing the gaseous solvent molecules onto chilled surfaces. When this type of solvent recycling is done effectively, a dry cleaner can operate for a long time on the same supply of solvent.

10

Rising Industrial Laundry Market in Hotel Industry

The hotel industry is witnessing a growing trend towards outsourcing its laundry. India is expected to add another 90,000 hotel rooms over the next five years, all of which are in the private sector, especially to meet the tourism demand. In 2010, 10 million people are expected to visit India.

The Indian Railways run approximately 12,000 trains every day. The capacity is to carry 1.4 crore passengers/day. It employs around 17 lakh employees (10 lakh in Group C), including 10,000 officers.

This presents a huge benefit to global players to quickly set up their laundries in India, and cater to the ever growing market.

The health care industry, the up coming and the existing, has started outsourcing laundry services. This sector which has been registering a growth of 9.3 per cent per annum between 2000 and 2009 is projected to grow by 15 per cent per annum by 2013. Laundry services in India are classified into Industrial Laundry and Retail Laundry. Industrial laundry is in its infant stage with major demand coming from hospitals and hotels which have their in-house laundry. Retail laundry is a much organised market with some professionally managed companies catering to the retail needs. Overall, the laundry market in India is still untapped and unorganised.

Industrial laundries generally require heavy capital investment in machinery and equipment for washing, spinning, ironing and drying besides land and property to set-up a laundry. Since laundry market in India is dominated by the small local laundry stores and local dhobis, they are not equipped to handle the huge capital requirement.

EQUIPMENT FOR INDUSTRIAL LAUNDRY

An industrial laundry would require equipment for:

- Washing
- Drying and
- Ironing.

The type of equipment to be purchased would be depend on the volumes that the laundry expects from potential clientele on a daily basis. Equipment for industrial laundries are available in different sizes with varying capacities. Equipment are available in the market for small, medium as well as large industrial laundries.

Equipment for industrial laundries should optimise the washing system considering criteria such as:

- Usage of appropriate washing machinery which would guarantee maximum efficiency with appropriate wash cycles, high spin capacity and minimum energy consumption
- Drier equipment should assure proper drying in the least amount of time with minimum energy consumption
- Flatwork ironers capable of absorbing the production of the driers to assure a high quality press
- Automation of the laundry handling processes in order to save personnel costs and increase productivity

STAGES IN INDUSTRIAL LAUNDRY

An industrial laundry generally involves five stages namely:

- Soiled Retrieval: The linen collected usually is dropped down a laundry chute. Laundry workers collect the soiled linen, in reserved carts and transport it to the laundry facility.
- Soil Sortint: The retrieved linen is unloaded and sorted. Different items often require different washing formulas. Heavy or biohazardous stains such as blood and faeces may require longer wash times and stronger formulas. Large institutions often use a production-line method for soil sorting, with several full-time employees assigned to the task. Since soiled linen may be contaminated with biohazards or sharp objects, employees involved in the sorting process are required to use personal protective equipment and standard safety precautions.
- Washing: The sorted linen is weighed according to the washing machine's load limit. Certified washer operator loads and unloads the large washing machines, decides what is to be washed according to the laundry's schedule and monitors the chemical levels in the water. Since modern tunnel washers monitor their own chemical levels and unload linen directly into the laundry's clean area, the operator is required only to load the linen. Over the past 20 years, many industrial laundries have switched from conventional washers to tunnel washers, also called continuous-batch washers. Since tunnel washers don't have to be stopped for loading and unloading of linen, they provide a more continuous flow of clean laundry.

Higher-volume facilities which may process over 15,000kg of linen per day often rely heavily on tunnel washers.

- Processing: The clean linen is dried, ironed and folded. Some items, such as towels and blankets, are put through a dryer until they are no longer damp, then sent to mechanical folders. Wetwork items, such as sheets, are sent through steam-powered ironers which dry, press and fold them.

Ironers use heavy steam-heated rollers to dry the linen while pressing out wrinkles. Some items, such as wash cloths, may be too small to be handled mechanically. These items must be packaged by hand.

- Packaging and Distribution: The processed linen is prepared for delivery. Individual orders are filled, based on the needs and requests of the laundry's customers and sent to the laundry's main distribution points and storage areas. Linen not used for orders is placed in storage areas, giving the facility a reserve of clean laundry.

Trained delivery people transport the clean linen back to the customers. This is a skilled position, since the delivery person must have a thorough knowledge of both laundry operation and the principles of good customer service.

In hospitals, delivery people must be familiar with patient relations, confidentiality policies. Large institutions will usually employ several full-time delivery people.

ECO-FRIENDLY CHEMICALS

Haylide Chemicals has launched a new range of eco friendly laundry chemicals. The complete professional range consists of 10 products in powder and liquid formulations. The Laundro Det and Boost-E is a powder detergent and booster; Laundro Mulse-E is a liquid emulsifier for F&B laundry; Laundro Bleach-O is a powder oxygen bleach for coloured and whites; Laundro Rinse is a liquid organic neutralising rinse; Laundro Complete is a powder all-in-one detergent and oxygen bleach for coloured and whites; Laundrokleen is a liquid all-in-one detergent for guest and domestic laundry; Laundro Soft is a liquid softener for towels and linen; Laundro Soft-N is a liquid 2-in-1 neutraliser and softener for towels and linen; Laundro Chlor-10 is a liquid chlorine bleach 10 per cent for white linen and Laundro Rinse-C is a liquid neutralizing rinse after chlorine bleaching.

The range is phosphate free. The base detergent is free from slurry based detergents and made from biodegradable surfactants. Haylide has used organic biodegradable acids in rinses and softeners in place of harmful, inorganic and traditional laundry rinses.

The oxygen bleaches and all-in-one single shot formulations reduce cycles of bleach and rinse. The softener range with combination of cationic and water soluble silicones provide softest results. The emulsifier for F&B stains is biodegradable and utilises denatured ethanol in place of IPA as a natural solvent.

HOTEL LAUNDRY – IN-HOUSE OR OUTSOURCED

Laundry and housekeeping are two of the most important functions in hotels, but often they are services put to the bottom of the priority list. Ironically, it's the unsung heroes in housekeeping that your guests will remember; the little touches when they return to their room after a day spent sight-seeing or in a long business meeting. Laundry quality leaves a lasting impression - you want it to be a fresh and clean one.

So, how do you ensure you are getting the best service? Processing your laundry in-house means you retain control, while outsourcing to a reputable laundry company can ensure consistency. For many, the answer to this age-old question is to do a bit of both.

"We have decided to continue with a mixture of in-house and outsourced laundry," says Julian Tomlin, group operations director at Exclusive Hotels, which is at the end of an internal laundry review across all its properties. "I believe you get a better top-end quality of linen through an in-house laundry." Though he is keen to add that he is very happy with his current laundry contractor, Watford Laundry.

Exclusive Hotels will send its flatware out and do towels, facecloths and robes in-house. "You have to ensure, however, that you have sufficient stock to let your laundry rest between uses," Tomlin adds. He would also like to find other like-minded hotels willing to share laundry delivery routes to cut down on costs and focus on the quality of the linen.

Cost and quality are two of the most important considerations for hoteliers. But for those who don't have the space, or the money to do both options, how do you decide which route to take?

Consistency is a major factor. You must be confident that standards will be maintained with your laundry contractor so that inferior laundry can be rejected without argument. Signing a contract based on the pristine laundry shown on signing day will not necessarily guarantee this level of quality continues. You need to factor in time to check your laundry deliveries - dark hairs can fall between the sheets from operatives' hair and flatbed iron marks can appear. Clear guidelines and terms need to be discussed at the start of the process if going down the outsourced route.

Matthew Drinkwater, deputy general manager at Audleys Wood hotel, Hampshire, which also uses a mixture of in-house and out-sourced laundry, incorporates this checking time into his managers' schedules.

Meanwhile London Hilton on Park Lane's laundry manager, Rebecca Still, believes combining outsourcing and on-site laundry processes offers the best of both worlds. "There is so much technology involved in laundry processing that it would be very difficult and expensive to keep up with these, and the maintenance of such equipment can be a financial drain," she says. "For our on-site service we couldn't live without our shirt finisher and collar and cuff machine, both of these dramatically cut the processing time of drying and pressing of shirts."

Any examination of tasks kept on site should include the initial equipment, ongoing running costs, high rental charges and replacing damaged linen.

A hidden cost is the investment required to train your staff to make best use of the equipment. Liz Smith-Mills, UK hotel consultant with Diversey, says: "Training is one of the most important factors to the quality of laundry within properties and language barriers and time spent in a country can impact on this being more or less effective."

Diversey is working in partnership with Electrolux to bring the benefits of in-house laundry to major lodging customers. Electrolux claims that a 200-bed hotel with 70 per cent occupancy switching to OPL could expect to report an additional £87,000 of profit on the bottom line on a five-year lease if it ran its laundry eight hours a day, seven days a week. In April 2010, four new washers from Electrolux Laundry Services (ELS) were installed at the Maison Talbooth hotel, Colchester, in its existing laundry room - it had some interesting results.

So, you've made your decision, one way or the other - or both, but have you considered the technological advances and the environmental impact?

Roger Oliver, managing director at the London Linen Group, claims that its steam-less laundry service uses 70 per cent less water and 25 per cent less gas and electricity when compared with conventional laundry services. It also offers a direct heated tunnel washer which uses thermal exchange to transfer heat from hot water to incoming cold water, reducing energy consumption.

Sunlight Textile Services UK and Ireland has three factories in south London and provides a laundry rental service for hotels including Starwood Hotel Resorts, the Hyatt Churchill and Holiday Inn. It is fortunate to have its own water from two bore holes on the site and believes this is one of the advantages to laundry being processed off-site - water costs are high on the list of disadvantages for hotels with on-site laundries.

Chris Hancock, regional service manager at Sunlight, says: "The space an on-site laundry takes up could be better used as a selling area for increased profits."

As you would expect, all of the above equipment, products, training and technologies come together to help achieve the main objective - the ultimate guest experience. Tomlin concludes: "For us, the quality of the linen and the sleep experience is a key differential for the customer experience."

Julian Tomlin's Laundry Tips:

- Remember to factor in your capital and operational costs as part of a review

- Review your maintenance contracts - make sure they include all laundry equipment
- Investigate a water re-use tank

IN-HOUSE VERSUS OUTSOURCED LAUNDRY

Lisa Williams is executive housekeeper at Park Plaza County Hall, London, and manages all the laundry in-house. She says: "I couldn't live without our two Miele washing machines and dryers. They are a good quality product and last for years. The quality of the laundry after washing is to a high-standard, too."

But she is familiar with both approaches. Here she offers her pro and cons of in-house versus outsourced laundry:

In-house/own linen:

- Choose your own quality
- You will not pay high rental costs
- Cost savings on purchasing and washing
- You have to do your own stock takes
- You have to replace damaged linen yourself with a cost implication
- Staff may take more care of your own linen
- Good quality linen can be sold to guests, extending the hotel experience

Outsourced/hired linen

- Quality/choice may not be up to your expectations
- High rental charges
- You do not have to do your own stock takes
- Reject linen is replaced, depending on service level agreement
- Linen replacement not always guaranteed by supplier
- Abused linen stock is charged for
- Damaged stock can also be charged for
- Staff may be less careful with the linen as it doesn't belong to the hotel

MAISON TOOLBOOTH HOTEL

The family owned Maison Talbooth hotel in Colchester is a well-established luxury hotel.

Owners, the Milsom Group, recently upgraded the laundry facilities and the results have revealed not only an increase in laundry efficiency, but also an improvement on the profit margin.

Each washer is equipped with Electrolux's Clarus control options to ensure water and energy savings. This inbuilt microprocessor co-ordinates timing, optimal water levels and temperature for a combination of superior performance and minimum water and energy consumption.

Four dryers and two ironers complete the replacement laundry equipment. The ironers speed up the laundry process as the sheets can be taken straight out of the dryers with the heated cylinder in the ironers drying and ironing table linen and bed sheets.

Since the update, the hotel laundry service has taken on the laundry requirements of all four hotels in the Milsom Group and Daniel Courtney, hotel manager, is delighted with the new facilities. "The laundry is working to full capacity", he states. "We have four laundry operators working from Monday to Friday, and during our busiest periods we can do the laundry, not only for the hotels, but also for a number of outside catering events a week."

The On Premises Laundry has enabled the laundry service to operate as a business in its own right, becoming a profit centre for the hotel and showing a significant increase in productivity.

COMMERCIAL LAUNDRY FACILITIES

Commercial, institutional and industrial (CII) laundry facilities clean large quantities of fabrics in a wide range of varieties and uses. Some are on-site facilities dedicated to washing fabrics used at the location; these are often referred to as an On Premises Laundry (OPL). OPLs are typically found in hotels, hospitals, nursing homes, prisons, universities, etc. Centralized contract laundries that launder fabrics from other businesses (such as uniforms, restaurant table cloths, bed linens, etc) are usually referred to as "Industrial Laundries". In either case, both types of facilities use vast amounts of water at varying degrees of efficiency. The potential for water conservation exists in most all facilities and should be part of every utility's CII water conservation strategy.

Water and wastewater costs represent more than 50 per cent of the total operating costs in the typical commercial laundry. The managers of these facilities are likely to be very interested in participating in any water conservation strategy deemed cost-effective.

Keep in mind that the quality of their service is paramount to the success of their business: all water conservation measures must maintain the effectiveness of cleaning the fabrics.

Commercial laundries deal with fabrics that are soiled beyond the level of typical residential clothes in both: (1) variety of dirt, grime, stains, food, chemicals, bacteria, grease, biological hazards; and (2) the concentration of these substances embedded in the fabric. You cannot compare the water use of residential clothes washers with commercial laundering equipment. Water is the universal solvent in the world, and there are practical limits to the reduction of water quantity and the ability to clean fabrics. The greatest water conservation opportunities often exist in the various methods of reusing or recycling water from the machines. The extent of a laundry's ability to recycle water usually lies in the facility's ability to filter, clarify and sanitize the effluent water from the washing machines.

While industrial laundries often use in-house staff to manage the total operations and maintenance of the washers, OPLs often rely on contractual service firms to: (1) supply the detergents and chemicals; (2) maintain the equipment; and (3) determines the wash formulas, whose components include the chemical recipe, type of cycle, duration of each cycle, water temperature, amount of water, and when each of these ought to occur for each wash classification and size of wash load.

Water utilities seeking to improve water efficiency must garner the cooperation of both the business owner and the chemical supplier and service contractor to achieve success. In some cases, these service providers own the washers and lease them to the business.

WASHER-EXTRACTOR

Small to medium size laundries mostly rely on equipment referred to as washer-extractors. These look and operate somewhat similar to a residential front-loading clothes washer, except washer-extractors are 3 to 30 times larger. The name 'washer-extractor' is derived from the high speed spin cycles used between wash and rinse cycles to extract the water and detergent from clothes using centrifugal force.

The largest models are huge; allowing workers to easily stand up inside the wash drum for service and maintenance. The fabrics are washed in batches, similar to a residential washer.

Washer-extractor efficiency is usually measured in gallons per pound of fabric, as opposed to residential machines that measure efficiency in gallons per cubic foot of capacity. The typical washer-extractors require 3 to 4 gallons (11.3 L to 15.1 L) of water per pound of fabric cleaned. The most efficient machines have built-in water recycling capabilities; storing the rinse water from the previous load to supply wash water in the subsequent load, using less than 2.5 gallons per pound (9.5 L) of fabric.

For washer-extractors without built in recycling features, there are auxiliary recycling systems available that can be attached to washer-extractors to filter and sanitize the rinse water to be reused or the wash water supply. These systems vary in quality, size and efficiency. Many OPL are installed in relatively small spaces, where the washers, dryers, chemical storage, and folding/stacking/sorting benches fill most of the available space.

The space does not always accommodate additional recycling equipment and related water storage tanks. Recycling the water requires adjustment in chemicals and detergents used in the wash and rinse water to maintain the quality of the washing process. This requires the chemical supply contractor to be involved in planning any such retrofits.

TUNNEL WASHERS

Tunnel washers (sometimes called "continuous batch washers") are very different than washer extractors; long chambers (8' × 8' × 30' (2.4 m × 2.4 m × 9.1 m) and larger) constructed with a series of compartments, called "pockets", through which a large internal auger (similar in shape of a large corkscrew) slowly turns to pull the laundry through the different pockets. The first few pockets mix detergent and chemicals (bleach, sanitizers, degreasers, etc) in the water and fabric to soak and wash.

Augers move the fabric to subsequent pockets, dedicated to rinse functions. Water moves in a counter flow direction to the laundry and is therefore used several times before being sent to the drain.

At the end of the tunnel the washed fabric is removed automatically in the form of a large cake, mechanically compressed before being fed into the line of dryers. Water consumption rates typically found in these washers are approximately 2.0 gallons (7.5 L) per pound of wash, or about two-thirds that of the typical washer-extractors.

These units are very expensive and are only used in the largest OPLs; most often they are found in industrial laundries with very high production rates. Tunnel washers are inherently water-efficient and are highly automated to maximize the throughput of the laundry. The high cost of water and wastewater has induced many industrial laundries build on-site water filtering and treatment facilities on the premises. There are no known pre-packaged systems available to improve water efficiency at these industrial laundries. Any improvements require a site specific, engineered system.

11

Working Process of Laundry Management

Laundry is the washing of clothing and linens.Laundry processes are often done in a business, room or area in a home or apartment building, reserved for that purpose; this is also sometimes referred to as a *laundry*. The material that is being washed, or has been laundered is also generally referred to as *laundry*.

HISTORY

WATERCOURSES

Laundry was first done in watercourses, letting the water carry away the materials which could cause stains and smells. Laundry is still done this way in some less industrialized areas and rural regions. Agitation helps remove the dirt, so the laundry is often rubbed, twisted, or slapped against flat rocks. Wooden bats or clubs could be used to help with beating the dirt out. These were often called washing beetles or bats and could be used by the waterside on a rock (a beetling-stone), on a block (battling-block), or on a board. They were once common across Europe and were also used by settlers in North America. Similar techniques have also been identified in Japan.

When no watercourses were available, laundry was done in water-tight vats or vessels. Sometimes large metal cauldrons were filled with fresh water and heated over a fire; boiling water was even more effective than cold in removing dirt. Wooden or stone scrubbing surfaces set up near a water supply or portable washboards, including factory-made corrugated metal ones, gradually replaced rocks as a surface for loosening soil.

Once clean, the clothes were wrung out — twisted to remove most of the water. Then they were hung up on poles or clotheslines to air dry, or sometimes just spread out on clean grass. ÿþ

WASHHOUSES

Before the advent of the washing machine, apart from watercourses, laundry was also done in communal or public washhouses (also called washhouses or wash houses), especially in rural areas in Europe or theMediterranean Basin. Water was channelled from a river or spring and fed into a building or outbuilding built specifically for laundry purposes and often containing two basins - one for washing and the other for rinsing - through which the water was constantly flowing, as well as a stone lip inclined towards the water against which the washers could beat the clothes. Such facilities were much more comfortable than washing in a watercourse because the launderers could work standing up instead of on their knees, and were protected from inclement weather by walls (often) and a roof (with some exceptions). Also, they didn't have to go far, as the facilities were usually at hand in the village or at the edge of a town.

These facilities were public and available to all families, and usually used by the entire village. The laundry job was reserved for women, who washed all their family's laundry (or the laundry of others as a paid job). As such, washhouses were an obligatory stop in many women's weekly lives and became a sort of institution or meeting place for women in towns or villages, where they could discuss issues or simply chat, equated by many with gossip, and equatable to the concept of the village pump in English. Indeed, this tradition is reflected in the Catalan idiom *"fer safareig"* (literally, "to do the laundry"), which means to gossip, for instance. Many of these washhouses are still standing and even filled with water in villages throughout Europe. In cities (in Europe as of the 19th century), public washhouses were also built so that the poorer population, who would otherwise not have access to laundry facilities, could wash their clothes. The aim was to foster hygiene and thus reduce outbreaks of epidemics.

THE INDUSTRIAL REVOLUTION

The Industrial Revolution completely transformed laundry technology. The mangle (wringer US) was developed in the 19th century — two long rollers in a frame and a crank to revolve them. A laundry-worker took sopping wet clothing and cranked it through the mangle, compressing the cloth and expelling the excess water. The mangle was much quicker than hand twisting. It was a variation on the box mangle used primarily for pressing and smoothing cloth.

Meanwhile 19th century inventors further mechanized the laundry process with various hand-operatedwashing machines. Most involved turning a handle to move paddles inside a tub. Then some early 20th century machines used an electrically powered agitator to replace tedious hand rubbing against a washboard. Many of these were simply a tub on legs, with a hand-operated mangle on top. Later the mangle too was electrically powered, then replaced by a perforated double tub, which spun out the excess water in a spin cycle.

Laundry drying was also mechanized, with clothes dryers. Dryers were also spinning perforated tubs, but they blew heated air rather than water.

CHINESE LAUNDRIES IN NORTH AMERICA

In the United States and Canada in the late 19th and early 20th century, the occupation of laundry worker was heavily identified with Chinese Americans. Discrimination, lack of English-language skills, and lack of capitalkept Chinese Americans out of most desirable careers. Around 1900, one in four ethnic Chinese men in the U.S. worked in a laundry, typically working 10 to 16 hours a day.

New York City had an estimated 3,550 Chinese laundries at the beginning of the Great Depression of the 1930s. In 1933, with even this looking to many people like a relatively desirable business, the city's Board of Aldermen passed a law clearly intended to drive the Chinese out of the business. Among other things, it limited ownership of laundries to U.S. citizens. The Chinese Consolidated Benevolent Association tried fruitlessly to fend this off, resulting in the formation of the openly leftist Chinese Hand Laundry Alliance(CHLA), which successfully challenged this provision of the law, allowing Chinese laundry workers to preserve their livelihoods.

The CHLA went on to function as a more general civil rights group; its numbers declined strongly after it was targeted by the FBI during the Second Red Scare (1947–1957).

LAUNDRY PROCESSES

Laundry processes include washing (usually with water containing detergents or other chemicals), agitation, rinsing, drying and pressing (ironing). The washing will often be done at a temperature above room temperature to increase the activities of any chemicals used and the solubility of stains, and high temperatures kill micro-organisms that may be present on the fabric.

Chemicals: Various chemicals may be used to increase the solvent power of water, such as the compounds in soaproot or yucca-root used by Native American tribes, or the ash lye once widely used for soaking laundry in Europe. Soap, a compound made from lye and fat, is an ancient and common laundry aid. Modernwashing machines typically use synthetic powdered or liquid laundry detergent in place of more traditional soap.

Dry cleaning: Dry cleaning is any cleaning process for clothing and textiles using a chemical solvent other than water. The solvent used is typically tetrachloroethylene (perchloroethylene), which the industry calls "perc". It is used to clean delicate fabrics that cannot withstand the rough and tumble of a washing machine and clothes dryer; it can also obviate labour-intensive hand washing.

LAUNDRY HYGIENE

For laundry hygiene see under hygiene.

APARTMENTS

In some parts of the world, including North America, apartment buildings and dormitories often have laundry rooms, where residents share washing machines and dryers. Usually the machines are set to run only when money is put in a coin slot. They turn on when the money is inserted and they run for as long as you pay.

In other parts of the world, including Europe, apartment buildings with laundry rooms are uncommon, and each apartment may have its own washing machine. Those without a machine at home or the use of a laundry room must either wash their clothes by hand or visit a commercial Self-service laundry.

RIGHT TO DRY MOVEMENT

Some organizations have been campaigning against legislation which has outlawed line-drying of clothing in public places, especially given the increased greenhouse gas emissions produced by clothes dryers.

Legislation making it possible for thousands of American families to start using a clothesline in communities where they were formerly banned was passed in Colourado in 2008. In 2009, clothesline legislation was debated in the states of Connecticut, Hawaii, Maryland, Maine, New Hampshire, Nebraska, Oregon, Virginia, and Vermont. Other states are considering similar bills.

Many homeowners' associations and other communities in the United States prohibit residents from using a clothesline outdoors, or limits such use to locations that are not visible from the street or to certain times of day. Other communities, however, expressly prohibit rules that prevent the use of clotheslines.

Florida is the only state to expressly guarantee a right to dry, although Utah and Hawaii have passed solar rights legislation.

A Florida law explicitly states: "No deed restrictions, covenants, or similar binding agreements running with the land shall prohibit or have the effect of prohibiting solar collectors, clotheslines, or other energy devices based on renewable resources from being installed on buildings erected on the lots or parcels covered by the deed restrictions, covenants, or binding agreements." No other state has such clearcut legislation. Vermont considered a "Right to Dry" bill in 1999, but it was defeated in the Senate Natural Resources and Energy Committee. The language has been included in a 2007 voluntary energy conservation bill, introduced by Senator Dick McCormack. Similar measures have been introduced in Canada, in particular the province of Ontario.

COMMON PROBLEMS

Novice users of modern laundry machines sometimes experience accidental shrinkage of garments, especially when applying heat. For wool garments, this is due to scales on the fibres which heat and agitation cause to stick together. Other fabrics are stretched by mechanical forces during production, and can shrink slightly when heated (though to a lesser degree than wool). Some clothes are "pre-shrunk" to avoid this problem.

Another common problem is colour bleeding. For example, washing a red shirt with white underwear can result in pink underwear. Often only like colours are washed together to avoid this problem, which is lessened by cold water and repeated washings.

Laundry symbols are included on many clothes to help consumers avoid these problems.

ETYMOLOGY

The word laundry comes from Middle English lavendrye, laundry, from Old French lavanderie, from lavandier.

DRY CLEANING

Dry cleaning is any cleaning process for clothing and textiles using a chemical solvent other than water. The solvent used is typically tetrachloroethylene (perchloroethylene), which the industry calls "perc" or "PERC". It is used to clean delicate fabrics that cannot withstand the rough and tumble of a washing machine and clothes dryer; it can also eliminate labour-intensive hand washing.

HISTORY

The ancient Romans used ammonia (derived from urine) and fuller's earth to launder their woollen togas. *Fullonicae* were very prominent industrial facilities, with at least one in every town of any notability, and frequently the largest employer in a district. These laundries obtained urine from farm animals, or from special pots situated at public latrines. The industry was so profitable that fuller's guilds were an important political constituency, and the government taxed the collection of urine.

Modern dry cleaning uses non-water-based solvents to remove soil and stains from clothes.

The potential for using petroleum-based solvents such as gasoline and kerosene was discovered in the mid-19th century by French dye-works owner Jean Baptiste Jolly, who noticed that his tablecloth became cleaner after his maid spilled kerosene on it. He subsequently developed a service cleaning people's clothes in this manner, which became known as "nettoyage à sec"—*i.e.*, dry cleaning.

Flammability concerns led William Joseph Stoddard, a dry cleaner from Atlanta, to develop Stoddard solventas a slightly less flammable alternative to gasoline-based solvents. The use of highly flammable petroleum solvents caused many fires and explosions, resulting in government regulation of dry cleaners. After World War I, dry cleaners began using chlorinated solvents. These solvents were much less flammable than petroleum solvents and had improved cleaning power.

Shift to tetrachloroethylene: By the mid-1930s, the dry cleaning industry had adopted tetrachloroethylene (perchloroethylene), or "perc" for short, as the ideal solvent.

It has excellent cleaning power and is stable, non-flammable, and gentle to most garments. Perc, however, was incidentally the first chemical to be classified as acarcinogen by the Consumer Product Safety Commission (a classification later withdrawn). In 1993, the California Air Resources Board adopted regulations to reduce perc emissions from dry cleaning operations; the same year, the U.S. Environmental Protection Agency (EPA) followed suit. The EPA updated its regulation in 2006 to reflect the availability of improved emission controls.

The dry cleaning industry is in the process of replacing perc with other chemicals and/or methods. Between 2006 and 2011, the dry cleaning industry had an average market of $7.5 billion, 22,000 firms, and employed approximately 150,000 workers. A typical dry cleaning firm employs 7 workers and brings in $330,000 per year.

Traditionally, the cleaning process was carried out at centralized factories; high street cleaners shops received garments from customers, sent them to the factory, and then had them returned to the shop, where the customer could collect them. This was due mainly to the risk of fire or dangerous fumes created by the cleaning process. At this time, dry cleaning was carried out in two different machines—one for the cleaning process itself and the second to dry the garments.

Machines of this era were described as *vented*; their fumes and drying exhausts were expelled to the atmosphere, the same as modern tumble-dryer exhausts. This not only contributed to environmental contamination but also much potentially reusable perc was lost to the atmosphere. Much stricter controls on solvent emissions have ensured that all dry cleaning machines in the Western world are now fully enclosed, and no solvent fumes are vented to the atmosphere. In enclosed machines, solvent recovered during the drying process is returned condensed and distilled, so it can be reused to clean further loads or safely disposed of. The majority of modern enclosed machines also incorporates a computer-controlled drying sensor, which automatically senses when all traces of perc have been removed. This system ensures that only the smallest amount of perc fumes will be released when opening the door at the end of the cycle.

PROCESS

A dry-cleaning machine is similar to a combination of a domestic washing machine, and clothes dryer. Garments are placed in the washing or extraction chamber (referred to as the "basket" or "drum"), which constitutes the core of the machine. The washing chamber contains a horizontal, perforated drum that rotates within an outer shell. The shell holds the solvent while the rotating drum holds the garment load. The basket capacity is between about 10 and 40 kg (20 to 80 lb).

During the wash cycle, the chamber is filled approximately one-third full of solvent and begins to rotate, agitating the clothing. The solvent temperature is maintained at 30 degrees Celsius (86 degrees Fahrenheit), as a higher temperature may damage it. During the wash cycle, the solvent in the chamber (commonly known as the "cage" or "tackle box") is passed through a filtration chamber and then fed back into the "cage". This is known as the cycle and is continued for the wash duration. The solvent is then removed and sent to adistillation unit consisting of a boiler and condenser. The condensed solvent is fed into a separator unit where any remaining water is separated from the solvent and then fed into the "clean solvent" tank. The ideal flow rate is roughly 8 liters of solvent per kilogram of garments per minute, depending on the size of the machine.

Garments are also checked for foreign objects. Items such as plastic pens will dissolve in the solvent bath and may damage textiles beyond recovery. Some textile dyes are "loose" (red being the main culprit), and will shed dye during solvent immersion.

These will not be included in a load along with lighter-colour textiles to avoid colour transfer. The solvent used must be distilled to remove impurities that may transfer to clothing. Garments are checked for dry cleaning compatibility, including fasteners. Many decorative fasteners either are not solvent proof or will not withstand the mechanical action of cleaning. These will be removed and restitched after the cleaning, or protected with a small padded protector. Fragile items, such as feather bedspreads or tasseled rugs or hangings, may be enclosed in a loose mesh bag. The density of perchloroethylene is around 1.7 g/cm at room temperature (70 per cent heavier than water), and the sheer weight of absorbed solvent may cause the textile to fail under normal force during the extraction cycle unless the mesh bag provides mechanical support.

Not all stains can be removed simply by dry cleaning. Some need to be treated with spotting solvents—sometimes by steam jet or by soaking in special stain-remover liquids—before garments are washed or dry cleaned. Also, garments stored in soiled condition for a long time are difficult to bring back to their original colour and texture. Natural fibres such as wool, cotton, and silk of lighter colours should not be left in dirty or soiled condition for long amounts of time as they absorb dirt in their texture and are unlikely to be restored to their original colour and finish.

A typical wash cycle lasts for 8–15 minutes depending on the type of garments and degree of soiling. During the first three minutes, solvent-soluble soils dissolve into the perchloroethylene and loose, insoluble soil comes off. It takes 10-12 minutes after the loose soil has come off to remove the ground-in insoluble soil from garments. Machines using hydrocarbon solvents require a wash cycle of at least 25 minutes because of the much slower rate of solvation of solvent-soluble soils. A dry cleaning surfactant "soap" may also be added.

At the end of the wash cycle, the machine starts a rinse cycle wherein the garment load is rinsed with fresh distilled solvent from the pure solvent tank. This pure solvent rinse prevents discoloration caused by soil particles being absorbed back onto the garment surface from the "dirty" working solvent.

After the rinse cycle, the machine begins the extraction process, which recovers the solvent for reuse. Modern machines recover approximately 99.99 per cent of the solvent employed. The extraction cycle begins by draining the solvent from the washing chamber and accelerating the basket to 350-450 rpm, causing much of the solvent to spin free of the fabric. Until this time, the cleaning is done in normal temperature, as the solvent is never heated in dry cleaning process. When no more solvent can be spun out, the machine starts the drying cycle.

During the drying cycle, the garments are tumbled in a stream of warm air (60-63°C/140-145°F) that circulates through the basket, evaporating any traces of solvent left after the spin cycle. The air temperature is controlled to prevent heat damage to the garments. The exhausted warm air from the machine then passes through a chiller unit where solvent vapours are condensed and returned to the distilled solvent tank. Modern dry cleaning machines use a closed-loop system in which the chilled air is reheated and recirculated. This results in high solvent recovery rates and reduced air pollution. In the early days of dry cleaning, large amounts of perchlorethylene were vented to the atmosphere because it was regarded as cheap and believed to be harmless.

After the drying cycle is complete, a deodorizing (aeration) cycle cools the garments and removes the last traces of solvent, by circulating cool outside air over the garments and then through a vapour recovery filter made from activated carbon and polymer resins. After the aeration cycle, the garments are clean and ready for pressing and finishing.

SOLVENT PROCESSING

Working solvent from the washing chamber passes through several filtration steps before it is returned to the washing chamber. The first step is a button trap, which prevents small objects such as lint, fasteners, buttons, and coins from entering the solvent pump.

Over time, a thin layer of filter cake (called "muck") accumulates on the lint filter. The muck is removed regularly (commonly once per day) and then processed to recover solvent trapped in the muck. Many machines use "spin disk filters", which remove the muck from the filter by centripetal force while it is back washed with solvent.

After the lint filter, the solvent passes through an absorptive cartridge filter. This filter is made from activated clays and charcoal and removes fine insoluble soil and non-volatile residues, along with dyes from the solvent. Finally, the solvent passes through a polishing filter, which removes any soil not previously removed. The clean solvent is then returned to the working solvent tank.

To enhance cleaning power, small amounts of detergent (0.5 per cent-1.5 per cent) are added to the working solvent and are essential to its functionality. These detergents emulsify hydrophobic soils and keep soil from redepositing on garments. Depending on the machine's design, either an anionic or a cationic detergent is used.

Since the solvent recovery is less than 100 per cent, and because dry cleaning does not remove water-based stains well, entrepreneurs have developed the wet cleaning process, which is, in essence, cold-water washing and air drying, using a computer-controlled washer and dryer. In general, wet cleaning is regarded as being in its infancy, although low-tech versions of it have been used for centuries.

SYMBOLS

The international GINETEX laundry symbol for dry cleaning is a circle. It may have the letter P inside it to indicate perchloroethylene solvent, or the letter F to indicate a flammable solvent (Feuergefährliches Schwerbenzin). A bar underneath the circle indicates that only mild cleaning processes should be used. A crossed-out empty circle indicates that dry cleaning is not permitted.

DRY-CLEANING WASTE

Cooked muck: Cooked powder residue is the name for the waste material generated by cooking down or distilling muck. It is a hazardous waste and will contain solvent, powdered filter material (diatomite), carbon, non-volatile residues, lint, dyes, grease, soils, and water. This material should be disposed of in accordance with local law.

Sludge: The waste sludge or solid residue from the still contains solvent, water, soils, carbon, and other non-volatile residues. Still bottoms from chlorinated solvent dry cleaning operations are hazardous wastes. Still bottoms from machines using other solvents may also be hazardous due to toxic constituents in fabric dyes and notions.

Filters: Filters used in perchloroethylene based machines are also regulated hazardous waste in the United States.

Separator water: Water will separate from the dry cleaning solvent, and must be removed. This waste water, from machines using perchloroethylene, is a regulated hazardous waste in the United States.

TOXICITY AND ENVIRONMENTAL EFFECTS

Perc is classified as carcinogenic to humans by the United States Environmental Protection Agency and must be handled as a hazardous waste. To prevent it from getting into drinking water, dry cleaners that use perc must take special precautions.

When released into the air, perc can contribute to smog when it reacts with other volatile organic carbon substances. California declared perchloroethylene a toxic chemical in 1991, and its use will become illegal in that state in 2023. A recent study conducted at Georgetown Universityshows that perc is retained in dry-cleaned clothes and that perc levels increase with repeat cleanings.

Some alternatives such as CO_2 offers a solution to perc, however CO_2 is inferior in removing some forms of grime.

SOLVENTS USED

Modern:

- Glycol ethers (dipropylene glycol tertiary-butyl ether) (Rynex, Solvair, Lyondell Impress) are in many cases more effective than perchloroethylene (perc) and in all cases more environmentally friendly. Dipropylene glycol tertiary butyl ether (DPTB) has a flashpoint far above current industry standards, yet at the same time possesses a degree of solvency for water-soluble stains that is at least equivalent to, and in most cases better than, perc and the other glycol ether dry cleaning solvents presently in commercial use. A particular advantage of the DPTB-water solutions of the Rynex product in dry cleaning is that they do not behave like a typical mixture, but, rather, the behaviour is the same as a single substance. This permits a better-defined separation upon azeotropic distillation at a lower boiling point, facilitates reclamation more effectively (at a level of 99 per cent or greater), and also enhances purification using conventional distillation techniques.
- Hydrocarbon is most like standard dry cleaning but the processes use hydrocarbon solvents such as Exxon-Mobil's DF-2000 or Chevron Phillips' EcoSolv. These petroleum-based solvents are less aggressive than perc and require a longer cleaning cycle. Although flammable, these solvents do not present a high risk of fire

or explosion when used properly. Hydrocarbon also contains volatile organic compounds (VOCs) that contribute to smog.

- Liquid silicone (decamethylcyclopentasiloxane or D5) is gentler on garments than perc and does not cause colour loss. Requires a license be obtained to utilize the property of GreenEarth Cleaning. Though considerably more environmentally friendly, the price of it is more than double that of perc and GreenEarth charges an annual affiliation fee. Degrades within days in the environment to silica and trace amounts of water and CO_2. Produces non-toxic, non-hazardous waste. Toxicity tests by Dow Corning shows the solvent to increase the incidence of tumors in female rats (no effects were seen in male rats), but further research concluded that the effects observed in rats are not relevant to humans because the biological pathway that results in tumour formation is unique to rats. (170.6 °F/77 °C flash point).
- Modified hydrocarbon blends (Pure Dry)
- Brominated Solvents n-Propyl Bromide (DrySolv).
- Perchloroethylene has been in use since the 1940s, perc is the most common solvent, the "standard" for cleaning performance, and most aggressive cleaner. It can cause colour bleeding/loss, especially at higher temperatures, and may destroy special trims, buttons, and beads on some garments. Better for oil-based stains (which account for about 10 per cent of stains) than more common water-soluble stains (coffee, wine, blood, etc.). Known for leaving a characteristic chemical smell on garments. Non-flammable. A recent study conducted at Georgetown University shows perc, classified as carcinogenic to humans by the EPA, is retained in dry-cleaned clothes and that levels increase with repeat cleanings.
- Liquid CO_2 - Consumer Reports rated this method superior to conventional methods, but the Drycleaning and Laundry Institute commented on its "fairly low cleaning ability" in a 2007 report. Another industry certification group, America's Best Cleaners, counts CO_2 cleaners among its members. Machinery is expensive—up to $90,000 more than a perc machine, making affordability difficult for small businesses. Some cleaners with these machines keep traditional machines on-site for the heavier soiled textiles, but others find plant enzymes to be equally effective and more environmentally sustainable. CO_2-cleaned clothing does not off-gas volatile compounds. CO_2 cleaning is also used for fire- and water-damage restoration due to its effectiveness in removing toxic residues, soot and associated odors of fire. The environmental impact is very low. Carbon dioxide is almost entirely non-toxic, it does not persist in clothing or in the

environment, and its greenhouse gas potential is lower than that of many organic solvents.

- Wet cleaning is a system that uses water and biodegradable soap. Computer-controlled dryers and stretching machines ensure that the fabric retains its natural size and shape. Wet cleaning is claimed to clean a majority of "dry clean only" garments safely, including leather, suede, most tailored woollens, silk, and rayon. Most perc cleaners use wet cleaning on some garments, but there are only about 20 exclusive wetcleaners in the United States.

Historical:

- Carbon tetrachloride — Highly toxic.
- Trichloroethane — Overly aggressive and harsh.
- Stoddard solvent — Very flammable and explosive, 100°F/38°C flash point.
- CFC-113 - Freon — Ozone destroying CFC.

HOME DRY CLEANING

Various consumer-grade products in the marketplace today, such as Procter and Gamble's Dryel, allow portions of the dry cleaning process to be performed at home using home laundry machines. Even though the use of these products does not follow all the steps of the commercial process, such use does work for certain types of garments.

INDUSTRIAL LAUNDRY

Large institutions that require a constant flow of clean linen, working-clothing or uniform, will often employ the services of an industrial laundry. Hospitals, prisons and hotels, for instance, will usually have their own laundry departments. The organized collection, laundering and timely delivery of textiled service ware is essential to the operation of the institution. Employees in uniforms reassure customers that they represent the company. From day-to-day counter work to service representatives making residential calls, customers trust uniformed employees and rely on them for dependable and positive reinforcement.

Stages of Operation: When linen is sent to be laundered, it goes through six stages. The first three stages are called "soiled side" operations, since they occur before the linen is actually washed. The last three are called "clean side" operations, since they involve the handling of clean linen.

1. Soiled Retrieval: In this step, the institution's linens are collected by laundry personnel and returned to the laundry facility. Members of the institution's housekeeping staff will place the soiled linen at a collection point, usually by dropping it down a laundry chute. Laundry

workers will then collect the soiled linen, place it in carts reserved for soiled linen and transport it to the laundry facility.

Linen retrieval poses a problem, especially in health care institutions. Soiled linen can be contaminated with bloodborne and airborne pathogens. For this reason, employees who retrieve soiled linen are required to use personal protective gear and standard safety precautions. This problem is especially prevalent in hospitals. Prior to sorting, the linen must be covered to prevent the spread of airborne germs.

2. Soil Sorting: At this stage, the retrieved linen is unloaded and sorted according to item type. Different items often require different washing formulas. Also, later stages in the process require the linen to be pre-sorted, since it is handled batch by batch. Heavy or biohazardous stains such as blood and feces may require longer wash times and stronger formulas. Thus it is inadvisable to mix different items of linen in the same wash batch. Large institutions often use a production-line method for soil sorting, with several full-time employees assigned to the task.

   Since soiled linen may be contaminated with biohazards or sharp objects, employees involved in the sorting process are required to use personal protective equipment and standard safety precautions.

   Smaller items tend to "hide" among larger items. For this reason, some sorting goes on during the washing, processing and packaging stages.

3. Washing: This is the stage in which the laundry is actually washed. The sorted linen is weighed according to the washing machine's load limit. Large washing machines are used, usually operated by a certified washer operator. The washer operator loads and unloads the washer, decides what is to be washed according to the laundry's schedule, and monitors the chemical levels in the water. Since modern tunnel washers monitor their own chemical levels and unload linen directly into the laundry's "clean area", the operator is required only to load the linen.

   Proper washing depends on five factors: Water quality, mechanical Agitation, Time, Chemical concentration and Heat. Washer operators use the acronym WATCH. These five factors work together. The purer the water and the fresher the chemicals, the cleaner the laundry will be. Mechanical action exposes the surface area of the linen to the water and chemicals, ensuring that the item is thoroughly soaked. Mechanical also tends to dislodge stains. Heat helps the chemicals to react with the stains. The longer the item is exposed to heat, chemicals and mechanical action, the cleaner it will be.

Over the past twenty years, many industrial laundries have switched from conventional washers to tunnel washers, also called continuous-batch washers. Since tunnel washers don't have to be stopped for loading and unloading of linen, they provide a more continuous flow of clean laundry. Higher-volume facilities, which may process over 15,000 pounds of linen per day, often rely heavily on tunnel washers.

4. Processing: In this stage, the clean linen is dried, ironed and folded. Some items, such as towels and blankets, are put through a dryer until they are no longer damp, then sent to mechanical folders. "Wetwork" items, such as sheets, are sent through steam-powered ironers which dry, press and fold them.

   Dryers use hot air and mechanical action to evaporate the moisture and chemicals from the linen prior to folding. Heated air is forced through pores into a spinning central cylinder called the drum. As the cylinder constantly spins, the linen inside tumbles, exposing the surface area to heat which evaporates the moisture. The air temperature must be carefully controlled. If it isn't hot enough, the linen won't be thoroughly dried. If it is too hot, the linen may overdry, damaging the product and creating a fire hazard.

   Ironers use heavy steam-heated rollers to dry the linen while pressing out wrinkles.

   Folders use mechanical action to fold the linen into shapes that are easily stored and handled. Folders come in two varieties: large-piece for blankets and other large items, and small-piece for smaller items such as towels or pads. The more compact the shape into which the item is folded, the greater the amount of linen that can be packed into a limited storage space.

   Some items, such as wash cloths, may be too small to be handled mechanically. These items must be packaged by hand.

5. Packaging: In this step, the processed linen is prepared for delivery. Individual orders are filled, based on the needs and requests of the laundry's customers, then sent to the laundry's main distribution points and storage areas. Linen not used for orders is placed in storage areas, giving the facility a reserve of clean laundry.

6. Distribution: In this step, trained delivery people transport the clean linen back to the customers. This is a skilled position, since the delivery person must have a thorough knowledge of both laundry operation and the principles of good customer service. In hospitals, delivery people must be familiar with patient relations, confidentiality policies and hospice. Large institutions will usually employ several full-time delivery people.

OCCUPATIONAL HAZARDS

The most common accidents in industrial laundries involve chemical exposure, sharp objects left in soiled linen, slips from wet floors, exposure to pathogens in contaminated linen, and body parts being stuck in machinery. While these problems can usually be avoided by standard precautions and a little common sense, they can and do happen. Production workers have a saying: "Common sense isn't that common."

Exposure to soil and pathogens can be limited by two things. One, of course, is the use of personal protective equipment: barrier gowns, gloves, eyewear, foot coverings and face masks. These items should be worn when handling soiled linen. Infections can also be eliminated by proper hand-washing with antibacterial soap. Employees should wash their hands after handling any linen, whether soiled or clean.

Since the noise levels in industrial laundries can be quite high, earmuffs and disposable earplugs are often issued. Hearing protection is essential.

Exposure to chemicals is also common. Since washers require a constant stream of detergent, bleach and other chemicals, the supply must be constantly replenished. Laundries are required to provide a material safety data sheet, or MSDS, for all chemicals used in the facility. Many laundries require their machine operators to be familiar with HAZMAT, if not fully certified.

With the constant workload and harsh working conditions, employees can easily become short-tempered. This occasionally leads to problems withviolence and workplace bullying. For this reason, laundry managers must be competent disciplinarians, ready to deal with employees who have attitude problems.

Laundry machines use high-pressure steam and dangerous chemicals. Poor maintenance can cause injuries such as severe burns and chemical exposures. Hoses, steam lines and other machine parts must be checked and replaced regularly.

PRODUCTION PROBLEMS

Communication: Like any good business, a laundry's operation depends on good communication. Customers must file their orders in a timely manner. Delivery people and order fillers must keep records of the types and quantities of linens used. Managers must be informed of production difficulties and attitude problems. Any breakdown in communication will hinder the laundry's productivity.

Cross-contamination: Clean linen and soiled linen should never be mixed. For this reason, most laundry facilities have two major work areas, the "soiled area" and the "clean area". These areas are usually separated by a wall. Separate carts are designated for clean and soiled linen. Linen usually passes from the soiled area to the clean area through the washers. Any clean linen that comes into contact with soiled linen or with carts used to transport soiled linen is considered soiled and must be re-washed. Laundry workers who handle soiled linen are required to wash their hands before working with clean linen.

Wet linen storage: Wet or soiled linen that is allowed to sit for an extended period of time may become permanently wrinkled. Worse, wet linen stored in a humid area maymildew, requiring replacement.

Dust: Dust can and does settle on clean linen. For this reason, clean linen left on shelves and in delivery carts should be covered. While many laundries use dust covers specifically made for this purpose, others will improvise, using sheets or blankets.

Cart Space: Every laundry, regardless of size, has a limited amount of cart space for storing linen. For this reason, the laundry's carts must be constantly recycled. The moment a cart is emptied, it is returned to the laundry to be filled with another order. If it is designated for soiled linen, it should be emptied at the laundry facility, then sent back to the collection point for another load.

Replacement linens: Each trip through the wash cycle places wear and tear on the linen. Thus, a major laundry facility needs a constant stream of new linens coming in to replace worn-out items. Items that are not too badly damaged may be set aside for something other than their original purpose. (Permanently stained or torn blankets, for instance, may be used to line floor areas being waxed.) However, they will still need to be replaced in the linen stream.

Maintenance: From its major computerized machines down to the wheels on its carts, every laundry facility depends on mechanical and electric devices. These devices require a range of constant maintenance by skilled and certified technicians. Poorly maintained equipment can limit productivity and may even cause or contribute to injuries.

Rework: As in any business, any job that was not done properly the first time must be redone. Items that weren't thoroughly cleaned must be rewashed. Orders that were filled using the wrong supplies must be re-filled. These are two of the many examples of rework in a laundry.

Overstuffing: In recent years, it has become standard practice in prisons for prisoners to deposit personal laundry in mesh bags. The advantage of this system is that the mesh bags keep personal items separate in large loads during the wash cycle. The disadvantage is that prisoners tend to overstuff the bags. This inhibits mechanical agitation while preventing water and chemicals from reaching soiled linen. The result is poorer quality linen.

Tunnel jams: If tunnel washers have one noteworthy defect, it is the tendency for the tunnel to become blocked when the washer is overloaded. When the tunnel is blocked, the washer must be stopped and allowed to drain, then the blockage must be removed manually. A tunnel jam may cost the laundry several hours of production time. Operators can prevent tunnel jams by paying strict attention to the washer's load limits.

IRONING

Ironing is the use of a heated tool (an iron) to remove wrinkles from fabric. The heating is commonly done to a temperature of 180–220 °Celsius, depending on the fabric. Ironing works by loosening the bonds between the long-chain polymer molecules in the fibres of the material. While the molecules are hot, the fibres are straightened by the weight of the iron, and they hold their new shape as they cool. Some fabrics, such as cotton, require the addition of water to loosen the intermolecular bonds. Many modern fabrics (developed in or after the mid-twentieth century) are advertised as needing little or no ironing. Permanent press clothing was developed to reduce the ironing necessary by combining wrinkle-resistant polyester with cotton.

The first known use of heated metal to "iron" clothes is known to have occurred in China. The electric iron was invented in 1882, by Henry W. Seeley. Seeley patented his "electric flatiron" on June 6, 1882 (U.S. Patent no. 259,054).

EQUIPMENT

Iron: The iron is the small appliance used to remove wrinkles from fabric. It is also known as a clothes iron, flat iron, or smoothing iron. The piece at the bottom is called a sole plate. Ironing uses heat energy, chemical energy, electrical energy, and mechanical energy.

Ironing board: Most ironing is done on an ironing board, a small, portable, foldable table with a heat resistant surface. Some commercial-grade ironing boards incorporate a heating element and a pedal-operated vacuum to pull air through the board and dry the garment.

On 16 February 1858 W. Vandenburg and J. Harvey patented an ironing table that facilitated pressing sleeves and pant legs. A truly portable folding ironing board was first patented in Canada in 1875 by John B. Porter. The invention also included a removable press board used for sleeves. In 1892 Sarah Booneobtained a patent in the United States for improvements to the ironing board, allowing for better quality ironing for shirt sleeves.

Ironing Board Cover Sizes

Size	Inches	Centimetres
A	43 × 12	110 × 30
B	49 × 15	124 × 38
C	49 × 18	124 × 45
D	53 × 18	135 × 45
E	53 × 19	135 × 49

Tailor's ham: A tailor's ham or *dressmakers ham* is a tightly stuffed pillow in the shape of a ham used as a mold when pressing curves such as sleeves or collars.

Commercial equipment: Commercial dry cleaning and full-service laundry providers usually use a large appliance called a steam press to do most of the work of ironing clothes. Alternatively, a rotary iron may be used. Historically, larger tailors' shops included a tailor's stove, a stove used by tailors to quickly and efficiently heat multiple irons. In many developing countries a cluster of solid irons, heated alternatively from a single heating source, are used for pressing cloths at small commercial outlets.

CLOTHES IRON

A clothing iron, also called a flatiron or simply an iron, is a small appliance: a handheld piece of equipment with a flat, roughly triangular surface that, when heated, is used to press clothes to removecreases. It is named for the metal of which the device is commonly made, and the use of it is generally calledironing. Ironing works by loosening the ties between the long chains of molecules that exist in polymer fibre materials. With the heat and the weight of the ironing plate, the fibres are stretched and the fabric maintains its new shape when cool. Some materials, such as cotton, require the use of water to loosen the intermolecular bonds. Many materials developed in the twentieth century are advertised as needing little or no ironing.

The electric iron was invented in 1882 by Henry W. Seeley, a New York inventor. Seeley patented his "electric flatiron" on June 6, 1882. His iron weighed almost 15 pounds and took a long time to warm up. Other electric irons had also been invented, including one from France (1882), but it used a carbon arc to heat the iron, a method which was dangerous.

HISTORY AND DEVELOPMENT OF FLATIRONS

Metal pans filled with hot water were used for smoothing fabrics in China in the 1st century BC.From the 17th century, *sadirons* or *sad irons* (from an old word meaning *solid*) began to be used. They were thick slabs of cast iron, delta-shaped and with a handle, heated in a fire. These were also called flat irons. A later design consisted of an iron box which could be filled with hot coals, which had to be periodically aerated by attaching a bellows. In Kerala in India, burning coconut shells were used instead of charcoal, as they have a similar heating capacity. This method is still in use as a backup device, since power outages are frequent. Other box irons had heated metal inserts instead of hot coals.

Another solution was to employ a cluster of solid irons that were heated from a single source: As the iron currently in use cooled down, it could be quickly replaced by a hot one. In the late nineteenth and early twentieth centuries, there were many irons in use that were heated by fuels such as kerosene, ethanol, whale oil, natural gas, carbide gas (acetylene, as with carbide lamps), or even gasoline. Some houses were equipped with a system of pipes for distributing natural gas or carbide gas to different rooms in order to operate appliances such as irons, in addition to lights. Despite the risk of fire, liquid-fuel irons were sold in U.S. rural areas up through World War II. In the industrialized world, these designs have been superseded by the electric iron, which uses resistiveheating from an electric current. The hot plate, called the *sole plate*, is made of aluminium or stainless steel. The heating element is controlled by a thermostat that switches the current on and off to maintain the selected temperature.

The invention of the resistively heated electric iron is credited to Henry W. Seeley of New Yorkin 1882. In the same year an iron heated by a carbon arc was introduced in France, but was too dangerous to be successful. The early electric irons had no easy way to control their temperature, and the first thermostatically controlled electric iron appeared in the 1920s.

Later, steam was used to iron clothing. Credit for the invention of the steam iron goes to Thomas Sears.

The first commercially available electric steam iron was introduced in 1926 by a New York drying and cleaning company, Eldec, but was not a commercial success. The $10 Steam-O-Matic of 1938 was the first steam iron to achieve any degree of popularity, and led the way to more widespread use of the electric steam iron during the 1940s and 1950s.

Types and names: Historically, irons have had several variations and have thus been called by many names:

- Flatiron or smoothing iron: The general name for a hand-held iron consisting simply of a handle and a solid, flat, metal base, and named for the flat ironing face used to smooth clothes.
- Sad iron or sadiron: Mentioned above, meaning "solid" or heavy iron, where the base is a solid block of metal, sometimes used to refer irons with heavier bases than a typical "flatiron".
- Box iron, ironing box, charcoal iron, ox-tongue iron or slug iron: Mentioned above; the base is a container, into which you can insert hot coals or a metal brick or slug to keep the iron heated. The ox-tongue iron is named for the particular shape of the insert, referred to as an ox-tongue slug.
- Goose, tailor's goose or, in Scottish, gusing iron: A type of flat iron or sad iron named for the goose-like curve in its neck, and (in the case of "tailor's goose") its usage by tailors.

FEATURES

Modern irons for home use can have the following features:

- A design that allows the iron to be set down, usually standing on its end, without the hot soleplate touching anything that could be damaged;
- A thermostat ensuring maintenance of a constant temperature;
- A temperature control dial allowing the user to select the operating

temperatures (usually marked with types of cloth rather than temperatures: "silk", "wool", "cotton", "linen", etc.);

- An electrical cord with heat-resistant silicone rubber insulation;
- Injection of steam through the fabric during the ironing process;
- A water reservoir inside the iron used for steam generation;
- An indicator showing the amount of water left in the reservoir,
- Constant steam: constantly sends steam through the hot part of the iron into the clothes;
- Steam burst: sends a burst of steam through the clothes when the user presses a button;
- (advanced feature) Dial controlling the amount of steam to emit as a constant stream;
- (advanced feature) Anti-drip system;
- Cord control: the point at which the cord attaches to the iron has a spring to hold the cord out of the way while ironing and likewise when setting down the iron (prevents fires, is more convenient, etc.);
- (advanced feature) non-stick coating along the sole plate to help the iron glide across the fabric
- (advanced feature) Anti-burn control: if the iron is left flat (possibly touching clothes) for too long, the iron shuts off to prevent scorching and fires;
- (advanced feature) Energy saving control: if the iron is left undisturbed for several (10 or 15) minutes, the iron shuts off to save energy and prevent fires.
- Cordless irons: the iron is placed on a stand for a short period to warm up, using thermal mass to stay hot for a short period. These are useful for light loads only. Battery power is not viable for irons as they require more power than practical batteries can provide.
- (advanced feature) 3-way automatic shut-off
- (advanced feature) self-cleaning

COLLECTIONS

One of the world's larger collection of irons, encompassing 1300 historical examples of irons from Germany and the rest of the world, is housed in Gochsheim Castle, near Karlsruhe, Germany.

The collections of irons are possessed by many ethnografical museums all around the world. In Ukraine, for example, about 150 irons are the part of the exhibition of the Radomysl Castle (Radomyshl, Ukraine).

LINEN

Linen is a textile made from the fibres of the flax plant, *Linum usitatissimum*. Linen is labour-intensive to manufacture, but when it is made into garments, it is valued for its exceptional coolness and freshness in hot weather.

The word "linen" is of West Germanic origin and cognates with the Latin name for the flax plant *linum*, and the earlier Greek (*linon*). This word history has given rise to a number of other terms in English, the most notable of which is the English word *line,* derived from the use of a linen (flax) threadto determine a straight line.

Textiles in a linen weave texture, even when made of cotton, hemp and other non-flax fibres are also loosely referred to as "linen". Such fabrics generally have their own specific names other than linen; for example, fine cotton yarn in a linen-style weave is called Madapolam.

The collective term "linens" is still often used generically to describe a class of woven and even knittedbed, bath, table and kitchen textiles. The name linens is retained because traditionally, linen was used for many of these items. In the past, the word "linens" was also used to mean light weight undergarments such as shirts, chemises, waistshirts, lingerie (a word also cognate with *linen*), and detachable shirt collars and cuffs, which were historically made almost exclusively out of linen.

The inside cloth layer of fine composite clothing garments (as for example jackets) was traditionally made of linen, and this is the origin of the word *lining.*

Linen textiles appear to be some of the oldest in the world: their history goes back many thousands of years. Fragments of straw, seeds, fibres, yarns, and various types of fabrics which date back to about 8000 BC have been found in Swiss lake dwellings.

Dyed flax fibres found in a prehistoric cave inGeorgia suggest the use of woven linen fabrics from wild flax may date back even earlier to 36,000BP.

Linen was sometimes used as currency in ancient Egypt. Egyptian mummies were wrapped in linen because it was seen as a symbol of light and purity, and as a display of wealth. Some of these fabrics, woven from hand spun yarns, were very fine for their day, but are coarse compared to modern linen. Today, linen is usually an expensive textile, and is produced in relatively small quantities. It has a long "staple" (individual fibre length) relative to cotton and other natural fibres.

Many products are made of linen: aprons, bags, towels (swimmers, bath, beach, body and wash towels), napkins, bed linens, linen tablecloths, runners, chair covers, and men's and women's wear.

ETYMOLOGY

The word linen is derived from the Latin for the flax plant, which is *linum*, and the earlier Greek (*linon*). This word history has given rise to a number of other terms:

- Line, derived from the use of a linen thread to determine a straight line;
- Lining, because linen was often used to create a lining for wool and leather clothing
- Lingerie, via French, originally denotes underwear made of linen
- Linseed oil, an oil derived from flax seed
- Linoleum, a floor covering made from linseed oil and other materials

In addition, the term in English, *flaxen-haired*, denoting a very light, bright blonde, comes from a comparison to the colour of raw flax fibre.

HISTORY

In ancient Mesopotamia, flax was domesticated and linen was produced. It was mainly used by the wealthier class of the society like priests. The Sumerian poem of the courtship of Inanna and Dumuzi (Tammuz), translated by Samuel Noah Kramer and Diane Wolkstein and published in 1983; mentions flax and linen.

It opens with briefly listing the steps of preparing linen from flax, in a form of questions and answers between Inanna and her brother Utu. In ancient Egypt, linen was used for mummification and for burial shrouds. It was also worn as clothing on a daily basis; white linen was worn because of the extreme heat.

Linen fabric has been used for table coverings, bed coverings and clothing for centuries. The significant cost of linen derives not only from the difficulty of working with the thread, but also because the flax plant itself requires a great deal of attention. In addition flax thread is not elastic, and therefore it is difficult to weave without breaking threads. Thus linen is considerably more expensive to manufacture than cotton.

There is a long history of the production of linen in Ireland. The Living Linen Project was set up in 1995 as an oral archive of the knowledge of the Irish linenindustry, which was at that time still available within a nucleus of people who formerly worked in the industry in Ulster.

The discovery of dyed flax fibres in a cave in Georgia dated to 36,000 BP suggests that ancient people used wild flax fibres to create linen-like fabrics from an early date.

The use of linen for priestly vestments was not confined to the Israelites; Plutarch wrote that the priests of Isis also wore linen because of its purity.

In December 2006, the General Assembly of the United Nations proclaimed 2009 to be the International Year of Natural Fibres in order to raise people's awareness of linen and other natural fibres.

Antiquity: When the tomb of the Pharaoh Ramses II, who died 1213 BC, was discovered in 1881, the linen wrappings were in a state of perfect preservation after more than 3000 years.

In the Belfast Library there is the mummy of "Kaboolie,' the daughter of a priest of Ammon, who died 2,500 years ago. The linen on this mummy is also in a perfect state of preservation. When the tomb of Tutankhamen was opened, the linen curtains were found to be intact.

Earliest linen industry: The earliest records of an established linen industry are 4,000 years old, from Egypt. The earliest written documentation of a linen industry comes from the Linear B tablets of Pylos, Greece, where linen is depicted as an ideogram and also written as "li-no" (Greek: ëßîíí, *linon*), and the female linen workers are cataloged as "li-ne-ya" (*lineia*).

The Phoenicians, who, with their merchant fleet, opened up new channels of commerce to the peoples of the Mediterranean, and developed the tin mines of Cornwall, introduced flax growing and the making of linen intoIreland before the common era. It is not until the twelfth century that we can find records of a definite attempt to systematize flax production.

When the Edict of Nantes was revoked, in 1685, many of the Huguenots who fled France settled in the British Isles, and amongst them was Louis Crommelin, who was born and brought up as a weaver of fine linen, in the town of Cambrai. He fled to Ulster, and eventually settled down in the small town of Lisburn, about ten miles from Belfast. Belfast itself is perhaps the most famous linen producing center throughout history; during the Victorian era the majority of the world's linen was produced in the city which gained it the name Linenopolis.

During the First World War Cambrai became well known as one of the centers of the most desperate fighting. The name "cambric" is derived from this town.

Although the linen industry was already established in Ulster, Louis Crommelin found scope for improvement in weaving, and his efforts were so successful that he was appointed by the Government to develop the industry over a much wider range.than the small confines of Lisburn and its surroundings. The direct result of his good work was the establishment, under statute, of the Board of Trustees of the Linen Manufacturers of Ireland in the year 1711.

Religion: In the Jewish faith, the only law concerning which fabrics may be interwoven together in clothing is one which concerns the mixture of linen and wool. This mixture is called *shaatnez* and is clearly restricted in Deuteronomy 22:11 "Thou shalt not wear a mingled stuff, wool and linen together" and Leviticus 19:19, "'...neither shall there come upon thee a garment of two kinds of stuff mingled together.'" There is no explanation for this in the Torah itself and is categorized as a type of law known as *chukim*, a statute beyond man's ability to comprehend. Josephus suggested that the reason for the prohibition was to keep the laity from wearing the official garb of the priests, while Maimonides thought that the reason was because heathen priests wore such mixed garments. Others explain that it is because God often forbids mixtures of disparate kinds, not designed by God to be compatible in a certain way, with mixing animal and vegetable fibres being similar to having two different types of plowing animals yoked together. And that such commands serve both a practical as well as allegorical purpose, perhaps here preventing a priestly garment that would cause discomfort (or excessive sweat) in a hot climate. Linen is also mentioned in the Bible in Proverbs 31, a passage describing a noble wife. Proverbs 31:22 says, "She makes coverings for her bed; she is clothed in fine linen and purple." Fine white linen is also worn by angels in the Bible.

FLAX FIBRE

Description: Linen is a bast fibre. Flax fibres vary in length from about 25 to 150 mm (1 to 6 in) and average 12-16 micrometers in diameter. There are two varieties: shorter tow fibres used for coarser fabrics and longer line fibres used for finer fabrics. Flax fibres can usually be identified by their "nodes" which add to the flexibility and texture of the fabric.

The cross-section of the linen fibre is made up of irregular polygonal shapes which contribute to the coarse texture of the fabric.

Properties: Linen fabric feels cool to the touch. It is smooth, making the finished fabric lint-free, and gets softer the more it is washed. However, constant creasing in the same place in sharp folds will tend to break the linen threads. This wear can show up in collars, hems, and any area that is iron creased during laundering. Linen has poor elasticity and does not spring back readily, explaining why it wrinkles so easily.

Linen fabrics have a high natural luster; their natural colour ranges between shades of ivory, ecru, tan, or grey. Pure white linen is created by heavy bleaching. Linen typically has a thick and thin character with a crisp and textured feel to it, but it can range from stiff and rough, to soft and smooth. When properly prepared, linen fabric has the ability to absorb and lose water rapidly. It can gain up to 20 per cent moisture without feeling damp.

It is a very durable, strong fabric, and one of the few that are stronger wet than dry. The fibres do not stretch and are resistant to damage from abrasion. However, because linen fibres have a very low elasticity, the fabric will eventually break if it is folded and ironed at the same place repeatedly.

Mildew, perspiration, and bleach can also damage the fabric, but it is resistant to moths and carpet beetles. Linen is relatively easy to take care of, since it resists dirt and stains, has no lint or pilling tendency, and can be dry-cleaned, machine-washed or steamed. It can withstand high temperatures, and has only moderate initial shrinkage.

Linen should not be dried too much by tumble drying: it is much easier to iron when damp because of its growth pattern. Linen wrinkles very easily, and so some more formal linen garments require ironing often, in order to maintain perfect smoothness. Nevertheless, the tendency to wrinkle is often considered part of the fabric's particular "charm", and many modern linen garments are designed to be air-dried on a good hanger and worn without the necessity of ironing.

A characteristic often associated with contemporary linen yarn is the presence of "slubs", or small knots which occur randomly along its length. These slubs used to be considered as defects associated with low quality. However many contemporary Linen fabrics, particularly in the decorative furnishing industry, slubs are intentionally included as part of the aesthetic appeal of a natural product and do not compromise integrity of the fabric thus not considered as a defect. The finest linen has very consistent diameter threads, with no slubs.

Measure: The standard measure of bulk linen yarn is the lea, which is the number of yards in a pound of linen divided by 300. For example a yarn having a size of 1 lea will give 300 yards per pound. The fine yarns used in handkerchiefs, etc. might be 40 lea, and give 40x300 = 12,000 yards per pound. This is a specific length therefore an indirect measurement of the fineness of the linen, *i.e.* the number of length units per unit mass. The symbol is NeL.(3) The metric unit, Nm, is more commonly used in continental Europe. This is the number of 1,000 m lengths per kilogram. In China, the English Cotton system unit, NeC, is common. This is the number of 840 yard lengths in a pound.

Production method: The quality of the finished linen product is often dependent upon growing conditions and harvesting techniques. To generate the longest possible fibres, flax is either hand-harvested by pulling up the entire plant or stalks are cut very close to the root. After harvesting, the seeds are removed through a mechanized process called "rippling" or by winnowing.

The fibres must then be loosened from the stalk. This is achieved through retting. This is a process which uses bacteria to decompose the pectin that binds the fibres together. Natural retting methods take place in tanks and pools, or directly in the fields. There are also chemical retting methods; these are faster, but are typically more harmful to the environment and to the fibres themselves.

After retting, the stalks are ready for scutching, which takes place between August and December. Scutching removes the woody portion of the stalks by crushing them between two metal rollers, so that the parts of the stalk can be separated. The fibres are removed and the other parts such as linseed, shive, and tow are set aside for other uses. Next the fibres areheckled: the short fibres are separated with heckling combs by 'combing' them away, to leave behind only the long, soft flax fibres.

After the fibres have been separated and processed, they are typically spun into yarns and woven or knit into linen textiles. These textiles can then be bleached, dyed, printed on, or finished with a number of treatments or coatings.

An alternate production method is known as "cottonizing" which is quicker and requires less equipment. The flax stalks are processed using traditional cotton machinery; however, the finished fibres often lose the characteristic linen look.

Producers: Flax is grown in many parts of the world, but top quality flax is primarily grown in Western Europe. In very recent years bulk linen production has moved to Eastern Europe and China, but high quality fabrics are still confined to niche producers in Ireland, Italy and Belgium, and also in countries including Poland, Austria, France, Germany, Sweden, Denmark, Lithuania, Latvia, the Netherlands, Italy, Spain, Switzerland, Britain and Kochi in India. High quality linen fabrics are now produced in the United States for the upholstery market.

Uses: Over the past 30 years the end use for linen has changed dramatically. Approximately 70 per cent of linen production in the 1990s was for apparel textiles, whereas in the 1970s only about 5 per cent was used for fashion fabrics.

Linen uses range from bed and bath fabrics (tablecloths, dish towels, bed sheets, etc.), home and commercial furnishing items (wallpaper/wall coverings, upholstery, window treatments, etc.), apparel items (suits, dresses, skirts, shirts, etc.), to industrial products (luggage, canvases, sewing thread, etc.). It was once the preferred yarn for handsewing the uppers of moccasin-style shoes (loafers), but its use has been replaced by synthetics.

A linen handkerchief, pressed and folded to display the corners, was a standard decoration of a well-dressed man's suit during most of the first part of the 20th century.

Currently researchers are working on a cotton/flax blend to create new yarns which will improve the feel of denim during hot and humid weather.

Linen fabric is one of the preferred traditional supports for oil painting. In the United States cotton is popularly used instead as linen is many times more expensive there, restricting its use to professional painters. In Europe however, linen is usually the only fabric support available in art shops; in the UK both are freely available with cotton being cheaper. Linen is preferred to cotton for its strength, durability and archival integrity.

Linen is also used extensively by artisan bakers. Known as a couche, the flax cloth is used to hold the dough into shape while in the final rise, just before baking. The couche is heavily dusted with flour which is rubbed into the pores of the fabric. Then the shaped dough is placed on the couche. The floured couche makes a "non-stick" surface to hold the dough. Then ridges are formed in the couche to keep the dough from spreading. It sort of looks like where the "o" is the dough and the is the folded couche.

In the past, linen was also used for books (the only surviving example of which is the Liber Linteus). Due to its strength, in the Middle Ages linen was used for shields and gambeson (among other roles such as use for a bowstring), much as in classical antiquity it was used to make a type of body armour, referred to as a linothorax. Also because of its strength when wet, Irish linen is a very popular wrap of pool/billiard cues, due to its absorption of sweat from hands. Paper made of linen can be very strong and crisp, which is why the United States and many other countries print their currency on paper that is made from 25 per cent linen and 75 per cent cotton.

LAUNDRY ROOM

A laundry room (also called a utility room) is a room where clothes are washed. In a modern home, a laundry room would be equipped with an automatic washing machine and clothes dryer, and often a large basin, called a *laundry tub*, for hand-washing delicate articles of clothing such as sweaters, and an ironing board. A typical laundry room is located in the basement of older homes, but in many modern homes, the laundry room might be found on the main floor near the kitchen or upstairs near the bedrooms.

Another typical location is adjacent to the garage and the laundry room serves as a mudroom for the entrance from the garage. As the garage is often at a different elevation (or grade) than the rest of the house, the laundry room that serves as an entrance from the garage that may be sunken from the rest of the house. This avoids or minimizes the need for stairs between the garage and the house.

Laundry rooms may also include storage cabinets, countertops for folding clothes, and, space permitting, a small sewing machine.

Most houses do not have laundry rooms; the washing machine and dryer are typically located in the kitchen or garage.

12

Cleaning and Stain Removal

TIPS FOR REMOVING STAINS

The toxins found in everyday cleaning products not only have an effect on our health — children, especially, are vulnerable — but also the well-being of our planet. We as re-sponsible consumers need to know what's in the products we use, and how they affect those around us.

It is possible to achieve a sanitary and pleasant cleanliness in the home without owning an arsenal of c-hemically laced cleaning products. Even though stains can be tough to remove in general, check out these green cleaning fabric stain tips to learn an alternate way to remove them.

First up, the ever-frustrating ink stain.-

Ink stains are some of the most common types of stains we get on our clothing — and are among the most stubborn to remove. Like a lot of the stains mentioned here, ink can be tackled with three of our Fantastic Four items: salt, baking soda, and lemon juice.

Back in the day, we used to spray aerosol hair spray on our clothes to make ink stains dissolve. It was certainly a smelly option and probably not the best for our clothes (or, considering the fumes coming from the aerosol cans, ourselves). But there certainly are other home remedies to try. For one, sprinkle a fresh stain with salt and then soak the entire garment in milk; afterwards, launder as usual.

Another method involves making a paste of lemon juice and cream of tartar. You should first test the fabric for colourfastness: Paint the mixture onto a hidden area of the fabric and let it sit for 20 minutes. If the colour is fine, then it's full steam ahead! Cover the stain with the paste and again let it sit for 20 minutes.

Then check that the stain is removed before laundering the item as usual. An alternative method would be to cover the stain with cream of tartar and drizzle a little lemon juice onto it. Rub the mixture in and let it sit for a minute or two, then brush off any excess cream of tartar. Launder the item as usual.

Here's a tip for removing ink from white fabric: Apply the cream of tartar and lemon juice paste and then lay the fabric flat outside in a sunny spot. The paste will remove the stain, and the sun will brighten the white fabric. Then, of course, wash as usual.

Say you're at a party, and you've managed to swipe your pen on your shirt. Since most people don't carry cream of tartar and lemon juice everywhere they go, here's a trick to use in a pinch: Plain club soda helps keep stains from setting. Dip the stained area into the club soda and then dab with a hand-kerchief or other lint-free cloth. If the stain is serious, follow the methods mentioned already, or just launder as normal.

Red wine can be removed from fabrics in some of the same ways as ink stains. Or, try this: Soak the stained area in water, then make a pouch in the cloth where the wine stain is. Next, pour cream of tartar into the pouched area. Tie the ends of the pouch and then let the garment soak. After soaking, dip it in and out of hot water, then launder as usual.

Say it's a dinner party, and somebody got a little exuberant in conversation. If the red wine stain is fresh, soak up the spill by immediately sprinkling it with baking soda. Next, as soon as possible, stretch the stained fabric over a large bowl or kettle, secure the fabric, and pour boiling water through the stain. Similarly, you can use salt for this purpose by sprinkling it on a spill immediately and letting it soak up the stain. Afterwards, soak the stained area in cold water and then launder the garment as usual.

Bloodstains on cotton, linen, or other natural fibre fabrics should be soaked in cold salt water for one hour, then washed using warm water and your usual laundry soap. If you have a fresh bloodstain, cover it with salt and blot it with cold water. Add fresh water and blot until the stain is gone.

Handle with cold, then heat. First, place an ice cube on the wax. When the wax is hardened, remove it with a dull knife. Next, get rid of any remaining wax by putting a piece of thick paper (such as a paper bag) flat over the stain. Then press the area with a warm iron; the wax will melt into the paper.

DYNAMIC DUO VS. STUBBORN STAINS

If you've got a very stubborn stain, try this method: Mix equal parts white vinegar and lemon juice in a laundry tub or dishpan. Drop the stained garment in and let it soak for 30 minutes to an hour. Check the stain and launder as usual. After washing, check the stain again. If any stain remains, repeat the process above. Do not put the item into the dryer until the fabric is clean, as the heat will set the stain. -

Rust stains give us another laundry situation where cream of tartar is a great green hero — it has an acidic quality that enables it to break down rust. First, cover the rust stain with cream of tartar. Next, tie up the area surrounding the stain, making the fabric into a pouch. Soak the entire pouch in very hot water for about five to ten minutes, then untie it and launder as usual. Salt and vinegar also work well as rust removers on fabric. Combine salt and vinegar into a thin paste and then spread the paste onto the stained area of the fabric. Next, lay the item out in the sun to bleach it. If sun is not an option, stretch the fabric over a large bowl or pan, secure the fabric, and pour boiling water through the stained area. Whether you use sun bleaching or the hot water method, allow the item to dry on its own. Run the item through a rinse cycle in your washing machine, or give it a good hand rinsing, and then check the stain again. If any of the stain remains, repeat the treatments. Never put the fabric through the dryer until you're certain the stain is gone.

Make a thin paste of lemon juice and salt; spread the paste on mildew stains. Lay out the fabric in the sun to bleach it. Afterwards, rinse and dry. Mildew stains on fabric can also be tackled with a paste of salt, vinegar, and water. If the stain is extensive, you can use up to full-strength vinegar.

Some garments may still retain a musty, mildewy smell even after washing. Get rid of the smell by soaking the garments in lemon juice and water and then letting them dry in the sun.

Dropping a bit of greasy gravy on your clothes can be a disaster, but not if you act quickly. Immediately after it happens, cover the fresh gravy stain with salt, letting it absorb as much of the grease as possible. Gently brush off the salt. If the stain is still visible, dab it with a cloth dipped in straight vinegar. This method can work for any fresh greasy spot.

If you have an article of clothing with set-in coffee or tea stains, don't despair. Just soak it in a solution of 1 unit vinegar to 2 units water and then hang the item to dry in the sun. Still, the best treatment for coffee or tea stains is to get them when they're fresh. When you tackle the problem right away, the stains usually rinse out eas-ily with some cold water (depending upon the fabric).

Reddish fruit juices of any kind — cherry, cranberry, blueberry — can be removed from bleach-safe garments by soaking them in a solution of 1 unit vinegar and 2 units water. Afterwards, launder as usual.-

As anyone who likes to spend time outdoors or has rambunctious children can tell you, trying to remove grass stains from white clothing with the usual laundering techniques can be a challenge. Try soaking the stained item in full-strength vinegar for a half hour or more before washing, then wash as usual.

First, soak the clothing in a solution of hot water and distilled white vinegar. If the fabric is delicate, change the water temperature to cold instead. Let it sit for a half hour, then rinse and wash as usual.

REMOVING STAINS: THE BASICS

There is no single technique or product that takes care of every spot and spill, but with the right information and supplies, many stains can be removed.

If a garment isn't washable, the safest thing is to take it to a dry cleaner, although there are some treatments you can try at home. If you stain a washable garment, the golden rule is: Act quickly. For a liquid, gently blot up any excess with a white cloth, working from the outside in, so you don't spread the stain; do not press hard or rub. Sprinkle an oily stain with cornstarch. If it's a dollop of something, like ketchup, scoop off any excess. Dab the area with cool water, which will lighten most spots and remove others altogether.

Textile and stain experts recommend certain stain removal supplies for each problem. Start small, using cotton swabs and eyedroppers. Often, you'll start with one treatment, then follow up with another, since many stains have more than one component: With lipstick or tomato sauce, for example, you have to treat the oil in the stain, then remove the colour. After using a remedy, always wash the garment as you normally would, but look at the area you treated before you dry it; repeat the treatment if necessary, or try another.

Always test stain-removal techniques in a hidden area of the garment, like an inside seam. There are no guarantees — sometimes stain-removal techniques do more harm than good — so if you have a particularly vexing stain or a valuable, delicate piece of clothing, take it to a professional. And unfortunately, some things just won't come out. With permanent ink, for example, the operative word is "permanent."

CARPET CLEANING

Chem-Dry has become a trusted name in carpet cleaning for thousands of households and businesses for good reason. Chem-Dry's carpet cleaning services are based on the three pillars we believe are a vital part to providing customers with the safe, long lasting, quality carpet cleaning they deserve.

Drier. Since the Chem-Dry cleaning process uses 80 per cent less water than typical steam cleaning, carpets dry within hours, not days. So you and your family can get back to enjoying your home sooner. Cleaner. Just like club soda, our primary solution is carbonated and penetrates deep into your carpets fibres, giving you the most thorough clean. And it doesn't contain harsh chemicals, so no dirt-attracting residue is left behind and carpets stay cleaner, longer.

Healthier. Our low-water, faster drying clean means less risk of mold and mildew growth under your carpet that can result from the excessive water used by most steam cleaners. And our main carpet cleaning solution is green-certified, so it's completely safe and non-toxic for your family and pets. That adds up to a healthier, safer carpet cleaning that lasts.

COMPARE OUR PACKAGES

Find out below how Chem-Dry's Carpet Protectant Package and Healthy Home Package (professional strength deodorizer and sanitizer) can help protect your home from everyday stains, unhealthy allergens and bacteria.

FIGHT STAINS WITH CARPET PROTECTANT PACKAGE

Your carpets get a lot of use, spills are inevitable. Over time, the factory-applied stain resistant becomes less effective and fades away leaving your carpets susceptible to staining. Chem-Dry Protectants refreshes the performance of stain resistant carpets, creating a barrier around the carpet fibres to resist soiling and staining by allowing spills to be removed before staining can occur.

Protect Package: A trio of protectants to revitalize the stain resistant power of your carpet:

- PowerGuard Protectant®- This revolutionary carpet stain protectant not only gives a boost to your carpet's stain-resisting powers, but works well with solution-dyed carpets.
- Repel Protectant- Repel Protectant works with all kinds of carpets by forming a protective shield around each carpet fibre. This liquid-repelling carpet solution doesn't give stains the chance to set in.
- Wool Protectant- Chem-Dry's Wool Protectant is a water-based solution specifically designed to enhance the stain resistant qualities of wool carpets and rugs. It defends against most liquid spills to stop stains in their tracks.

SANITIZE AND DEODORIZE TO REDUCE ALLERGENS AND BACTERIA WITH HEALTHY HOME PACKAGE

Does someone in your home suffer from allergies? Do you have children who love to roll around and play on the carpet? Unfortunately, carpets absorb and collect common allergens and germs that can spread illness, cause allergies and make asthma symptoms worse for you and your family. Chem-Dry professional strength Deodorizer and Sanitizer reduce tough odors and allergens, leaving your carpets clean and healthy and your family safer.

Healthy Home Package: Deodorizer/Sanitizer:

- Sanitizes home to eliminate unhealthy bacteria that can spread illness
- Reduces common allergens from dust mites, pests, pet dander, mold, pollen and more
- Special deodorizer reaches odors absorbed in your carpets so they aren't just masked – they're eliminated

STAIN REMOVAL

Stain removal is the process of removing a mark or spot left by one substance on a specific surface like a fabric. A solvent or detergent is generally used to conduct stain removal and many of these are available over the counter.

STAIN PREVENTION

If a stain has "set", it has become chemically bonded to the material that it has stained, and cannot be removed without damaging the material itself. It is therefore important to avoid setting stains that one wants to remove. This can be done by avoiding heat (by not pressing or ironing the stain), sponging stained materials as quickly as possible, using the correct solvent (some solvents will act as catalysts on certain substances and cause the stain to set more quickly), and avoiding rubbing the stain. This has been edited.

STAIN REMOVAL

Most stains are removed by dissolving them with a solvent. The solvent to use depends from two factors: the agent that is causing the stain, and the material that has been stained. Different solvents will dissolve different stains, and the application of some solvents is limited by the fact that they not only dissolve the stain, but also dissolve the material that is stained as well. Another factor in stain removal is the fact that stains can sometimes comprise two separate staining agents, which require separate forms of removal. A machine oil stain could also contain traces of metal, for example.

Also of concern is the colour of the material that is stained. Some stain removal agents will not only dissolve the stain, but will dissolve the dye that is used to colour the material.

Solvents: These are some of the solvents that can be used for stains, with some examples of the stains that they are capable of removing:

Oxidising solvents: Household bleach generally removes a stain's colour, without dissolving the stain itself. Hydrogen peroxide is also a bleaching agent that can be used to treat stains.

Lacquer solvents: Acetone is good for removing some glues, nail polish, ink stains, rubber cement, and grease. Nail polish remover may contain acetone, however for general use it is best to obtain bottled acetone from a hardware store. It can be diluted with water.

Detergents: Surfactants (detergents) are molecules that have one polar end and one non-polar end and can be used for stain removal. They can help to emulsify compounds that are not usually soluble in water. For example, if you put oil in water, they tend to stay separated. If you put oil, detergent, and water together and shake them up, then you get a mixture that can help to remove stains.

Acids: Lemon juice, containing citric acid which is the active bleaching agent, can effectively remove stains. Its action can be accelerated by exposing the stain to sunlight, or some other UV source, while soaking. Various Acids were used in the past such as Phosphoric acid as used in Calcium Lime Rust Remover (CLR) and Hydrofluoric acid as used in the Australian Product made in Queensland called "Rustiban".

Both of these Acids have been removed from sale to the general public due to toxicity concerns. Both of these Acids were used primarily to remove Rust. Other Rust removal Acids are oxalic acid.

Alkalis: Sodium Hydroxide Is also commonly used in drain cleaners. It allows Grease and other oils to dissolve into Aqueous solution. *i.e.* Water. Other Alkalis such as Potassium Hydroxide (much stronger than Sodium Hydroxide) are also used. Both of these are hazardous chemicals and react with animal flesh. High enough concentrations, as in industrial cleaners, and/ or significant exposure time without adequate protection of the exposed area will cause serious chemical burns.

OTHERS

Club Soda: This can be used for pet stains and out of doors.

Glycerine: This can be used to soften "set" stains, especially on wool and non-water-washable fabrics.

APPLICATION OF SOLVENTS

There are four ways to apply a solvent to a fabric for removing stains:

- Soaking
- Application of pressure
- Front sponging

This is the most common way of treating non-washable fabrics. The front of the fabric is sponged with a sponge that is soaked in the solvent being used. The rear of the fabric should be backed up with a clean, absorbent, material. The stain is rubbed with the sponge radially, from the centre of the stain towards its edge. It is important not to rub the sponge in a circular motion, as that causes the stain to spread in rings.

Back sponging: The stained side of the material is placed face down on a clean, absorbent, material. The back of the fabric is then sponged with a sponge that is soaked in the solvent being used.

It is important not to rub the material with the sponge, but to use a padding motion, so as not to spread the stain. The solvent dissolves the stain, which is deposited on the absorbent material beneath. To completely remove the stain it may be necessary to use more than one absorbent pad.

HAIR DYE STAINS

Hair colouring products are commonly used to cover gray, look more attractive of keep up with fashion, yet they pose a challenge for many women. Because of the length of time the hair dye must be on the hair to achieve deep, even results, it often seeps or drips down onto the hairline, ears or neck, causing unsightly and irritating stains on the skin.

Dye users are not universally affected—some persons have a tendency to get stains while others do not—most likely due to the variations in lipid or natural oil composition on the skin surface from one person to the next.

Many salons and stylists advocate the use of petroleum jelly to prevent stains. Placing a rim of petroleum jelly around the hairline creates a physical barrier to prevent the dye from running down onto the skin of the forehead and neck, and fills the pits and recesses within the epidermal layer.

Chemistry: Human hair is composed largely of keratin protein, which has a negative ionic charge, giving hair a negative ionic charge as well. As chemistry dictates, oppositely charged compounds attract and compounds with the same charge repel each other. Most hair dyes are positively charged, helping them attach to the negative sites in hair and contributing to a better bond between the dye and the hair.

Unfortunately, like hair, human skin is made of keratin and contains sites with a negative charge, and therefore, it also attracts the dye. Skin also has pores and other pits and recesses which allow dye to get physically trapped in the epidermal layer. These both contribute to the development of stains on the skin.

The dye itself can be directly absorbed through the skin and into the bloodstream. The stratum corneum (the outermost layer of skin also called the "horny layer") contains a "lipid domain" that allows the dye to pool and provide opportunity to diffuse into the body. Some hair dyes can also irritate the skin with prolonged exposures. As a result, quickly removing or minimizing skin exposure to dye is often considered desirable.

Removal methods: While many home remedies exist to attempt to remove the stains from skin, there are very many products distributed in traditional drugstore or discount channels for this purpose. The home remedies vary in effectiveness and carry the risk of skin irritation and abrasion as a result of excessive scrubbing, plus eye irritation if allowed to drip or run into the eye. Some of the more common home remedies include: bleach, ammonia, acetone, and rubbing alcohol.

The following are risks of the common removal methods:

Acetone: The CDC reports that repeated and prolonged exposure of the eyes to acetone has the potential to cause permanent vision problems resulting from corneal clouding.

Ammonia: (ammonia is also contained in many hair dyes) Hair colours containing ammonia have been safely used for years. However, ammonia exposure can cause conjunctiva irritation of the eyes.

Bleach: Traditional bleach contains chlorine and/or hydroquinone. Chlorine can irritate and burn skin, as can skin-bleaching products. In the United States, the FDA has proposed a ruling to remove all skin bleaching products from being available over the counter. Isopropyl Alcohol: Concentrated isopropyl alcohol has been shown to irritate skin, and prolonged inhalation of the vapors can impair coordination and cause headaches. While it may be an effective stain remover, it must be used gently to avoid abrasion of skin.

TYPES OF STAINS AND FIRST STEP CLEANING ACTIONS

OIL-BASED

(grease, tar, cooking oil, milk, cosmetics)

An oil-based stain will darken the stone and normally must be chemically dissolved so the source of the stain can be flushed or rinsed away. Clean gently with a soft, liquid cleanser with bleach OR household detergent OR ammonia OR mineral spirits OR acetone.

ORGANIC

(coffee, tea, fruit, tobacco, paper, food, urine, leaves, bark, bird droppings) May cause a pinkish-brown stain and may disappear after the source of the stain has been removed. Outdoors, with the sources removed, normal sun and rain action will generally bleach out the stains. Indoors, clean with12 per cent hydrogen peroxide (hair bleaching strength) and a few drops of ammonia.

METAL

(iron, rust, copper, bronze)

Iron or rust stains are orange to brown in colour and follow the shape of the staining object such as nails, bolts, screws, cans, flower pots, metal furniture. Copper and bronze stains appear as green or muddy-brown and result from the action of moisture on nearby or embedded bronze, copper or brass items. Metal stains must be removed with a poultice. Deep-seated, rusty stains are extremely difficult to remove and the stone may be permanently stained.

BIOLOGICAL

(algae, mildew, lichens, moss, fungi)

Clean with diluted (1/2 cup in a gallon of water) ammonia OR bleach OR hydrogen peroxide. Do Not Mix Bleach Andammonia! This Combination Creates A Toxic And Lethal Gas!

INK

(magic marker, pen, ink)

Clean with bleach or hydrogen peroxide (light coloured stone only!) or lacquer thinner or acetone (dark stones only!)

PAINT

Small amounts can be removed with lacquer thinner or scraped off carefully with a razorblade. Heavy paint coverage should be removed only with a commercial "heavy liquid" paint stripper available from hardware stores and paint centers. These strippers normally contain caustic soda or lye. Do not use acids or flame tools to strip paint from stone. Paint strippers can etch the surface of the stone; re-polishing may be necessary. Follow the manufacturer's directions for use of these products, taking care to flush the area thoroughly with clean water. Protect yourself with rubber gloves and eye protection, and work in a well-ventilated area. Use only wood or plastic scrapers for removing the sludge and curdled paint. Normally, latex and acrylic paints will not cause staining. Oil-based paints, linseed oil, putty, caulks and sealants may cause oily stains. Refer to the section on oil-based stains.

WATER SPOTS AND RINGS

(surface accumulation of hard water)
Buff with dry 0000 steel wool.

FIRE AND SMOKE DAMAGE

Older stones and smoke or fire stained fireplaces may require a thorough cleaning to restore their original appearance. Commercially available "smoke removers" may save time and effort.

ETCH MARKS

Etch marks are caused by acids left on the surface of the stone. Some materials will etch the finish but not leave a stain. Others will both etch and stain. Once the stain has been removed, wet the surface with clear water and sprinkle on marble polishing powder, available from a hardware or lapidary store, or your local stone dealer. Rub the powder onto the stone with a damp cloth or by using a buffing pad with a low-speed power drill. Continue buffing until the etch mark disappears and the marble surface shines. Contact your stone dealer or call a professional stone restorer for refinishing or re-polishing etched areas that you cannot remove.

EFFLORESCENCE

Efflorescence is a white powder that may appear on the surface of the stone. It is caused by water carrying mineral salts from below the surface of the stone rising through the stone and evaporating. When the water evaporates, it leaves the powdery substance. If the installation is new, dust mop or vacuum the powder. You may have to do this several times as the stone dries out. Do not use water to remove the powder; it will only temporarily disappear. If the problem persists, contact your installer to help identify and remove the cause of the moisture.

SCRATCHES AND NICKS

Slight surface scratches may be buffed with dry 0000 steel wool. Deeper scratches and nicks in the surface of the stone should be repaired and re-polished by a professional.

POULTICES

MAKING AND USING A POULTICE

A poultice is a liquid cleaner or chemical mixed with a white absorbent material to form a paste about the consistency of peanut butter. The poultice is spread over the stained area to a thickness of about 1/4 to 1/2 inch with a wood or plastic spatula, covered with plastic and left to work for 24 to 48 hours. The liquid cleaner or chemical will draw out the stain into the absorbent material. Poultice procedures may have to be repeated to thoroughly remove a stain, but some stains may never be completely removed.

POULTICE MATERIALS

Poultice materials include kaolin, fuller's earth, whiting, diatomaceous earth, powdered chalk, white molding plaster or talc. Approximately one pound of prepared poultice material will cover one square foot. Do not use whiting or iron-type clays such as fuller's earth with acid chemicals. The reaction will cancel the effect of the poultice. A poultice can also be prepared using white cotton balls, whitepaper towels or gauze pads.

CLEANING AGENTS OR CHEMICALS

OIL-BASED STAINS

Poultice with baking soda and water OR one of the powdered poultice materials and mineral spirits.

ORGANIC STAINS

Poultice with one of the powdered poultice materials and 12 per cent hydrogen peroxide solution (hair bleaching strength) OR use acetone instead of the hydrogen peroxide.

IRON STAINS

Poultice with diatomaceous earth and a commercially available rust remover. Rust stains are particularly difficult to remove. You may need to call a professional.

COPPER STAINS

Poultice with one of the powdered poultice materials and ammonia. These stains are difficult to remove. You may need to call a professional.

BIOLOGICAL STAINS

Poultice with dilute ammonia OR bleach OR hydrogen peroxide. Do Not Mix Ammo-nia And Bleach! This Combinationcreates A Toxic And Lethal Gas!

APPLYING THE POULTICE

Prepare the poultice. If using powder, mix the cleaning agent or chemical to a thick paste the consistency of peanut butter. If using paper, soak in the chemical and let drain. Don't let the liquid drip.

Wet the stained area with distilled water.

Apply the poultice to the stained area about1/4 to 1/2 inch thick and extend the poultice beyond the stained area by about one inch. Use a wood or plastic scraper to spread the poultice evenly. Cover the poultice with plastic and tape the edges to seal it.

Allow the poultice to dry thoroughly, usually about 24 to 48 hours. The drying process is what pulls the stain out of the stone and into the poultice material. After about 24 hours, remove the plastic and allow the poultice to dry.

Remove the poultice from the stain. Rinse with distilled water and buff dry with a soft cloth. Use the wood or plastic scraper if necessary.

Repeat the poultice application if the stain is not removed. It may take up to five applications for difficult stains.

If the surface is etched by the chemical, apply polishing powder and buff with burlap or felt buffing pad to restore the surface.

ADHESIVE REMOVAL

HOW TO REMOVE DUCT TAPE FROM CLOTHES

Removing duct tape from clothes is easy. But you need to put more effort to remove the residue off the cloth while keeping the fabric and colours intact.

Try Simple First: Some people scrape off the sticky glue with their fingernails. Others just soak their clothes in detergent water for about 30 minutes and follow it up with light scrubbing. Of course these simple measures work at times.

But sometimes some duct tapes leave behind rigid stains. Then we need to look for chemical options such as adhesive remover.

Chemical Options: In the case of non-washable fabrics, just scrapping off the glue may work. If any stain remains, use either Afta Cleaning Fluid or K2r Spot Lifter

If the fabrics are washable, there are various ways to be done away with the messy glue.

One of the much followed practices is rubbing alcohol on the affected part. Even nail polish which contains acetone or paint thinner which contains toluene is used to get rid of sticky stains. However, these chemicals may not safeguard the colour of the fabric.

It is always safer to try any chemical solvent on an inconspicuous part of the cloth before applying it on the duct tape residue in more visible areas.

People have experimented with solvents like De-Solv-It, or Goo Gone to remove the glue with good results. It is advisable to work it a little at a time with the solvent and should not be too abrasive while scrubbing. The glue should be scrubbed out before the fabric gets dry. Or else, we should re-soak the cloth. Once the glue is gone, rinse the cloth before washing. Some people claim Goo Gone can remove any residue, no matter how sticky it is. Another solvent called Desolve is also recommended by some users.

There are others who have successfully used Hhirspray to remove stains. Again, the advice is - try it on a hidden spot of the cloth first. The removal process consists of saturating the affected part with hairspray and then washing it with warm water and mild detergent. If the stain is not washed away in one attempt, repeat the process – treat the spot with hairspray and then wash it.

One can also use WD-40 instead of hairspray. WD-40 softens the glue, making it easy to come off. The adhesive remover Un-Do can also be used for that purpose and it is relatively inexpensive. Un-Do works well in taking off price tags and stickers as well.

REMOVE ADHESIVE FROM WOOD FLOORS

Hardwood floors are beautiful and rare to have in modern homes but many have been covered by carpet and getting to them will mean having to learn how to remove adhesive. For whatever reason, people used to cover beautiful hardwood floors with carpet or linoleum. When you discover a hardwood floor under such drab coverings it is like finding a buried treasure. Unfortunately when you remove carpet or vinyl from hardwood floors you will find that adhesive is left behind. This is definitely an unsightly scene which makes knowing how to remove adhesive very important. The article that follows will teach you how to remove adhesive from wood floors naturally.

- *Step 1:* Clean the Floor: There is most likely a lot of grime and dirt left on the wood floor when the carpet or vinyl has been removed. This grime can easily prevent the removal of the adhesive even though you may not be able to see it with your eyes. Mix the water with the soap to make the water soapy. Apply it to the wood floor and scrub hard to clean it. This may remove a good amount of the adhesive from the wood floor as well as remove oils and dirt that could hinder the removal of adhesive.
- *Step 2:* How to Remove Adhesive with Peanut Butter: The best and easiest way in how to remove adhesive is by using peanut butter. It is crucial that you use only all-natural peanut butter; organic and made only from peanuts. The natural oils found in the peanut butter work against the bonding agent found in the adhesive. Use your finger and rub some of the peanut butter over the adhesive. Apply considerable pressure as you rub the adhesive into the wood in a circular motion.

The adhesive will begin to come up and form tiny balls. Use this method as long as you can before wiping the peanut off with a rag and soapy water.

- *Step 2:* Icing the Adhesive: Adhesive forms a strong molecular bond with the wood which can be interfered by freezing the molecules. Make sure that the area is dry before moving forward. Place a thin rag on top of the adhesive and place ice on top of the rag. After about ten minutes the adhesive should be frozen. Remove the rag with the ice in it and start to rub the adhesive with your finger or use the putty knife to carefully remove the frozen adhesive.
- *Step 3:* Mineral Spirits: Depending on the finish of the wood using mineral spirits could damage it so use it as a last resort for tough adhesives. Pour some of the mineral spirits onto a towel and rub the adhesive. Scrub it thoroughly to hopefully remove the majority of the adhesive. You may not be able to remove as much of the adhesive as you like with the rag. In this case switch to using the scrubbing brush to firmly scrub the floor.

REMOVE ADHESIVE FROM A CONCRETE FLOOR

Adhesives on concrete floors add an ugly look to the floors. Removing adhesive from concrete floors is a tedious and difficult task; knowing how to remove adhesive from concrete floor can help maintain the beauty of concrete floors.

- *Step 1:* Pour Hot Water: Boil water and pour on the surface to be cleaned off the adhesive. Let the hot water remain on the surface for few minutes. This will soften the adhesive and makes it supple. Chemical adhesive removers can also be used to soften the adhesive on concrete floor. Citrus based adhesive removers are commonly used to remove adhesive from concrete floors. Wait for around 30 minutes after applying adhesive removers on concrete floors.
- *Step 2:* Scrape the Adhesive: Scrape the softened adhesive using flooring razor scraper and dispose it. There are also tile and glue removertools available in the market. The tile and glue remover tool has an 8-inch long blade which scraps the surface moving back and forth. Be careful not to scrape with a sharp instrument that can scratch or gouge the floor.
- *Step 3:* Wash the Floor: After scraping the adhesive from concrete floor, wash the surface with sufficient water. Wipe ups any loose adhesive with an absorbent cloth.

REMOVE WAX FROM FURNITURE

If you plan to remove wax from furniture, you have to remember to what purpose it was originally applied to the piece of furniture. Furniture wax is often used as a polish, wood finish, and finish protector. In general, the purpose of furniture wax is to moisturize and patinate the wood. Wordsof Advice: When removing wax build-up, try not to strip the surface of the piece. Stripping removes not only the wax but also its original finish. If the furniture happens to be an antique piece, stripping it would significantly decrease the value of the piece. You don't remove the paint on your car just because you cannot remove a dried layer of turtle wax that you spot on the surface. The same holds true when you wish to remove wax from a piece of furniture. You have to realize that wax buildup is an indication that your finish needs an appropriate of cleaning, and not a full-blown stripping.

There are two ways to remove wax from furniture, depending on the degree of staining. You may first try to buff the piece of furniture and if you don't get visible results, you can use a wax removal product.

- *Step 1:* Buff the Furniture: First, you may buff the surface of your piece using a soft cloth. The rag has to be lint-free. Old, 100 per cent wool clothes would also do. You have to wipe off accumulated dust and buff in circles while you apply some pressure to the surface of the piece. Continue until the surface has become less sticky and dull. If your wipe gets stained, you need to replace it with a clean one. Keep in mind that your aim is to remove any excess wax on the surface of your piece of furniture. You do not want to reapply the excess wax instead. The cleaning process may completed by buffing with another cloth.
- *Step 2:* Remove Excess Wax: In case that the wax build-up turns old and therefore hard, you have to remove the excess wax. Purchase a product that is designed specifically for wax removal. There is wide variety on the market, and you will find a product of your choice in every good furniture store. Wax removal products are intended to eliminate excess dirt, wax, and oils. You don't risk harming your furniture's finish as long as you follow the directions. You have to apply a thin layer of the wax removal product on a clean cloth and not directly onto the surface of your piece of furniture. Then, you need to buff the wood surface as you did in the first part of the cleaning process. Keep doing that until you notice visible results. After treatment with the wax removal product, you can polish your piece of furniture with beeswax or carnuba wax.

WAX REMOVER TIPS FOR HARDWOOD FLOORS

Hardwood floors are a very beautiful addition to any home, but wax and wax build-up may require special techniques or wax removerproducts. Treated hardwood floors are one of the easiest floors to maintain and keep clean. Even spilled melted wax is easy to remove from hardwood, provided you have the right materials and technique. Read on to learn several wax remover tips, tricks and warnings.

Do Not Remove Hot Wax: Accidents happen, and when you move a candle from shelf to shelf, you may spill some hot wax onto the hardwood floor. Your initial reaction might be to quickly grab a towel to wipe it up. This method will remove some of the wax, but you will also spread the remainder of the hot wax outward. This will cause the thin layer of wax to harden. Wax remover chemicals will not help you here, and the only way to remove this hardened wax could damage your hardwood floors.

Instead of rushing to clean the hot wax, just leave it alone. Let the wax cool and harden. This will make removing it much easier. You can also fill a bag with ice and hold it over the hot wax. This will speed up the cooling time.

Be Mindful of the Chemicals Used: There are many wax remover chemicals on the market, but you must use only those that are safe for hardwood floors. The most important thing is to avoid ammonia or products labeled as wax strippers. Many hardwood floors are sealed with polyurethane or another type of shellac or hard shell finish. Ammonia or wax stripper will cause the hard finishes to melt from the chemical reaction and turn white in tint.

Simple is Better: There are dozens of wax remover products on the market designed for use on hardwood. These products can range from a couple dollars in upwards of $10 to $20.

Rather than spend money, you can create your own effective clean-up solution. Place a few drops of oil-free soap and a splash of white distilled vinegar into a bucket, and then fill with hot water. Use a sponge mop and clean the floor as you normally would.

Scrape Away Wax: When you remove wax from a hardwood floor, note that it is easy to needlessly damage the floor. A putty knife is the best tool as its edge is tapered and thin. Put the edge at the wax line, and push with even pressure to easily remove the wax. When the wax is removed, buff the area with a terrycloth towel.

REMOVE SILICONE CAULK FROM GLASS

The use of silicone caulk as a sealant can result in traces of the substance accidently coming into contact with glass and remaining there to harden. Follow the steps below to easily remove the caulk and return the glass to its original state.

- *Step 1:* Inspection: Examine the entire pane or sheet of glass to locate every point from which silicone caulk needs to be removed. If necessary, stick a small piece of masking tape next to each instance so that you do not lose track of it. This inspection will also help you to determine how much work will be required to complete the job.

- *Step 2:* Remove Excess: Depending on how firmly the silicone caulk is fixed in place, you may be able to remove the majority of it with either a scraper or a razor blade. If you have both, begin by using the scraper as it will be safer and easier to use. Position the center of the blade against the base of the caulk where it meets the glass. Attempt to cut the caulk away by firmly applying some pressure while holding the scraper at a 45-degree angle. If this does not work or only removes the excess, carefully make use a razor in the same way as the scraper. To enable it to be gripped properly, it should have a casing on one edge.
- *Step 3:* Apply Heat: In the event that the silicone caulk proves difficult to remove and you are concerned about the risk of scraping the glass, make the job easier by first applying some heat. Though a hot air gun can be hired from a tool hire company, a hairdryer may prove just as useful for the task. On a high heat, train the nozzle of the hairdryer onto the caulk for a few moments before using a scraper to test whether it has softened. If the substance gives easily, continue with the scraping process to remove it.
- *Step 4:* Remove Traces: Whether there were only ever traces of caulk on the glass or some remains after the excess has been removed, you may find it necessary to undertake further cleaning work to remove it. Begin by applying some heat and scraping away as much of the caulk as possible, thereafter dampen a sponge with some rubbing alcohol or mineral spirit and wipe the affected section of the glass. This will help to melt the caulk so that you can make the remainder easier to scrape it away. If the glass remains cloudy, use a cloth dampened with alcohol to rub the glass with to clean it.

Finish off the task of cleaning the glass with some household soap dissolved in water and a clean cloth, rinse the glass with clean water before drying it thoroughly.

HOW TO GET LATEX CAULK OFF OF BRICK

Latex caulk is a very useful material for many reasons. It is waterproof, and easy to install. It tends to stay where you put it. However, this can be a problem if you need to replace it. Working on latex caulk is tricky, and getting all of it off of a surface can be difficult, particularly if you are working on a rough surface like brick.

If you use the right strategies, you can get caulk off even the most difficult of surfaces.

- *Step 1:* Softening the Caulk: Use your hair dryer on the caulk you plan to remove for a decent period of time, but not on one section continuously. This will soften the caulk up and make it easier to remove. In the event that you have a heat gun already, you should use that instead.

Alternatively, you can use caulk remover to soften the caulk. This involves purchasing caulk remover, and is much slower. If you choose this method, you must plan to apply the caulk remover, then leave it to sit overnight while it does its work.

Whichever method you choose, it will soften the caulk enough that you can work on it.

- *Step 2:* Removing Large Pieces: Once your caulk is soft enough to work on, use a utility knife to remove it. Slide the knife in between the caulk and the wall, and then separate it. Do this to both edges of the caulk seal. Once the caulk has been cut free of the wall on both sides, you should be able to lever it out completely. Do this as slowly as possible, as the more force you use, the more likely you are to make a mistake. You can use a razor or any dedicated scraping tool in place of a utility knife.

  Unfortunately, it is likely that there will be pieces of caulk that are too small to cut off without damaging the surrounding surface. Do not attempt to scrape them off.

- *Step 3:* Removing Small Pieces: Once you have removed all you can with your scraping or cutting tool, dampen a sponge and use it to clean the area with any remaining pieces of caulk on it. Rinse the sponge regularly as you work to remove caulk fragments from it.

  Once you have removed any loose fragments, apply isopropyl alcohol to any areas that still have caulk on them. Let the isopropyl alcohol sit for several minutes, and monitor it carefully, as it is flammable. During this time, the alcohol will cause the caulk to swell up and detach from your bricks.

- *Step 4:* Finishing the Job: After the isopropyl alcohol does its job, you should be able to remove the remaining caulk. Get out your sponge again and wipe away the fragments that have been left behind. Rinse the sponge often, and be sure to wipe every area that has had alcohol on it clean.

HOW TO REMOVE LATEX CAULK FROM WOOD

Latex caulk is used to keep the moisture out of wood joints. However, over time the latex caulk will dry out and will need to be replaced. This means you need a method for removing the latex caulk from the wood to leave it clean so you can apply a new layer of this practical adhesive.

It's a simple job using tools that, in most instances, you probably already own. Ensure you leave the wood clean when you finish.

- *Step 1:* Cleaning: The very first thing to do is to clean the wood and the old caulk thoroughly. Use a good wood cleaner for this, making sure you do a thorough job. This is important since it will help you remove the old latex caulk more cleanly. Allow the wood to dry completely before you move on to the next step.
- *Step 2:* Heat Gun: If you don't own a heat gun, it's worthwhile buying a small one since they have many uses including the removal of old latex caulk. Set the heat gun on low so the temperature is no higher than 300 degrees F.

  You don't need to hold the gun too close to the caulk since you don't want to scorch or burn it. Move the heat gun across the entire surface of the latex caulk so that you soften and loosen it. Don't let the heat focus on a single spot for too long. Stop when the caulk is loose and you can press and move it easily with your fingers.
- *Step 3:* Removing Caulk: With the caulk soft, you can begin to remove it using a single edged razor blade (make sure you always push the blade away from yourself in order to avoid any possible injury). Alternatively, you can purchase a special caulk removal tool which is designed to penetrate corners and small spaces in order to remove all the caulk more easily.

  As it cools, the caulk will stiffen again so you might need to use the heat gun once more in order to soften it and then remove the remaining latex caulk with the razor blade.

  You will need to remove all the old latex caulk and this can be achieved by inspecting your work and making sure that you dig down into all the cracks and deep into the joints to pry it all out. Stop only when all the old latex caulk has been removed. Wipe clean with an old rag.
- *Step 4:* Denatured Alcohol: Now that the old latex caulk has all gone, you need to prepare the surface for new caulking. Put some denatured alcohol on a rag and clean the wood, making sure you remove any old caulk that might still be lying on the wood. The advantage of using denatured alcohol for this process is that it evaporates rather than soaks into the wood, meaning you don't need to wait for the wood to dry before applying the new latex caulk.

BATHROOM AND KITCHEN CLEANING

HOW TO GET MOLD OUT OF GROUT

Mold and mildew tend to develop in areas where there is excess moisture.

Over time the moisture can develop into a bacterial growth that is not only unhygienic and potentially dangerous, but difficult to remove. Mold that has settled intobathroom grout can be particularly hard to clean. By following some simple steps using typical household items, you can kill the entire growth and eliminate the chances of it regenerating.

- *Step 1:* Put on your rubber gloves to protect your skin. The grout cleaning mixture can potentially discolour your clothing if it touches the fabric so it is also best to wear an old set of clothes while you are working.
- *Step 2:* Combine 1 cup of bleach and 3 cups of warm water in a bucket. Remove the spray top of your bottle. Place your funnel into the top of the bottle and carefully pour the bleach mixture from the bucket into the container. Attach the spray top to the bottle and ensure that the top is tightly secured. Use a permanent marker to label your spray bottle "Bleach Mixture."
- *Step 3:* Spray the affected areas with the mixture being careful to keep the liquid away from your skin. Use your brush to vigourously scrub at the mold and mildew. For small areas, use your tooth brush to remove the mold and mildew. Rinse the area with cool, clear water. Repeat the spraying and scrubbing process if necessary. Be sure to store the bleach mixture spray bottle in a safe place for further use. Keep it up on a shelf and out of the reach of children.
- *Step 4:* Fill a small bowl with vinegar. Lay three or four sheets of paper towel into the vinegar to soak them. Place the paper towels over any grout areas that require extra help to clean. Press the towels firmly until they are fully in contact with the grout. Leave the paper towels in place for about eight hours. If the paper begins to dry out, apply more vinegar to keep them saturated. Remove the paper towels from the grout and use your brush to scrub any remaining mold or mildew. Rinse the area with cool, clear water.
- *Step 5:* You can prevent further growth of mold and mildew in your bathroom grout by applying lemon juice to the surfaces where it grows after showers and baths. After bathing, dry the shower area with a towel to remove excess water and moisture. Open the shower door or curtain to allow for air circulation in the room. Apply a liberal amount of lemon juice to your sponge. Rub the sponge over the grout and allow the lemon juice to sit for about fifteen minutes. Finally, rinse the area with cool, clear water.

BATHROOM CLEANING TIPS

Windows and Mirrors: In a 32 oz. spray bottle, add 1/3 cup white (clear) vinegar and 1/4 cup rubbing alcohol. If you absolutely must have another cleaner, add 1 tablespoon automatic dishwashing detergent. Tubs and Shower Stalls: Alkaline deposits in the water cause those not so pretty spots on your glass doors and shower walls. Apply a car wax to the walls and doors, but not the floor or it gets real slick. Both fibreglass and glass are porous. The car wax seals those pores, which makes cleaning easier and keeps water spots away. Reapply twice yearly.

Squeegee or wipe down your shower after each use to further prevent buildup. If you're tired of fighting the soap scum buildup, switch to liquid soap, natural soap or Dove. It's the talc in most bar soaps that causes the buildup. Changing soap can eliminate the buildup. You still need to clean the shower once a week, but the job is easier.

Clean the showers once a week with an orange citrus based cleaner. Spray on and give it ten minutes to dissolve the dirt. Why do all that scrubbing when your product does it for you?

OK, so the soap scum refuses to budge and friends are coming for a visit. Use your orange based cleaner concentrated. Pour plenty on an old dishrag and wipe on the walls and doors. Use can use boiling hot white vinegar (wear gloves) but you must keep applying it as the white vinegar dries. It takes time to dissolve that buildup.

Patience now becomes a virtue. Wait and wait and wait some more. Go clean the rest of the house. If the cleaner starts dripping down the walls, wipe it back on. Check the walls with a fingernail. If the residue removes easily, round one is about over.

Use a white bristle pad to scrub. They look like fibres and are glued to a sponge. Use the white ones only. The coloured scrubbers are coarser and do scratch. Test a spot to make sure it won't scratch the fibreglass. Dampen the pad, keeping it good and wet and gently scrub. This removes the soap buildup and most of the white mineral deposits on the glass doors. Nothing removes the etch marks themselves, but further damage is halted. Reapply the orange citrus cleaner if necessary.

Plastic shower curtains can be machine washed. Remove, spray with your diluted orange based cleaner and wait about 10 minutes. Wash with your rags and they come out quite clean. Air dry. If the curtain is long enough, cut off the seam at the bottom to prevent mildew buildup down there.

Toilets: Ring around your toilet? Again, alkaline deposits cause those nasty rings. Depending on the hardness of your water, pour one or two cups of white vinegar into the toilet once a month to eliminate the problem.

Toilet bowl rings - Here I take a deep breath and plead with you to follow these instructions. Repeat. Follow these instructions. Do not deviate or you will scratch the inside of your toilet bowl.

Turn off the water flow to the toilet and flush to remove the water. Saturate a couple of heavy duty paper towels with white vinegar or the Orange Citrus

Cleaner. Place around the edges making sure all areas are covered. Keep the towels damp for several hours, even overnight, until the water spots start dissolving. Then scrub with a stiff nylon brush.

If the white vinegar does not dissolve the whole ring, go to a janitorial supply store or a hardware store and purchase a pumice stone and a stiff toothbrush. Dampen one end of the pumice stone and keep it wet.

Gently, very gently, rub the pumice stone across the lines. When enough pumice builds on the sides, switch to a stiff bristle brush to continue working. Rub gently until the deposit disappears. Pumice will scratch the toilet. Use it only one time and cautiously.

Sinks: Once a month, pour one cup of baking soda, followed by one cup of white vinegar down the drain. Wait an hour and flush with warm water. The combination fizzles away most of the buildup. Works for shower, tub and kitchen sink drains as well.

Faucets: Water deposits build up around faucets and drain areas. Use a paper towel soaked in white vinegar and place around the faucet. Plug the drain and pour 1/2 cup white vinegar in the sink and wait. It takes time for the white vinegar to dissolve the alkaline deposits. Scrub using a stiff bristled nylon toothbrush.

Do not use orange based or powdered cleansers on brass or gold plated faucets. These fixtures corrode and scratch quickly. Dry these faucets after each use to prevent water spot damage.

Mildew: Keep ahead of mildew so it doesn't become a problem. Every six months spray your bathroom ceiling with a 50/50 solution of hydrogen peroxide and water. Peroxide is a safe bleach and won't harm the environment or your lungs. Find larger quantities of peroxide at beauty or medical supply stores.

Spray the mixture on and leave it. No need to rinse or scrub. If you currently have mildew, follow the above directions. Wait two hours and respray. Then wait 24 hours and spray a third time if necessary.

CLEANING YOUR GAS STOVE AND OVEN

Regular cleaning of your gas cook stove will keep it looking as good as the day you bought it, but you need to take care with the cleaning products you use on your gas stove or oven. Many commercial cleansers and abrasives will cause discoloration and can scratch gas stove and oven surfaces.

Before cleaning any gas stove or oven surface, be sure the unit is off and completely cooled. Steam burns can occur from wiping a hot surface with a wet cloth or sponge. Follow these guidelines for care and cleaning without damaging your gas stove or gas oven surfaces.

Surface Burners and Burner Box: Most newer gas stove models have sealed stovetop burners. This means they are completely sealed off from the burner box (area of the stovetop below the metal cook top). Sealed burners should never be removed by home owners - it's a job only for professionals during installation and service. Sealed burners also mean that food and spills cannot spill into the burner box, so removing the burners is not necessary in order to clean the stovetop. If you have an older model stove with a lift-up cook top, follow your manufacturer's instructions for opening the surface for cleaning.

Regular cleaning of spills will lessen your cleaning work load. Wipe your stovetop after each use when it has cooled. Clean burners with dish soap and a plastic scouring pad. Stubborn cooked-on spills can be cleaned with a mild abrasive cleanser and a cloth, or make a paste from baking soda and water for a mild homemade alternative. Wash removable burner grates in a sink full of warm, soapy dishwater with a plastic scouring pad. Rinse all parts with warm clear water and dry. Be careful to avoid the gas ports on your burners. If they should become plugged with debris, poke the ports clean with a toothpick or straight pin, or brush gently with a soft-bristled brush. For pilot-less stoves, check the port and area below the igniter wire and clear it as well. Debris left under the igniter can keep the gas burner from lighting.

Clean the solid cook top surface with soapy water. Avoid abrasives and harsh chemicals as they can damage the surface of stove top finishes like porcelain enamel. Rubbing alcohol and household ammonia diluted with water (1:1 ratio) are other good stove top cleansers that will leave your top shining.

Controls: Remove control knobs and wash them in warm, soapy water. For clocks and display areas, wipe with a damp cloth and dry. If you are cleaning the display with glass cleaner, spray it first on a cloth and not directly on the surface to avoid cleaner seeping inside the mechanisms. Replace controls after they are cleaned and turn each one on briefly to ensure proper replacement.

Oven Door: The oven door on nearly all ovens is removable for easier cleaning. Avoid soaking the door or window with excessive amounts of water; it can seep inside and caused staining or discoloration. Wash the door and window with soap and water and rinse with clear water. Use glass cleaner only if sprayed on a cloth first. Do not use abrasive pads, powdered cleaners, or steel wool on glass and enamel, or the surfaces will be scratched.

Oven Interior: Mild abrasive cleaners and plastic pads can be used inside the oven. Metal scouring pads will scratch the oven's surface. Commercial oven cleaners should be used according to manufacturer's instructions.

Acidic spills (like tomato and milk bases) should be wiped up as soon as possible to prevent discoloration of the porcelain. To absorb a spill when it is hot, pour salt on it and wipe it up when the oven has cooled. A mildly abrasive baking soda and water paste can be used in the oven, too. Remove oven racks and clean them in warm, soapy water. Stubborn messes can be cleaned by using mild abrasive cleansers or a soap filled scouring pad. Rinse and dry the racks before returning them to the oven. For easier cleaning of oven racks, soak and wash them in the bathtub - they fit much better into a bath.

Trim: Spills and drips from fat, grease, and acidic foods like tomatoes should be wiped up immediately using a paper towel to keep your trim and finishes from discoloring.

Metal trim can be cleaned with glass cleaners or mild cleansers, soap and water. Abrasives or cleaners made for oven interiors should not be used. Plastic trim pieces are best cleaned with a glass cleaner on a soft cloth. Any abrasives and harsh cleansers can cause pitting and discoloration to oven surfaces, and so should not be used.

For a good, general, all-around cleaner for your gas stove and gas oven, use warm, soapy water. Avoid anything that is very caustic or abrasive. Baking soda and water pastes are good back-up, mild abrasives. When using commercial cleansers, read the manufacturer's directions to be sure it is safe for use on your stove's finishes. Consistent care and cleaning of your gas stovetop and oven will keep your appliance shining and new looking.

HOW TO CLEAN THE KITCHEN SINK

The kitchen sink should be one of the cleanest surfaces in our home. Unfortunately, quite often, it's full of germs. After all, the kitchen sink sees a lot of action.

We rinse our fruits, vegetables, fish, meat, poultry, and almost anything we can think of in the sink. We drain our pots and pans into it. We wash dishes, glasses, and silverware there.

Sometimes, we even toss a child or two in it for a nighttime bath. Maybe we even rinse the pet's dishes and toys.

Unfortunately, simply rinsing the kitchen sink until it looks clean is not going to keep it germ free. Regular cleaning and sanitizing should take place in order to protect your family from germs and bacteria. Different types of sinks require different types of cleaning solutions. However, they can all benefit from a simple sanitizing procedure that works to deter germs and bacteria from taking roost.

To sanitize the kitchen sink, you have three basic options. You can purchase a commercial disinfectant and use it according to the directions on the label. Commercial disinfectants are available in most home improvement stores, discount stores, supermarkets, and online.

For ceramic and cast iron sinks, you can prepare a solution of one part liquid chlorine bleach to sixteen parts water. You cannot use this solution on stainless steel sinks. Additionally, you need to exercise caution when using a solution that includes liquid chlorine bleach. Pour it slowly and be careful not to get any on surfaces that will undergo damage. An application of undiluted white vinegar on the sink is another option that you can use. For the best results, apply the vinegar using a clean cloth to ensure that the entire sink is treated with it.

Stainless Steel Sinks: Stainless steel sinks should always be thoroughly rinsed after every use, not only to keep them clean, but also, to prevent potential pitting. Acids and salts can damage the finish of a stainless steel sink, so it is important to avoid leaving foods that contain these in the sink.

Mild soap and a nylon sponge can be used for daily cleaning of a stainless steel sink. Also, an all purpose cleaner or a glass cleaner can be used. Always rinse the sink clean after using a cleaner or soap and then dry it with a soft cloth.

If spots are a problem with your sink, a clean cloth soaked in vinegar can help to remove these. To keep the finish at its finest, avoid using bleach, ammonia, and abrasive cleaners. Also, you should avoid using abrasive sponges and steel wool pads on stainless steel, as they tend to damage the finish.

Wetting the entire surface of the sink and liberally sprinkling baking soda onto the surface is the best way to deal with stubborn stains. Use a nylon scrubbing sponge to work the baking soda in and then rinse thoroughly clean.

Stubborn mineral residue can be dealt with by lining the entire sink with paper towels soaked in white vinegar. Allow the vinegar to sit undisturbed for several minutes, up to a half hour, and then toss them in the trash. Use a nylon scrubbing sponge saturated with soapy water to scrub the area clean. Rinse the sink completely when finished. Remember to dry the sink with a clean soft cloth for the best results.

Stubborn stains can be dealt with by using a commercial stainless steel cleaner according to the directions included with it. Rinse and dry the sink afterwards.

Cast Iron Sinks: Cast iron sinks should be thoroughly rinsed after each use in order to promote cleanliness. Moreover, this type of sink benefits from a thorough drying with a clean cloth after it has been rinsed. To clean a cast iron sink thoroughly, wet the entire surface and liberally sprinkle baking soda onto the sink's surface.

Use a clean nylon cleaning sponge to scrub the baking soda onto the sink. Rinse the sink clean from all baking soda residue. Avoid abrasive cleaners when cleaning cast iron. The best way to treat stains in a cast iron sink is to avoid them in the first place. Never place any item into the sink that might leave a stain on the finish. Avoid leaving dirty dishes, pots, or pans in the sink. Additionally, do not leave tea bags, coffee grounds, or cans in the sink.

Ceramic Sinks: Ceramic sinks can easily be cleaned with a cleanser in a gel or creamy solution. This helps avoid scratches. It is important not to use abrasive cleaners on ceramic sinks. For stubborn stains, repeat the cleaning with a bit more effort. If the stain persists, remove it using a clean cloth soaked in club soda.

Faucets and Handles: Faucets and handles can easily be cleaned with a mild soapy solution. If fingerprints or water spots remain, use a clean cloth soaked in white vinegar and wipe them clean. The vinegar also sanitizes the faucets and handles.

TOILET BOWL BRUSH HOLDERS: CHIC AND SANITARY

It is hard to conceive of a toilet bowl brush being both chic and sanitary, but nowadays it's true. Product designers are creating more imaginative designs that are fashionable and aesthetically pleasing for the most utilitarian of objects, even the lowly toilet bowl brush.

Clean and Sleek: The next time you visit a store in search of a toilet bowl brush, it is possible you may walk right by them on the shelf. While you can still get classic bowl brushes, the traditional designs are becoming something of the past with new stylish, modern designs quickly replacing them. These new designs of both bowl brushes and toilet brush holders camouflage something that many homeowners have long considered unsightly and wanted to keep hidden. Scrub and Flush: Additionally, new designs consider the dirty job that a toilet bowl brush must do. Disposable wand style toilet bowl brushes are a big hit allowing the scrubbing brush to be flushed when done cleaning. This is a welcome option, leaving no dirty or germ laden toilet brush behind to be stored.

REMOVING RUST STAINS FROM TOILET FIXTURES

Rust stains on toilet fixtures and bowls are a common occurrence. These annoying stains occur because of the minerals in hard water, especially water with a high concentration of iron. Rust stains can be difficult to remove, because generic household cleaners do not work on them. However, by using the right cleaner and cleaning method, you can remove rust stains in toilets.

- *Step 1:* Prepare the Surrounding Area: Before you set about cleaning the rust from your toilet fixtures, remove all surrounding objects to avoid caustic cleaners from splashing onto them. Move away carpet from the nearby area as well. Wear a pair of thick gloves. Open the bathroom window to air out any fumes or odors that may emanate as a result of the cleaning. Wear a protective jacket to avoid damage to your clothes and protect your feet with thick shoes.
- *Step 2:* Apply Concentrated Lemon Juice or White Vinegar on the Rusted Parts: Using a sponge, generously apply a coating of lemon juice or white vinegar on the rusted fixture. Scrub thoroughly and apply another coating. Wait for about 30 minutes and wipe off the stain. If needed, repeat the process a couple of times. If the rust stain is not completely removed, proceed to the next step.
- *Step 3:* Use Baking Soda or Borax: Baking soda is also effective in removing rust stains. Make a thick paste of baking soda with white vinegar or lemon juice. To avoid chemical reactions, avoid using a plastic container to mix the paste together. Apply the paste onto the

rusted surface. Let it sit for about 1/2 an hour. Wipe of the paste and scrub the area. If there is some rust still remaining, repeat the process and scrub clean. If this method does not remove all the rust, you will have to try a chemical cleaning product that is not as environmentally friendly.

- *Step 4:* Use a Commercial Cleaning Product: Several commercial cleaning products can effectively remove rust from toilet fixtures. However, these options must be tried last, because they are generally toxic in nature. You must be very careful when using such products. Keep young children and pets a safc distance away. These cleaners are not recommended for those households that have a septic system.

Zud® Heavy Duty Cleanser is a potent cleaner that can effectively remove all rust stains from toilet fixtures. Read the package instructions thoroughly before use. Apply the solution or powder onto the affected area as per directions. Wait for 1 hour and then scrub it off with a brush. Avoid using steel wool or other harsh cleaners that can scratch the surface. Flush the toilet or rinse off the fixture with water. Hydrochloric acid is another component that is effective in ridding your toilet of rust stains. It is found in another popular cleaning brand called The Works®. You can try the toilet bowl cleaner or the tub and shower cleaner. Spray on the solution and wait for the recommended amount of time before rinsing it off.

CLEANING SHOWER DOOR GLASS: HARD WATER STAIN REMOVAL

Cleaning shower door glass can be difficult, especially if you have resilient hard water stains to remove. However, consider the tips and advice below to efficiently clean your shower door glass in addition to removing those tough water stains.

Clean the Glass Daily: A great way to prevent hard water stain and keep your glass immaculate is to clean it daily. Hard water stain can be very difficult to remove once set onto the glass. By using a squeegee or a paper towel and Windex, you will can quickly erase any stains before they settle and keep your glass clean.

Try Rubbing Alcohol: If you notice minor build-up on your glass, try spraying it with some rubbing alcohol and wipe with a damp cloth. Be aware that this method is most effective for stains that have recently accumulated. For major build-ups that have occurred over time, you may want to use a stronger chemical.

Try Fabric Stain Removers: Another method, often over-looked, is to use fabric stain removers, like Shout or Resolve. Pour the liquid onto a damp cloth and scrub lightly over the hard water stains. This method should remove a good amount of the hard water stains and will bring a more pleasant odour to your bathroom. Try a Green Method: If you prefer a greener method, take a lemon and cut it in half. Next, rub the inside of the lemon over the shower door stain. For doors that need a little extra cleaning, allow the lemon juice to sit on the stains for a few minutes and then wipe away.

Use a Chemical Cleaner: If the above remedies aren't as effective as you'd like, then you can purchase a lime and hard water stain remover. You'll won't have to spend too much on this item and the instructions are very easy to follow. The cleaner should easily remove the stains although you may need to do a little scrubbing in order completely eliminate the stain.

BATHROOM CHROME CLEANING TIPS

Bathroom chrome, or chromium, is a common surface in most bathrooms, found in such items as the faucet, shower rod, shower drain and toilet handle. It can be a tough metal to keep clean, but this article will outline the most efficient process for a total bathroom chrome cleaning.

You will need ONE of the following:

- Chrome cleaning solution
- Soft metal cleaner
- White vinegar
- Rubbing alcohol

Step One - Pick a Cleaning Strategy: Many people clean their bathrooms object by object, starting at the sink and then going to the toilet before ending at the bath tub. Though this process works for general cleaning, it's efficient you plan to do all the chromium in the room at a sweep. First, get all of the non-chrome cleaning out of the way before you begin cleaning chrome, especially if this is your first time. Once you've done it, you can figure out your own process that is efficient and comfortable to you.

Step Two - Prepare the Materials: Make sure you have all of the items listed above. In both buckets, mix warm water with dishwashing soap to create a sudsy solution. In one bucket, add some of your preferred cleaning solution into the mix as well.

This will be the bucket you use for soaking smaller parts. Do not use abrasive cleaning materials such as household cleaners. Make sure to only use fresh water and soap.

Step Three - Attack the Sink: The chrome commonly found in sinks is the faucet, handles, drain and drain plug. Removing the sink plug may be tricky. Try unscrewing and removing it by hand first. Some models require a screwdriver for removal, and others may require you to go under the sink to remove the plug. Below your sink is a rod that can be removed by loosening the nut that holds it. Once the rod is removed, you should be able to remove the sink plug with ease. Depending on how your faucet knobs are set up, you may have to unscrew those as well.

Wipe down the surfaces with sudsy water. Use the toothbrush to clean any hard to reach surfaces, such as the inside of the faucet. The sink plug will likely be filthy, so let it soak in the cleaning solution bucket for a bit. When you're finished, dry the pieces and leave them unassembled on your sinktop.

Step Four - Clean the Toilet and Bath Tub: The toilet should be simple enough. Just wipe down the handle with sudsy water. You may want to shut off the water valve to your toilet so you don't accidentally flush and waste water when doing a thorough cleaning. A bath tub's chrome components vary by household, so make sure you get them all. The shower rod, bath tub handles, bath tub faucet, shower plug and overflow plate are likely chrome candidates. The shower plug and overflow plate will probably require a screwdriver to remove. Soak them in the chrome cleaning solution.

Just like the sink, wipe down every surface and use the toothbrush when necessary. Dry and set unassembled pieces on the sinktop.

Stepn Five - Polish and Reassemble: Polish down every chrome surface to remove the final tough stains. Reassemble all of your parts and make sure they work.

BRASS BATHROOM FAUCET CLEANING AND POLISHING

A brass bathroom faucet can be harder to maintain than other fixtures in the home, because it is a harder metal to clean. But you can keep your brass faucet looking vibrant, clean and new with a few tips for regular maintenance.

Routine Cleaning: Keeping brass clean isn't hard, but it does take regular cleaning and effort. To avoid tarnishing, make sure you make the cleaning part of your daily or weekly chores. Normally, a damp cloth is all it takes to shine up a brass faucet. Abrasive cleaners can actually damage brass, but if the damp cloth alone doesn't cut it, try a mix of warm, soapy water with the cloth. Also be sure you dry the brass completely once done cleaning, which will prevent water spots and further damage.

Tarnish: Some people enjoy the look of tarnish on some pieces. It can add a certain charm to some fixtures and pieces. But if you aren't going for an antique look, then tarnish can be a real challenge to remove. You can find special formulas in most hardware stores that promise to remove tarnish on brass. They can range from inexpensive to high-end, and you'll need to read the directions on the bottles carefully before purchase or use. Some of these products are designed to clean light tarnish, and others will require several steps and will remove heavier buildup.

If you prefer to try a natural cleaner, vinegar works great on tarnish. The vinegar will break down the tarnish and make it much easier to wipe away. For extra cleaning power, warm the vinegar up first.

Fingerprints: Did you know that if you touch brass, the oils on your skin can leave behind fingerprints that may not show up for months? When you are cleaning brass, be sure to wear gloves to avoid this problem. Ketchup: Yes, ketchup. The citric acid in ketchup does wonderful things for brass. It cleans and shines it without much effort. Use a soft, dry cloth that is free of lint to apply it. Put a small amount of ketchup on the cloth and gently rub it in to the brass fixture, then, with a clean cloth, rub the ketchup off completely. You may need to rinse away residue with some water, but make sure you have it dry before you walk away.

Homemade Polish Paste: Another wonderful, easy to make cleaner can be found in your kitchen cabinets. A teaspoon of salt, a half-cup of distilled vinegar and about three tablespoons of flour will make a paste you can use to polish metals such as brass. Dissolve the salt in the vinegar, and add the flour until a paste forms. Use this concoction by rubbing it onto the faucet or other fixture. Then, let it sit for about 10 minutes and wipe it away with a damp cloth. Your brass will be as clean and shiny as the day you installed it.

Keep It Dry: Since you're dealing with a bathroom faucet, keeping it dry may be a challenge, but can help keep the metal clean. Just keep a soft cloth nearby to wipe it down when you remember to. This will help prevent spotting and tarnish.

KITCHEN FAUCETS AND SINKS: CLEANING MATERIALS AND TIPS

Keep your kitchen faucets and sinks clean to improve the appearance of your eating and gathering space. Experts suggest that having a clean kitchen faucet and sink will also decrease stress levels and give you a "finished" feeling to the day. Here are a few tips to help you clean your kitchen faucets and sinks clean and shiny.

Cleaning Materials: The best cleaning materials for a kitchen sink is a soft cloth, warm water and an all-purpose cleaner. Stay away from any type of abrasive materials such as steel wool or cleaners with grit in them. These products can end up scratching the finish.

Rinse Down Sink First: Before you start spraying down your sink with cleaner, rinse the basin and wipe the area with a soft cloth. This will help you loosen and remove any dirt, grime or food residue.

Apply Cleaner to Rag: Instead of spraying your cleaner onto the sink itself, apply it to the rag. Doing it this way you are ensured of an even coating of cleaner instead of just streams of it. Apply Directly to Built-In Stain: Contrary to the previous tip, if you have a hard-to-remove or set stain, apply the cleaner directly to it. Let it set to help dissolve the stain before wiping it up. Wipe Sink and Faucet Dry: After cleaning the sink, wipe it completely dry. Any water that is left on the faucet or the sink will leave spots and cause water stains if left too long.

BATHROOM TILE GROUT: CLEANING IN THE CRACKS

Cleaning bathroom tile grout is easier than you think! When you don't want to spend a lot of time or money scrubbing in the cracks, follow these simple steps.

- *Step 1:* Prepare the Floor: Sweep and mop the floor to get rid of any debris. Leave the floor slightly damp, but not drenched. Spray a generous amount of non-abrasive bathroom cleaner onto the grout. Do not use an abrasive cleaner as it may remove not only dirt and grime, but part of the grout as well. Let the cleaner soak in for a few minutes.
- *Step 2:* Scrub the Grout: Fill the bucket with a mixture of hot water and a small amount of the bathroom cleaner and set it on the floor. If desired, wear knee pads. Wet the scrub brush with the hot water mixture and scrub the grout with a back and forth motion. At this point, you will notice the grout lightening in colour.
- *Step 3:* Rinse: The last thing to do is to mop the floor once more with clear, warm water. Once the floor is dry, your tile grout should be good as new!

REMOVE SILICONE CAULK FROM PORCELAIN

Removing and replacing silicone caulk is critical when renovating a bathroom. Silicone caulk is a product that is used in a bath or showerto keep water from creeping up, under or around the tiles. This messy substance is effective because it is glue and a flexible sealant. These contradicting characteristics are useful to seal a joint between dissimilar materials. In the damp environment such as a kitchen or bathroom, the silicone caulk keeps the water away and it serves its purpose in areas that need to be waterproofed. Moldy or cracked silicone caulk must be removed before it can be replaced in order to be effective, but it is a tough job as all traces of the old caulk must be gone before sealing with the new silicone caulk. Follow these steps to remove silicone caulk from porcelain:

- *Step 1:* Clean the Area around the Silicone Caulk: It's always best to clean the area before commencing any DIY job. Clean around the old caulk to let it do one last job preventing water from seeping into the porcelain. Clean the general area before getting down and dirty.
- *Step 2:* Remove the Old Silicone Caulk: Use a razor blade or box cutter to cut along the old silicone caulk. Cutting from both sides will break the seal with a porcelain fixture or the wall. Make a vertical cut in the silicone caulk with a putty knife and pry up an end of silicone caulk from the porcelain by hand, if possible. To assist, use the putty knife to loosen the caulk so that it is easier to grip the caulk. Go slowly to make sure that the silicone is lifted and removed as much as possible. You will find it pulls off in a strip, therefore using a blade may not be necessary.

- *Step 3:* Scrape Off the Final Bits: Use a razor blade without scratching the porcelain surface. Make sure there are no marks left. This may take a while to get all the silicone caulk removed as some final pieces are very stubborn and do not want to part with the porcelain.
- *Step 4:* Clean the Area Again: Use a rag, add rubbing alcohol and remove leftover residue of silicone caulk as well as cleaning grease, mold or anything else that may be breeding behind the silicone caulk. Vacuum the last pieces of caulk and spray a concentrated mildew killer to get rid of the last germs.

Once the porcelain is caulk-free, you can put a new layer on it, but it is necessary to make sure that the area is completely dry. Most silicone caulks cannot be painted, but you can buy a matching colour for your porcelain to compliment the decor. Silicone caulk is a great product, but beware that it causes eye infections, not to mention the mess. Most of this activity involves cleaning before and after the application.

CLEANING A BLACK BATHROOM SINK: SHINY AND STREAK-FREE

Bathroom sinks are subject to more abuse than virtually any other sink in the home. They accumulate everything from soap scum to mouthfuls of toothpaste. Black bathroom sinks can show scum worse than any other colour.

Protect Your Sink: Sinks are made for water. You should avoid draining trash or chemicals down your sink. Trash, such as used floss, lotion, or makeup should be thrown in the trash. Chemicals, such as hair spray or bathroom cleaner, should be disposed of appropriately along with other hazardous household materials.

Protect Yourself: Before cleaning your sink, and especially if you will be using harsh chemicals, put on a pair of gloves to protect your skin. Depending on the chemicals you will use, you may also need eye protection.

Remove The Worst Accumulation: Remove any hair, scum, or other accumulation that you can easily grasp or scrape with your fingers. You can just throw this accumulation in the trash or in a leftover plastic bag. Remove the plug from the sink and scrape all the scum on the plug into your trash bag.

Clean and Scrub: Use your bathroom cleaners to scrub off any residual build-up. This may take extra time and elbow grease, especially if you have an excessive build-up of lotion, makeup, toothpaste, or any other bathroom products. You can use paper towels, but to be even more environmentally friendly, use cleaning cloths or cleaning pads. Don't be afraid to scrub hard. Bathroom sinks are made of materials that can withstand the necessary assault required to clean the sink, and sometimes the only way to remove stains is with a lot of scrubbing. When you are finished, rinse the sink's entire surface with lukewarm water. This is also a good time to rinse your cleaning cloths in lukewarm water.

Dry: When you finish, wipe the sink dry with a paper towel or a dry cleaning cloth. Water spots can be noticeable on all types of sinks but especially on black sinks. They are created by drops of water that evaporate and leave behind a faint rim of minerals.However, water spots can be prevented by thoroughly drying the sink by hand.

Maintain: Maintain your sink's cleanliness by cleaning the sink at least once a week. Between cleanings, give the sink a quick wipe and dry with a paper towel or cleaning cloth every time you use it. You can store the cleaning cloths under the sink for quick access.

ANTIQUE CUPBOARD CLEANING AND MAINTENANCE

An antique cupboard can be a gorgeous addition to a home. When properly restored, antique cupboards maintain both the style and sensibility of their eras. However, antique cupboards are also an investment. They must be cleaned and maintained carefully to protect their value and their appearance.

Leave it Be: If you are in doubt of the best way to preserve your antiques, don't do anything at all. Your antique cupboard is the worst possible piece of furniture for trial-and-error techniques. If you do not know how to care for your antiques, but you want your cupboard to be restored or cleaned, take it to a specialist in antiques restoration. You can get the names of quality restoration specialists and furniture conservators by asking your local antiques dealers.

Faded is Fine: Furniture from the 18th or 19th century was often painted with a vibrant red or blue. Over time, the paint oxidizes, which fades the paint and gives it a mellow look. This look is highly desired among antiques collectors. Even if the paint begins to crack, it is still better left alone. That cracking gives you the warm comfort that it is original.

Avoid Oils on Wood: Many other antique pieces were originally stained rather than painted. In the 18th and early 19th centuries, many pieces were made from domestic woods and then stained to resemble exotic, expensive, imported woods. Oil may seem like it would help stained wood to shine, but oil is actually very bad for woods. It soaks into the grain, oxidizes, and turns the wood black. If you must add a protective covering to your cupboard, use wax. Wax creates a protective surface and is easy to remove, a feature that furniture conservators appreciate.

Fixing Damaged Finishes: What if your antique cupboard has already been stripped, varnished, or oiled? This leaves you with some options. You can leave it alone, or you can take it to a furniture conservator who can restore it to its original appearance. However, restoring furniture usually does not add to its value, so this may not be the best choice if you want to sell the cupboard. It can sometimes be a relief to own a piece that is not in its original condition, because you do not need to worry about what happens to it. If you have kids who frequently spill things or bang their belongings against the table, or if you have pets who might chew on the furniture, it may ease your mind if they are not destroying highly valuable furniture.

GLASS DOOR BEVERAGE REFRIGERATOR CLEANING AND MAINTENANCE

If you own a glass door beverage refrigerator for your home or business, you might wonder if there's a special way to clean it that won't cause damage. Learn how to clean and maintain your glass door beverage refrigerator to keep it running for a long time.

Steps to Clean Your Glass Door Fridge:

- if you have a glass door fridge, it is important to make sure that it is clean and running correctly. Before you clean, turn off and unplug the refrigerator. Empty the refrigerator of beverages and any parts that you can take out. Make a solution of baking soda and warm water and wash the inside of the refrigerator with the solution. Rinse the inside very well and dry with a clean towel.

You can wash the shelves that you removed in a detergent solution. Rinse them well then dry with a clean towel. While you are doing this, you should inspect the shelves carefully to make sure that there hasn't been any cracking or chipping. The difference in temperature may cause this kind of damage, so let the shelves get to room temperature before washing and use lukewarm water to clean.

Use the detergent solution to wash the door gasket, do this especially well in the cracks and crevices where bacteria, minerals and food can build up. Rinse well then dry.

Using the same detergent solution, you can wash the outside of the fridge. Again, rinse then dry. After this step, you might want to use a window cleaning product on the door only to remove any streaks or spots.

The plastics used in the refrigerator may be damaged by high temperatures. Never use hot water to clean. Household chemicals can be damaging to the refrigerator, so refer to your refrigerator's manual before using any cleaners on it. Use a mild detergent like dishwashing liquid with warm water, or a baking soda mixture. Avoid using abrasive cleaners and scrubbing pads or they will damage the refrigerator.

Between Cleanings: If you clean spills as they happen you can prevent staining, odors and build up of bacteria. Plastics are especially vulnerable to these things, especially if you are keeping dark coloured food and liquids.

Make sure that all food and beverages are stored in a sealed container and routinely remove outdated food to prevent odors.

To keep the refrigerator and all its parts running smoothly, you will want to vacuum dust from the condenser occasionally. Removing dirt and dust from the fan will allow it to run freely. A dirty fan is over worked, and will over heat causing damage to the parts of the motor. Remove the pan located under the refrigerator and wash it in your gentle detergent solution, rinse, dry and replace. This pan collects water from the automatic defroster.

Removing Refrigerator and Freezer Odors: By keeping the food and beverages sealed tight, immediately cleaning up spills, cleaning the drip pan and making sure that the fridge is free of outdated products you can keep odors from taking over your fridge. You should also check your food after any power outages.

CLEAN THE BATHTUB DRAIN IN FIVE STEPS

It may be a dirty job, but we all have to clean the bathtub drain at some point. When the water can't flow freely down the drain it backs up into the tub leaving soap scum and a bigger clean-up job. to clean the drain correctly, you should follow these important steps to help guide you through the process, and to ensure that your drain is clean and free from any clogs.

1. You need to first see what is clogging your drain and allowing the water to sit in the tub even after your have shut the water off hours ago. Unscrew the drain to see what is giving you this problem, and normally you will find hair wrapped around the drain or stuck deep inside. This is normally why the tub is clogged.
2. Remove the hair that is clogging the drain. Wear gloves if necessary.
3. Look in the drain to see if there is any mildew creeping around. This can also prevent the drain from functioning properly. Clean the mildew with a small sponge or damp towel. If there is a lot of dirt and grime stuck into or around your drain, try scraping if off to loosen it up.
4. Clean the tub and the drain with a cleaning agent suitable for bathtubs to get rid of the dirt and mildew that has been lurking in your tub. It is advised to clean not only the drain, but the entire tub as well. You want the entire bathtub to be clean and free of bacteria.
5. Pour Drano into the drain to diminish any clogs. You can normally use 1/5 of the bottle. However, if you have a stubborn clog it is best to pour at least half of the bottle down the drain. Wait 15 to 30 minutes, depending on the clog, before rinsing the drain with hot water. If you find that the drain is still clogged after doing this, then go ahead and pour the rest of the bottle in the drain and wait for 30 minutes before flushing out the drain.

Treating a clog in the bathtub drain may not be fun, but it doesn't have to be difficult. Keep cleaner and a can of Drano on hand in case of future clogs.

CLEANING A FRAMELESS GLASS SHOWER DOOR

If you are thinking about installing frameless glass shower doors to improve the décor of your bathroom, rest assured, it's a good decision. Keeping frameless glass shower doors clean is a simple process; much easier than keeping framed shower doors clean.

Prevention: The first thing you should think about when installing and learning to clean the glass shower doors is that prevention is the key to making the frameless glass shower door last a long time. Be sure to coat thoroughly with a layer of Transparent Polymer Coating (TPC) surface protector. This will work to fill all the pores of the glass, which will smooth it out and prevent any build-up.

Daily Cleaning: It doesn't take any effort to keep the frameless glass shower doors clean on a daily basis. Just keep a normal squeegee in the shower and use it before you leave the shower. This is simple yet truly effective in keeping glass door looking new.

Deep Cleaning: Although you shouldn't have to worry about deep cleaning very often at all if you've taken preventative steps, the occasion might still come up. For finger prints or general deep cleaning, use over-the-counter shower cleaner, there are plenty of environmentally friendly cleaners on the market now so you won't have to use harsh chemicals.

BEVERAGE STAIN REMOVAL

COFFEE STAIN REMOVAL HINTS

Coffee stains can be removed easily using this method. The stain can be removed much more easily if not allowed to dry. Blot the stain with a clean white cloth to remove any excess liquid. Mix a teaspoon of a good dishwashing detergent, such as Dawn, with a cup of lukewarm water. Sponge the area with the dishwashing solution, then blot again with your clean white cloth. Next, mix 1/3 cup of white vinegar with 2/3 cup of lukewarm water. Once again sponge the area with this solution, and blot again with a clean white cloth. Rinse with clean water, and launder as soon as possible, following the care label instructions. Carpeting can be cleaned using the above method and ingredients.

1. Mix one teaspoon of a mild ph balanced detergent (a mild non-alkaline non-bleaching detergent) with a cup of lukewarm water
2. Blot
3. Mix one third cup of white household vinegar with two thirds cup of water
4. Blot
5. Sponge with clean water
6. Blot

HOW TO REMOVE BLOOD STAINS FROM CLOTHING

You should remove blood stains from your clothing as soon as they get stained. The proteins in the blood make the stains especially problematic. Enzymes are efficient in breaking up organic matter, so enzymatic detergents are recommended in these cases. You should never use warm water or any other type of heating source on a blood stain. When heated, the proteins in the blood leave a permanent mark. There are several ways in which you can get rid of a blood stain. For instance, you can use salt or saliva. However, if the stain is larger and you are looking for a safer solution, you should wash the piece of clothing appropriately.

- *Step 1:* Absorb the Blood: As soon as you stained the fabric, press a white cotton rag or paper towels on the stain. The cotton rag is preferable because it has better absorbent properties. Try to absorb as much blood as possible to prevent it from spreading and making a larger stain.
- *Step 2:* Check the Composition of the Clothes: Find the label on the piece of clothing and carefully read the washing instructions and composition. In case of wool, silk, linen or dry-clean only clothing, you shouldn't proceed. Take the piece of clothing to your dry cleaner as soon as possible. You should not attempt cleaning the stains yourself because whatever pretreatment you might apply could permanently damage the material and the dry cleaner might not be able to remove the stain.
- *Step 3:* Use Detergent and Hydrogen Peroxide: In a small bowl, mix together 1 teaspoon laundry detergent and 1 cup of hydrogen peroxide. Soak a clean sponge or a clean white piece of cloth in the bowl. Wring out the sponge halfway, and rub it against the stain. You may also scrub the stain with your hands.

  On white clothing, you can pour hydrogen peroxide directly on the stain. Make a mixture with 50 per cent water. When you put hydroxide peroxide on a blood stain, it will start foaming. When it stops foaming, it means either that the stain is removed or that the fabric is very wet and needs wringing.
- *Step 4:* Soak in Sparkling Water: When you are done rubbing the clothing with hydrogen peroxide or detergent, put it in sparkling water. Let it soak for about half an hour.
- *Step 5:* Wring the Clothing: Wring the clothing and inspect the stained area in the light (preferably sunlight). The stain might be completely gone or it might still be a little yellowish.
- *Step 6:* Wash Clothing: Wash your clothing. If it can be machine-washed, set a low water temperature. In case it needs hand-washing, use a gentle detergent and cold water.
- *Step 7:* Air Dry: Let your clothing air dry. Do not use the drier; if the stain did not completely come out, heat will make it permanent and you will never be able to wash it out.

CLEAN JUICE STAINS

Removing juice stains can be accomplished by quickly rinsing with cool water. Don't use detergent on the stain - it will set it and make it impossible to remove. Instead, use white vinegar and blot to remove. Clear fruit juices, such as grapefruit, orange, or apple can be removed by blotting out as much of the juice as you can, and then rinsing with cool water. If needed, use a sponge and white vinegar to clean the spot, and then use a stain pretreater, such as Shout, and launder per the care label instructions. On dry clean only items, sponge on a little white vinegar, and rinse with cool water. If the stain persists, use a digestant enzyme paste on the stain, and let stand for 30 minutes. Rinse. Don't apply a digestant enzyme cleaner to silk or wool. These are best handled by a dry cleaning professional.

1. Blot up liquid
2. Mix one teaspoon of a mild pH balanced detergent (a mild non-alkaline non-bleaching detergent) with a cup of lukewarm water
3. Blot
4. Rinse with white household vinegar
5. Blot
6. Mix one teaspoon of a mild pH balanced detergent (a mild non-alkaline non-bleaching detergent) with a cup of lukewarm water
7. Blot
8. Sponge with clean water
9. Blot
10. If stain remains, blot with alcohol

REMOVE BLOOD STAINS FROM CARPET

The task of managing to remove blood stains may seem daunting, especially if such tough stains are on a carpet. However, if you follow the right methods and use suitable products and equipment, you should be able to completely remove the stain.

Follow the simple steps below to effectively remove blood stains from a carpet.

- *Step 1:* Tackle the Stain Immediately: As soon as you notice a blood stain you have to make it a point to act as soon as possible. If the blood is still fresh, you have a better chance of removing it. Though the materials list above are not uncommon in a kitchen, it is best to ensure that you have them on hand at all times in case you need to use them in an emergency.
- *Step 2:* Wet the Stain: First you have to wet the stain. Simply fill a cup with water, mix in some dishwashing liquid and pour it over the blood stain. You may need to pour more water until you see that the

area has been soaked well. Make sure not to use hot water as it may make the stain set even more.

- *Step 3:* Absorbing Process: Use a rag or an old towel to start absorbing the water and blood from the carpet. It is crucial to dab, not wipe or rub as this could further spread the blood. Keep dabbing and pressing until you see the blood getting absorbed.
- *Step 4:* Using a Laundry Cleaner: If the blood stain is not fresh, you can use other methods. For instance, you can rub some laundry cleaner onto the stain with your fingers, and allow some minutes for it to set. Make sure to use a laundry cleaner that does not contain harmful chemicals that could cause damage to your carpet. Then, use a soft sponge or a toothbrush to rub the area. Never use a scrubber or a brush as it may ruin the carpet's fabric. Finally, use a rag to remove the soapy residue.
- *Step 5:* Using Chemical Based Cleansers: If the above methods have not proved to be successful, you may need to use stronger chemical-based cleansers. This should only be used as a last resort as such cleansers may likely cause the carpet to fade. Some of these products include hydrogen peroxide or a solution of household ammonia mixed with warm water. In such cases, make sure to use a white rather than a coloured cloth to rub the area to avoid transferring colour onto the carpet. Spray the solution onto the blood stain, and then blot. Afterwards, rinse the area with water and allow to dry well. Pretesting the solution on an unnoticeable area of the carpet first is recommended.

Alternatively, you could attempt to use a commercial carpet cleaner. These products are usually ideal for a variety of stains, but mild ones may not be sufficient to remove a persistent stain such as blood. However, it is always worth a try before using the more dangerous solutions such as ammonia or peroxide.

BEER STAIN REMOVAL HINTS

Beer stains are fairly easy to remove. If the stain is still wet, blot up as much as you can with a clean white cloth or paper towels. Never rub a stain. Mix a teaspoon of a good dishwashing detergent, such as Dawn, with a cup of warm water. Spoon some of this detergent mixture onto the stain, and allow to stand for 5 minutes.

Rinse the stain with a little warm water, and carefully blot dry. If the stain is stubborn, mix one part of white vinegar to two parts water, and repeat the previous steps. If the stain is on clothing, always rinse the stain in cool running water from the back of the stain, and treat the stain as you would carpet. Vinegar will bleach clothing, so be sure to rinse right away, and wash according to care label instructions. Remember, the dark beers such as Guinness Lager will cause the worst stain due to its dark colouring.

1. Mix one teaspoon of a mild ph balanced detergent (a mild non-alkaline non-bleaching detergent) with a cup of lukewarm water
2. Blot
3. Mix one third cup of white household vinegar with two thirds cup of water
4. Blot
5. Sponge with clean water
6. Blot

REMOVE BLOOD STAINS FROM WOOD

If you cut yourself or suffer from some other type of injury, you may end up with blood stains somewhere in your home. In addition to being an unpleasant reminder of the injury or the other situation that caused the stain, you'll oftentimes find that blood is difficult to get out of certain surfaces. One of those surfaces that is notoriously hard to remove blood stains from is wood. Read on for a brief guide on how to clean up blood stains from a wooden surface like a hardwood floor, a wooden countertop, or a wooden piece of furniture.

- *Step 1:* Clean Up the Blood Before It Can Stain: If you happen to catch the wooden surface before the blood has a chance to set into it and cause a stain, you can oftentimes clean up the mess very quickly and with little in terms of repercussions. Soak up as much of the blood as you can with a paper towel. Remember that it's always most important to deal with and properly treat injuries first before you begin to clean up any other objects.
- *Step 2:* Clean the Blood With Wet and Dry Washcloths: Get the tip of one corner of a washcloth wet with cold water. The washcloth should not be too wet, as this could cause the blood to run and may just end up spreading the stain. Dab at the stained area with the wetted tip of the washcloth. Alternate treating the stained area with the wet washcloth and cleaning up any moisture that collects with a dry washcloth. As the wet washcloth becomes soaked and dirty, dip another corner of the washcloth into the cold water to continue. Keep going until the surface of the wood is as clean as possible.
- *Step 3:* Treat the Stain With Hydrogen Peroxide: It's likely at this point that there will be some blood left remaining on the surface, or that the stain will still be visible. In this case, you'll need to repeat the process from step 2, but use a washcloth with the tip dipped into hydrogen peroxide instead. Hydrogen peroxide is a better substance to use to clean up the blood and is a good option if water isn't sufficient to completely eliminate the stain.

- *Step 4:* If Necessary, Use Bleach: Before you begin to use bleach to clean up any especially persistent and tough stains, be aware of the fact that the bleach is likely to stain the wood. If you have a darker wood surface, it's best to avoid bleach. Lighter woods may still be discolored somewhat by the bleach. Use only a very small amount of bleach to dab at the surface with a soaked washcloth. Be sure to thoroughly wash off the surface of the wooden object with cold water after you've treated the stained area to your satisfaction.

EASY WINE STAIN REMOVAL

Wine stain removal can be a nuisance, especially with red wine. The best solution as with any stains is to use a wine stain removal solution right away. For wine stain removal on clothing or other fabrics, you can use white wine to remove it. If that wine stain removal process fails, you can create a solution for the fabric to pre-soak in:

- 1 Cup Dawn Dish Washing Liquid
- 1 Cup Hydrogen Peroxide

Allow the mixture to soak into the clothes before laundering. You should place a clean towel in between the stain and the back of the item of clothing to ensure it does not soak through. Wine Stain Removal For Carpeting: If you spill red wine on the carpeting, pour hydrogen peroxide over the stain and blot the stain away. In tougher stains or colourfast carpets you will want a wine stain removal solution consisting of luke warm water and vinegar. You can blot the majority of the stain away and then use a clean damp sponge and some elbow grease for the remainder.

HOW TO CLEAN FRUIT STAINS

NEW Method! Motstenbocker's Lift Off #1 is a a new biodegradable and water based product and is designed to specifically remove stains such as: coffee, tea, juice, soda, sauces, ketchup, mustard, blood, grass, pet stains, liquor, chocolate, jelly, barbecue and soy sauce and red wine. It can be used on: carpets, fabrics, rubber, metal, formica, tile, vinyl, wall coverings, clothes, furniture, plastic and delicates. It works better than existing products; it works in the same reactionary time; it is safe on all surfaces; it costs the same or less than other products; it is safe for the user and again, it is water based and biodegradable!

Old Method

1. Blot up all liquid
2. Mix one teaspoon of a mild pH balanced detergent (a mild non-alkaline non-bleaching detergent) with a cup of lukewarm water
3. Blot
4. Rinse with white household vinegar

5. Blot
6. Mix one teaspoon of a mild pH balanced detergent (a mild non-alkaline non-bleaching detergent) with a cup of lukewarm water
7. Blot
8. Sponge with clean water
9. Blot
10. If stain remains, blot with alcohol

SODA STAIN REMOVAL TIPS

Soda is a tasty drink we all enjoy, soda stain removal is something we do not. While all stains are a nuisance, soda stain removal does not have to be difficult. As with any stain, you should try to clean it right away, before it sets in.

The first step is to use a clean dry towel and blot the area, removing any excess liquid. Secondly for soda stain removal you should create a cleaning solution consisting of:

- ¼ Cup of Liquid Dish Detergent
- 1 Cup Cold water

Using the soda stain removal solution and a clean rag, blot the area first and then gently scrub it clean.

Stubborn Soda Stain Removal: If the soda stain is still showing after the above process, create a new soda stain removal solution and begin again:

- ¼ Cup Vinegar
- 1 Cup Luke Warm Water

Soda stain removal may be more difficult depending on the surface, but it is not impossible. You may have to put a little elbow grease in to the soda stain removal process to see the results you want.

HOW TO CLEAN MILK STAINS

Milk stains can be removed from machine washable garments by quickly blotting them up with cool water as promptly as possible. Soak the garment in cool water for 30 minutes or more.

Work undiluted liquid detergent into the stain, and rinse. Launder per care label instructions. If the garment is dry clean only, cover the stain with a sponge, and squirt cool water through the sponge with a medicine dropper. Blot dry with a clean white cloth.

If this fails to remove the stain, try working a bit of liquid detergent into the stain and carefully rinse. Finally, sponge with isopropyl alcohol to remove the detergent. Dilute the alcohol at a ratio of 2 to one with cool water, and be sure to test this solution on an area of the garment that is not seen, such as a seam allowance.

1. Mix one teaspoon of a mild pH balanced detergent (a mild non-alkaline non-bleaching detergent) with a cup of lukewarm water
2. Blot
3. Mix one tablespoon of household ammonia with a half cup of water
4. Blot
5. Mix one teaspoon of a mild pH balanced detergent (a mild non-alkaline non-bleaching detergent) with a cup of lukewarm water
6. Blot
7. Sponge with clean water
8. Blot

CLEAN SODA POP STAINS

Soda pop can be removed by using this method. Hydrogen peroxide is mixed at the ratio of 1/4 cup hydrogen peroxide to 3 cups of water. Using a spray bottle, spray on and let stand for 10 minutes. Rinse with 1/4 cup of white vinegar added to 3/4 cup of cold water, and blot dry. Boiling water is also reported to remove pop and juice stains from clothing if the stain has not set.

1. Mix one teaspoon of a mild ph balanced detergent (a mild non-alkaline non-bleaching detergent) with a cup of lukewarm water
2. Blot
3. Mix one third cup of white household vinegar with two thirds cup of water
4. Blot
5. Sponge with clean water
6. Blot

COFFEE STAIN REMOVAL

Coffee stain removal can be done easily if you follow a few simple tips. As with any stain, coffee stain removal should be done immediately if possible. The longer the stain has a chance to set, the harder it will be to remove.

Using a clean white cloth, blot the stain to remove any excess liquid. Coffee stain removal can also be done with a mixture of dishwashing liquid and luke warm water or with the use of 1/3 cup of white vinegar and 2/3 cups of luke warm water. You can use either coffee stain removal solution and sponge gently to remove the stain.

Once the stain has been lifted, you should rinse with cold water and launder according to the labeled instructions for care.

Coffee Stain Removal for Carpet: Coffee stain removal on carpet can be done in the same manner as above. Using the same solutions of dish detergent and water or vinegar and water, the area can be blotted, sponged, blotted, and rinsed. If the coffee stain removal left behind any excess discoloring, you can use your shampooer for further results.

REMOVE BLOOD STAINS FROM CEMENT SURFACES

If you have an accident that results in an injury, you may need to be prepared to remove blood stains from surfaces around your home. Blood can easily cause unpleasant looking stains on a variety of surfaces, from furniture to carpets to clothing and more. If you accidentally end up with a blood stain on a concrete surface, acting quickly is one of the best ways to ensure that the stain can be removed properly. Read on for a brief guide on how to remove blood stains from concrete or cement surfaces around your home.

- *Step 1:* Clean Up the Blood: If you're able to target the area immediately after the accident, the first thing that you should do is to clean up any extra blood that may be pooling on the ground. Use a clean cloth to dab at the area, but do not rub as this could spread the stain. Continue until you've eliminated all of the excess liquid from the ground. Wear gloves as you do this and be very careful, both so that you don't spread the blood around to make the stain larger and also because blood from someone else may be contaminated and capable of spreading disease.
- *Step 2:* Scrub the Stain: Use a brush with stiff bristles to scrub at the stained area. The goal is to get the particles of blood that have dried on the surface of the concrete to loosen and then become removed. Continue to scrub for about 10 minutes or until the stain becomes to chip off.
- *Step 3:* Sweep Up the Stain: If the particles of blood have become loosened, use a broom and dustpan to sweep them up. This will generally work well if the stain is older and has had a chance to thoroughly dry over the concrete surface. It may be messy if the accident just occurred. Discard the waste in a safe and healthy manner, following any legal guidelines regarding hazardous waste disposal in your area.
- *Step 4:* Apply a Detergent Mixture: In a small bowl, mix 1 part liquid dish detergent with 3 parts water, and stir until the contents are fully mixed. Pour a small amount of the mixture onto the stained area, and then continue to scrub at it vigourously with the stiff bristled brush. Take note whether the stain begins to become loose. Clean up the liquid with a clean cloth or paper towels.
- *Step 5:* Treat With Hydrogen Peroxide: If the stain still persists after you've completed all of the previous steps, pour a small amount of hydrogen peroxide on the stained area. Allow it to sit for about 15 minutes to begin to break down the stain itself, and then scrub at it once again with the stiff bristled brush. Clean up the peroxide with another clean cloth or a paper towel. Examine the stain; if it is still there, treat it with another portion of hydrogen peroxide as well.

REMOVING CRAYON STAINS FROM PAINTED WALLS

Crayon stains can appear to be very severe and problematic when they show up on walls or the floor. However, if you have a young child who has taken to drawing on walls with his or her crayons, you need not fear. Crayon stains can generally be removed entirely from painted walls. If you can't remove the stain completely, you can at the very least lighten it significantly so that it will not be as visible. Read on for a brief how-to guide on removing crayon stains from painted walls in your home.

- *Step 1:* Spray the Stain Down With Lubricant: Begin by spraying the stain with the lubricating fluid. Use a fair amount of the fluid so that you can be sure that the entire stain is covered. Do not spread the fluid around with a rag or other item at this point, but rather just let it wash over the stain completely. You'll need to allow the stain to completely soak up the fluid. This typically takes about 3 minutes.
- *Step 2:* Wipe the Stain: Use a clean cloth to thoroughly wipe down the stained area. This should clean up any of the lubricating liquid that was spilled in the area, as well provide you with a chance to remove the first layers of the stain. After you've completely wiped up the stained area, check the stain to see if you were successful at removing any of the crayon material from the painted wall. If the stain is gone or if it's sufficiently reduced, stop at this point; otherwise, continue to step 3.
- *Step 3:* Wash the Area With Liquid Dishwashing Detergent: Mix three parts warm water with one part liquid dishwashing detergent in a bowl. Use a cloth to apply the detergent mixture generously to the stained area. Before the detergent solution can sit on the stained area at all, use a large sponge to scrub at the stained area. Apply pressure with the sponge to really work into the wall so that you can successfully remove the stain.

When you're through, wash the wall with regular water and once again examine the stained area. If the stain still remains in some form, repeat this process again with a mixture that is half water and half liquid dishwashing detergent. Between these steps, most crayon stains will be thoroughly removed from a painted wall. Be sure to step back a few feet to be able to determine whether the crayon stain is still visible. In many cases, even a largely faded crayon stain will be acceptable, because you won't be able to see it from a distance. The tools necessary for this project are available at hardware and home improvement stores.

STEAM CLEAN A COFFEE STAIN FROM YOUR CARPET

A coffee stain is one of the most difficult to remove from any surface.

Removing coffee from carpet can be extremely difficult. With the combination of a little elbow grease and a steam cleaner, the stain can be completely removed. It is very important to remember that using cold water is essential to the removal of a coffee stain, as hot water will set the stain. Always test an inconspicuous area of the carpet before applying any product to the stain. This will insure that there will not be any removal of dye from the carpet fibres.

- *Step 1:* Keep Stain from Setting: If you can't completely remove the stain immediately, blot up as much of the liquid as possible with a clean white rag. Sprinkle some salt over the affected area to absorb as much of the coffee as possible. The key is to avoid the coffee stain from seeping through to the underlayment. If the coffee absorbs into the padding, it will continue to rise up and re-stain the carpet.
- *Step 2:* Use Steam Cleaner: Fill the steamer with cold water. Mix together a 50/50 solution of cold water and white vinegar. Pour mixture into a clean spray bottle. Spray vinegar/water solution onto the coffee stain. Blot excess moisture with a clean white rag. If it appears that the stain is gone, re-fill the steam cleaner with fresh cold water. Use the cleaner to remove excess vinegar. Both coffee and vinegar are acidic. Since vinegar is more acidic than coffee, by placing it on the coffee stain, it will break the bond that coffee has formed on the carpet fibres.
- *Step 3:* Remove Remaining Stain: If, after Step 2, some staining remains, use hydrogen peroxide on the area. Pour the hydrogen peroxide directly on the stain. With your hands, rub the hydrogen peroxide into the carpet fibres with a massaging motion. Allow the carpet to completely dry. As the hydrogen peroxide turns to water with sun exposure, there is no need for further steam cleaning. Repeat soaking and massaging the area with hydrogen peroxide until the coffee stain is gone when the carpet is completely dry.
- *Step 4:* More Tricks: Squirt some white shaving cream onto the stain. Massage fibres individually to remove coffee. Either steam residue with cold water or use a clean wet rag to blot up remaining shaving cream. Make a paste of baking soda and water (consistency of toothpaste). Apply the paste onto the stain. Allow to dry completely and vacuum.
- *Step 5:* What not to Do: Never use hot water on coffee stains as it will serve to set the stain permanently. Always use a blotting action, as rubbing will open the fibres and will make the stain worse. Never use soap on carpet. Soap will always leave a residue that will attract dirt to the carpet fibres. Never push down on the fibres, as this will force the stain deeper into the carpet. Always vacuum after a coffee stain removal is complete to restore carpet's fibres to normal.

REMOVING COFFEE STAINS FROM COUCH CUSHIONS

Coffee stains on couch cushions are considered difficult to remove, however, it is possible to have stain-free cushions without having to go to the drycleaner's. Ideally, you should act as soon as you have spilled the coffee. There are several solutions you can use staring from liquid detergent to baking soda and salt.

- *Step 1:* Remove Cushion Covers: Try to remove the cushion covers as soon as you have spilled the coffee to prevent the coffee from spreading on the rest of the cushion or cause a larger stain. If you don't have removable cushion covers, skip this step.
- *Step 2:* Remove Excess Liquid: Remove the excess liquid using a towel or a clean piece of cloth. It's important that the towel or the piece of cloth you use is white, as dyed fabrics may leave colour behind and cause additional staining.
- *Step 3:* Rinse Thoroughly: Put the cushion cover or the entire cushion under cold water and keep it there for at least 5 minutes. You may notice that part of the stain is gone.
- *Step 4:* Apply Liquid Detergent or Alternative Cleaning Solutions: Apply bleach-free liquid detergent on the coffee stain. Allow to settle for up to 10 minutes. Then, insert the cushion cover or cushion under warm water and soak for at least 30 minutes.

  Instead of the liquid detergent, you may use other substances as well.

  Baking soda and salt can be used, but in this case you will have to skip step 3. The powder should be applied on the cushion and left for 30 minutes.

  Club soda may be applied on the stain for 1 minute and then blotted with a towel. Ginger ale may be used in the same manner as club soda.
- *Step 5:* Rinse Again: Rinse with clean water. Avoid rubbing to remove coffee stains, as rubbing may only enlarge the stain or cause additional wear to the couch cushion. Also, rubbing may cause discoloration or a change of colour of the area.

  If you have applied baking soda and salt, you won't require rinsing, but you will have to vacuum the cushion or remove the powder with a clean towel.
- *Step 6:* Use Stain Remover: If the coffee stain on the couch cushion persists, you should get a commercial stain remover. Apply the solution on the cushion and then wash the cushion cover. If the cover is not removable, you may wash the entire cushion, but if this is filled with feathers, washing may not be a solution.

Instead of the stain remover, you may use diluted vinegar (1 part vinegar, 2 parts water) or diluted bleach (1 part bleach, 10 parts water), which may eliminate traces of coffee stain, but may cause slight discoloration. You may test the solution on a small area of the stained cushion to see if the discoloration is visible.

REMOVING COFFEE STAINS FROM CLOTHING

If you're an avid coffee drinker, it's almost a foregone conclusion that you'll have to deal with coffee stains at some point in your life. Coffee spills can result in stains on clothing, carpets, rugs, furniture and more. Fortunately, although you might not be able to remedy the fact that hot coffee spilled on your clothes may cause injuries and burns, you'll be able to deal with the stain if you act quickly enough. Read on for a brief overview of how to remove coffee stains from clothing in just a few simple steps.

- *Step 1:* Remove the Clothing and Rinse: Before you do anything, it's a good idea to remove the article of clothing that had coffee spill on it. Turn the clothing inside out so that the surface that came into contact with the coffee directly is not exposed. Turn on a cold water faucet in your sink and rinse the stained area off with cold water. Do not get any water on the front side of the item of clothing if you're able to prevent that from happening. Wring the clothing out to get rid of any excess water that has collected in the fabric.
- *Step 2:* Apply Clothing Detergent: Pour detergent on the stained area. It's a good idea to pour the detergent on the part of the clothing that actually came into contact with the coffee, so you might need to turn the clothing right side out once again in order to have the best access. Scrub the detergent into the clothing with a toothbrush until it begins to lather up somewhat.
- *Step 3:* Allow the Detergent to Soak In: The detergent should now be allowed to soak into the clothing. This will help it to remove the stain as much as possible. If you just recently spilled the coffee and the stain is fresh, allow the detergent to sit for about 10 minutes before you rinse it out. If the stain has already dried, let the detergent sit for about half an hour before you proceed to the next step.
- *Step 4:* Rinse the Detergent: Rinse the detergent off using only cold water. When the clothing dries a bit, check to see if the stain is still visible. If it is, you may either repeat the detergent application and rinsing process or opt to take your clothing in to a dry cleaning service for additional attention.

If the stain has been sufficiently lightened or removed from the clothing entirely, put it in the washing machine on a standard warm cycle. You can then allow the garment to air dry so that you can be sure that the stain has been eliminated properly. The faster that you're able to deal with a stain caused by coffee on an article of clothing, the greater the likelihood that you'll be able to remove that stain.

REMOVING COFFEE STAINS FROM SILK

The key to removing coffee stains from silk is to begin the process before the coffee dries. It will be much more difficult to remove a stain that has been allowed to set. If you cannot completely remove the stain immediately, at least begin the process to minimize damage to the garment. Do not dry the area, as this will permanently set the stain.

- *Step 1:* Blot Stain: If possible, remove the item of clothing. Being very careful not to allow the coffee to spread or splash onto other areas, blot the stain with a white paper towel or clean rag. If you do not have immediate access to the required materials, blot the area with cold water. This will keep the stain from setting until you can tend it it properly.
- *Step 2:* Dab the Stain with Vinegar Solution: The best method to remove coffee stains from silk is to mix equal parts of distilled white vinegar and water. Lay a clean white rag under the stained area. Dip a corner of a clean white rag into the vinegar/water solution. Carefully blot the stained area, working from the center to the edges. Do not allow the area to become too saturated, as this will spread the stain. Continue blotting, re-wetting different areas of the rag.
- *Step 3:* Stubborn or Set Stains: If the stain is especially stubborn, you may need to resort to steaming the coffee stains out of the garment. First, lay a folded clean white rag onto the ironing surface (table, ironing board). Lay the garment, stain side down onto the folded rag. Sprinkle cornstarch onto the stained area. Lay a clean white rag on top of the garment. With the iron set on "steam", set the iron onto the top rag. The silk will be protected by the rag layers. This will steam the coffee out of the garment.
- *Step 4*: Wash Garment: After the initial stain removal, hand wash your silk garment. Do not place it in the dryer or use any sort of heat to dry it. Heat drying will set any residual stain. Allow the garment to air dry, and inspect it thoroughly.
- *Step 5:* Soaking Especially Stubborn Stains: Should the coffee stains still be visible, soaking the garment in an oxygen based laundry detergent booster for 20-30 minutes may help. Mix oxygen stain lifter with water according to package directions. Soak the entire garment in the mixture. Remove, and wash by hand with an appropriate detergent. Allow the garment to air-dry. Inspect the stained area

closely. If necessary, repeat Steps 3-5 until you are satisfied with the appearance of the garment.

- *Step 6:* Last Resort: Ultimately, there is always the chance that the coffee stains will not completely come out of the garment. There is also the possibility that with the removal of the stain, some of the original dye may be removed, causing uneven colouring of the garment. If the problem is the former, take the garment to a reputable dry cleaner. Be sure to explain what the stain is and everything you used on the stain. If, on the other hand, the colour is now uneven, you may find it necessary to dye the garment.

LAUNDRY CHORES

CLEAN YOUR IRON

Cleaning your iron on a regular basis is essential to maintaining clean, crisp clothes. At first glance, you may wonder how it is that one goes about cleaning an iron. In fact, you may even avoid the task simply because you don't know how to go about it.

Fortunately, cleaning the iron is no more difficult than cleaning most other small appliances. All it takes is a little bit of time and a few simple tools.

Cleaning the Reservoir: The reservoir of your iron needs cleaning if it looks as though small deposits are being left in the small holes on the soleplate. Typically, the deposits are minerals from the water that you are using in the reservoir. The deposits may have a white colour, and they may resemble salt.

Cleaning the reservoir requires the use of white vinegar and a clean rag. Fill the reservoir of a cold iron at least one fourth of the way with white vinegar. Turn the iron on and place it on the steam setting. Steam iron the clean rag until the reservoir is completely empty.

If the deposits are still visible to you, you will need to fill the reservoir with clean water and steam iron a rag again. If the deposits are still visible to you after this, you will need to repeat the process with vinegar until the deposits are no longer apparent.

Rinse the reservoir thoroughly with clean water by filling it completely and then emptying it completely. In order to avoid mineral buildup and deposits, use only distilled or purified water in the reservoir. If you continue to use tap water, simply remember to clean the reservoir periodically.

Vinegar has a strong smell associated with it, especially when it is heated. Ventilate the area where you are working as much as possible, by opening windows, turning on vents or fans, or keeping the door open.

Cleaning the Soleplate: Unfortunately, the soleplate of an iron is prone to occasional build up. Therefore, the soleplate requires cleaning in order to avoid staining the clothes or fabrics. Avoid abrasive cleaning powders or scouring pads. Begin with a cold iron that is unplugged from the electrical outlet. Use a mild dish washing soap or laundry detergent to create a sudsy solution. Use a nylon mesh pad, sponge, or a clean cloth dipped in the solution to completely wipe off the soleplate of the iron. Wipe the soleplate clean with a damp cloth or rag.

If the soleplate is the victim of a starchy build up or corrosion of some form, you will need to use something a little stronger. Use a clean cloth dipped in white vinegar to remove the build up. Wipe the soleplate clean with a cloth dampened in clean water.

If this does not work, then you will need to heat a solution of white vinegar and salt until the salt dissolves. Using a clean cloth sipped in the heated solution, wipe the iron's soleplate clean. Continue wiping until you have removed all of the build up or corrosion. Remember to wipe the iron completely clean with a cloth dampened in clean water.

Cleaning the Exterior of the Iron: The exterior of the iron should be kept clean to avoid any unnecessary transfer of dirt onto the articles that are being ironed. Simply wipe the exterior clean with a damp cloth or sponge occasionally. If the iron does happen to pick up some form of residue on its exterior, then wipe it with a mild dish washing solution. Completing this task when you are cleaning the soleplate of the iron is an excellent time saver.

Storing the Iron: Whenever you are finished with the iron, you should empty the reservoir completely and allow it to dry out. This will also help to prevent mineral build up and lessen the frequency with which you need to clean the reservoir. Remember that the water in the reservoir may be hot since the iron was turned on. Empty the water slowly by tilting the iron over the sink or laundry tub. Store the iron in an upright position in a location where it won't be easily disturbed.

SETTING UP A CLOTHESLINE

With spring upon us, you may have considered a revamp of yourcleaning process at home. We all need to have clean clothes and there's no doubt modern washing machines and clothes dryers are a convenient way to have them, but at what cost? Now, no one wants to go back to boiling clothes in a cauldron or beating them on rocks down by the river, but the idea of an old fashioned clothesline is well worth considering. A clothesline will save you money and is kind to the environment. And as an added bonus, your dry clothes will actually smell as fresh as the outdoors.

Installing a clothesline isn't difficult; in fact, it's a good weekend project. Follow these steps to get clothes smelling like fresh spring air — the natural way.

- *Step 1:* Determine What Kind of Clothesline You Want: Your choice of clothesline will probably depend on how much space you have in your yard, as well as your opinion of the "beauty" of a clothesline. The old cross bar "T shape" made of metal or wood has been a standard for years, mainly because it works well. You might also want to consider installing an umbrella clothesline that folds up when it's not in use. A major benefit of an umbrella clothesline is you can remove it from your yard when it's not in use, so you don't have to look at it every day.

- *Step 2:* Decide Where to Put It: It's best to locate your clothesline away from trees and overhanging wires if possible. Also try to locate it away from walking or gardeningareas and where kids or pets run around.
- *Step 3:* Dig a Hole (Or Two): No mater what type of clothesline you install, you're going to have to dig a hole. But before you pick up your shovel, have your local utilities (phone, cable, power, water and gas company) come out and mark the location of their facilities for safety reasons.

A "T post" clothesline generally requires two holes (unless you're going to attach one end to the house or a tree) while an umbrella design only needs one. If you live in an area where the ground freezes in winter, dig down below the frost line — three feet should be enough even in the coldest climates. It's also a good idea to try to make the bottom of the hole slightly wider than the top. This helps to prevent any movement of the base when frost leaves the ground.

- *Step 4:* Prep the Holes: Since clotheslines need to support a lot of weight, you'll need to set your posts in cement. The easiest way is to use fence post cement that you just pour into the hole with water. Note that if your soil is dry it will literally suck water out of the concrete. Make sure that doesn't happen by spraying the hole with water before putting in any concrete. Fill the hole about 1/3 with cement, and add water.
- *Step 5:* Set the Posts: Stand your post in the center of the hole, and then fill the rest of the hole with cement. While it's best to use pressure treated wood for the poles and cross pieces, cedar or redwood also resist the elements, and give a more natural appearance.

Use a level to ensure your post is straight. Stake it in place and let the cement dry for a day.

Note: If you want your umbrella dryer to be removable, you will need a piece of plastic pipe slightly wider than the base pole. Cover one end of the tube and then stand it in the cement-filled hole, making sure the plastic tube sticks well up out of the ground so you can straighten it. Once the cement has set up, you can cut the tube off at ground level.

- *Step 6:* Install the Line: The next day after the cement has set up, install your clothesline pulleys and the clothesline itself. Try to position the lines so they're two or three inches above the head of the person who uses it most. At that height, they won't have to continually stretch above their head. After running your lines, don't forget to install a clothes line tightener (a metal bracket that fits between the lines and keeps them taut) so clothes won't drag on the ground.

REMOVING GREASE STAINS FROM CLOTHING

Nothing is more frustrating than discovering a grease stain on your favourite blouse or your son's best blazer. Grease stains come in all shapes and sizes and from a variety of sources. Whether your stain is from cooking oil or automotive grease, there are several ways to successfully remove the stain and have your clothing looking as good as new.

The best advice when dealing with grease stains is to treat them as soon as possible. Most treatments can work on set-in stains as well as fresh ones, but the sooner you tackle the stain, the easier it will be to remove it. Use the hottest water possible when washing out a grease stain. This gives the detergent the boost it needs to remove the grease. Check each time after washing to make sure the stain is completely removed before drying the garment. A stain that has gone through the dryer will be much more difficult to remove.

If you are dealing with thick automotive grease, the excess grease should be scraped from the stain with a knife before you treat it. Many people have found that absorbing as much oil from the stain as possible before treating it helps the stain removal process go more smoothly. This can be done using an absorbent powder.

Cornstarch, baby powder, and baking soda are some of the best products to use for this purpose. Simply apply the powder to the stain, working it in very slightly if necessary. Let it sit for a few hours or even overnight, and then brush it off. This method is especially useful when dealing with more delicate fabrics that may not be able to handle harsher treatments.

After absorbing as much of the grease as possible, you may need to move on to other treatments to completely remove the stain. A variety of products can be used for this. If you are someone who consistently has to deal with grease stains, you should stock up on products that are formulated to deal with tough grease stains on laundry.

Otherwise, these products aren't always necessary. Most people find that applying plain old dish soap to the stain will do a fine job of removing it. Just work a little soap into the stain, being careful not to spread the grease. Let the garment sit for at least a few minutes, and then lauder as normal. Liquid laundry detergent, dish washing detergent, and even shampoo can also be used in this way. You can also make a thick paste out of powder laundry detergent and water to pre-treat the stain. Hair spray and WD-40 have also been used to combat grease stains, but these methods are harsher and may not be suitable for all fabrics. Testing these products on a small, inconspicuous area of the garment will let you know if they are safe to use.

After treating a stain with these chemicals, treat the stain with detergent or soap and then launder as normal. Ammonia is also good for grease stains. If you have a whole load of greasy laundry, adding up to a cup of ammonia to the wash can help remove all of the stains.

CLEAN THE WASHER

Ah, the fresh scent of clean laundry tantalizes our nostrils and adds a bit of pleasantness to our day. That is, until we look at the laundry and notice that it isn't quite as clean as we thought it was. Maintaining a clean washer helps to ensure that the laundry looks its brightest and smells its freshest.

Follow a few simple strategies on a regular basis, and your washer will produce the results that you want. Probably the most important step you can take is to read the manual provided by the manufacturer with the washing machine. Use the methods described in the manual for proper maintenance and cleaning of your machine if any are provided for you.

Fortunately, most of these cleaning steps are only necessary on an as needed basis. If you prefer, complete most of them once a month for a sparkling clean washing machine. Follow these helpful pointers or the ones in your manual to produce a nice clean washer.

- Wipe the outside of your washer with a soft cloth and a mild solution of soap. This is especially important if you use the washer lid as a landing station for your laundry.
- Whenever a load of wash is extremely dirty and leaves a bit of residue on the interior or inner tub of your washer, use a clean, damp cloth to wipe it clean.
- If your washer is equipped with a lint filter, remove all lint accumulation on a regular basis such as after every wash cycle.
- Clean the bleach and fabric softener dispensers as soon as they show any sign of dirt or residue. Avoid using laundry detergent to clean the fabric softener dispenser since it may interact with the fabric softener the next time you use it.
- If desired, apply a coating of appliance wax following the instructions provided with the container. This helps to protect the exterior of your washer.
- If your washing machine is set up to drain into a laundry tub, you should have a strainer placed in the drain to gather all traces of lint and larger particles of dirt. If the plumbing becomes clogged, your

washer may not work properly. A clogged drain can prevent the water from draining properly. Remove any build-up in the strainer after each washing cycle.

- Clean the washing machine about once a month by running a hot water cycle with bleach. Be sure that you do not use more than the recommended dosage of bleach for your washer. This information may be visible on the bleach dispenser or in the washer's manual.
- Clean underneath the lid of the washer using a soft cloth or sponge and clean water or a mild soap solution. While you are at it, clean the top of the washer that sits beneath the lid as well.
- If you have hard water and mineral deposits have appeared on your machine, refer to your manual for removal instructions. If you do not have the manual, contact the manufacturer by telephone or e-mail. Additionally, you can search online for possible suggestions. Certain types of materials may not react well to specific cleaning methods; therefore, it is essential that you check before you use anything such as vinegar or a cleaning agent that includes vinegar.

CLEAN THE DRYER

Did you know that an improperly maintained dryer could cause a fire? Lint build up in the dryer and its exhaust duct can cause many problems. It can block the flow of air, preventing your clothes from drying properly. It can create excessive heat build up. It can even result in a fire in some models of dryers.

Fortunately, you can avoid all of these potential problems with a few preventative measures. A few precautions should be taken whenever you use the dryer. The first thing you should do if you have not already done so is to read the precautionary statements that are included with the dryer's manual.

Cleaning Steps

- Maintain a clutter free zone around the dryer. Don't use the top of the dryer as a storage place. Allow empty space to exist around all of the dryer's sides, as well as the back of the dryer.
- Avoid using the dryer for clothes that have been exposed to volatile chemicals including gasoline, cleaning solvents, cooking oils, and finishing stains or oils. Clothing with spills from any of these products should be hand rinsed before placing them into the washer.

Ideally, they should also be washed more than once. Moreover, it is best to hang them outside the home to air dry naturally. If you simply must use the dryer for these, place it on the lowest temperature setting. Remove the clothing immediately, and place it somewhere to cool down completely before putting it away.

- Another important step to take is to remove any lint buildup from the lint trap after every use. Although the lint buildup may not be excessive, this excellent habit will keep you from ever allowing the lint to build up to a dangerous point. In fact, lint is often carried by campers to use as a starter for their campfire.

Annual Cleaning Steps

- Remove the lint trap from the dryer. Use an attachment from a vacuum cleaner to eliminate all signs of accumulated lint from the trap. Vacuum every area of the lint trap that is accessible. You can also use a lint brush to remove as much lint as possible, but it will not be as efficient.
- Vacuum the floor beneath the dryer and the wall behind it to remove all traces of lint, dust, and dirt. To do this properly, you will need to remove the dryer from its location. Just pull it out far enough to allow you to complete the task. Exercise caution if you have a gas dryer and make sure that you don't disrupt the connection. If the floor is dirty, wet mop it now and allow it to dry before replacing the dryer.
- Make a visual inspection of the exhaust duct. When you are inspecting and cleaning the exhaust duct, you need to unplug the dryer from the electrical outlet. Use a vacuum cleaner attachment to remove all signs of lint accumulation from the duct.
- Make a visual inspection of the exhaust hood that is on the exterior of the home. For this step, you will need to turn the dryer on and then go outside to look at the exhaust hood. An ideal time to do this check is when you have a load of clothes in the dryer anyway. Inspect it to ensure that the flaps are moving properly and are not being blocked by something such as a nest or debris. If the flaps are working properly, they will be moving without restriction. If the location of the hood makes it difficult for you to see the flaps, use a hand mirror to see what is happening. If something is blocking the duct, remove it when the dryer is unplugged.
- If you do not have rigid duct material, then replace it. The plastic or foil accordion type ductwork traps lint more easily than a corrugated semi-rigid metal duct. They are also more susceptible to damage such as kinks and dents, which can reduce the air flow and increase drying time.

If you prefer, you can hire a professional to clean the dryer for you. If you decide to do so, have the cleaning service clean the interior of the dryer as well.

IRON A DUVET COVER

A duvet cover is large and cumbersome, making it difficult to clean and iron. If you are cleaning your duvet cover and searching for an easier way to smooth it out, consider the following alternative ironing methods. Folding and Ironing: Once the duvet cover is dry, carefully fold it in half and drape it over your ironing board. Ensuring that both halves of the duvet cover are smoothed out, gently iron the cover over low heat. Do not iron a crease into the duvet cover where it is folded, but rather hang your duvet cover from a shower curtain rod or over the back of a couch or bed until it has fully dried after ironing.

Hang Drying: If using an iron is not working properly, consider hanging the duvet cover to dry it. Allow it to begin the drying process in a dryer, but remove it after 10 to 15 minutes of drying. The cover should still be damp. Shake the wrinkles out of the cover, smooth it out over a table or bed, and hang the cover to dry by a clothesline or shower curtain rod.

IRON WITH STARCH

Although many people assume that it is difficult or expensive to iron with starch, the process is actually quite easy to accomplish cheaply at home. Professional dry cleaning services offer added convenience, but you can achieve a similarly crisp and starched clothing appearance with some simple techniques at home. Read on for advice about how to mix starch for ironing purposes and use it during your ironing.

How to Make Starch: Starch that is used for ironing purposes is typically a combination of cornstarch and water. Although you can purchase commercially manufactured ironing starches, which often contain additional scents and ingredients, you can just as easily create your own starch spray mixture at home.

Mix 1 tbsp. cornstarch with 1 cup of water. You can increase the concentration of the starch for added crispness in your clothing. Stir the cornstarch into the water until it is entirely dissolved, then transfer the mixture to a small spray bottle.

Ironing a Shirt: When ironing a shirt with starch, begin by ironing the back and front of the shirt body. Ensure that you have set the iron to the appropriate temperature for the type of fabric that you will iron. Lay the shirt over the ironing board so that the sleeves hang over the sides.

Begin by ironing out the large creases in the back of the shirt. Move the iron steadily but not too quickly. Do not stop the iron during the ironing process, as you run the risk of burning the shirt fabric. Be careful to iron the pleats of the shirt down along the pleat. Once you have ironed the surface of the shirt that is laid out upon the ironing board, move the shirt so that all other sections of the body are available for ironing. Take care while ironing the front of the shirt. Avoid ironing over the buttons, although you may iron between them safely. Continue by ironing the sleeves of the shirt. Lay them out flat upon the ironing board and iron around the buttons. Follow the crease from the shoulder of the shirt down, and try to iron along that crease all the way to the cuff of the sleeve. At this point, you are ready to starch your shirt.

Starching a Shirt: Begin by starching the collar of the shirt. Spread the shirt out and spray starch over the inside of the collar. Before it dries, iron the inside of the collar flat. Continue ironing the collar until the starch has dried completely.

Next, reposition the shirt so that the outside of the collar is over the ironing board. Repeat the process by spraying starch over the collar and ironing it flat until the starch has dried. A starched collar is less likely to fold under than an unstarched collar, even if it is ironed.

Next, iron the cuffs of the sleeves and the buttonholes. You can repeat the process of starching and ironing from the collar of the shirt. When you have finished, hang the shirt to dry. You will have a crisp, clean shirt that retains its shape over many hours of wearing.

REMOVING YELLOW STAINS FROM WHITE CLOTHES

If you are fond of clothes made from white fabric, it's always disheartening to discover yellow stains. However, by knowing what process to follow in order to remove them, you will realize that they are not as much of a hassle as they seem.

- *Step 1:* Identify Cause: Though the cause of yellow stains may not be immediately evident, you may find yourself able to work it out with a little investigative work. For example, if the staining occurs around the collar and cuffs, consider whether this may be due to a particular lotion or sunscreen that you use. However, if the entire garment has developed a yellow tinge then it is likely to be the fault of items it has been washed with. This will help you to determine what method to use to rectify it.
- *Step 2:* Spot Stains: Begin the process of treating yellow stains by mixing a thick solution of soda crystals and water in a clean empty container. Lay the garment out on a flat surface and apply the mixture directly to the stain. Using a toothbrush or nailbrush, gently scrub at the stain while continually checking the status of it to determine whether there is any change. When the staining disappears, rinse with warm clean water and laundry detergent before allowing it to dry. If this doesn't work, add some white vinegar to the above soda crystal solution. Leave the mixture in place on the garment to soak for at least half an hour before scrubbing the stain away.
- *Step 3:* Stubborn Stains: Where the yellow stains prove too stubborn to be removed by the above methods, use a mixture of lemon juice and salt. Cover the stains with salt before following this with lemon juice and scrubbing the mixture with a small stiff bristled brush. Rinse

it with warm water and standard laundry detergent before leaving it to dry in direct sunlight, if possible.

Where this does not work, mix a solution of peroxide lemon juice and water and apply it to the yellow stains. Begin by scrubbing the stain to determine whether this removes the stain and leaving the garment in direct sunlight, if this doesn't work.

If the material is suitable, apply a few drops of neat bleach or peroxide directly to the stains and scrub to remove the stains. Once the stain is removed, rinse the garment with laundry detergent.

- *Step 4:* Colour Change: If the staining have affected the white shade of the entire garment it will be necessary to soak it in a strong solution of Borax and hot water. Use this method initially before attempting the same with bleach if it does not work. After the garment has been washed and rinsed, allow it to dry in direct sunlight.

IRON SATIN

Satin is a dressy fabric made of polyester that comes in many beautiful colours, and is not difficult to iron to keep it looking great. Polyester is not a fabric that wrinkles easily, but you can apply an iron to it to make it look smooth and pressed, especially if they have not been worn for some time.

Iron Settings for Satin: Set you iron on low heat when you iron your satin garments. For satin garments that you packed away and want to get ready for wearing, use a setting of 4 on your iron. Otherwise, set your iron anywhere between 1 and 3. High temperatures will burn satin, so you will want to avoid damaging your good dresses if they are made of satin.

Ironing Satin: Place your satin garment on your ironing board. When you iron satin, move the iron quickly across the fabric. Polyester fabrics do not require heavy pressure from an iron. Use long, smooth strokes with your iron over the satin, moving the garment on the ironing board as you iron. When you are finished, turn off your iron and hang your satin garment up. If the satin garment is worn infrequently, place a plastic garment cover over it. This will protect it from dust in your closet.

IRON RAW SILK

Raw silk is a beautiful material for clothing but it can be difficult to care for when it comes time to clean garments made from this fibre. Raw silk is best cleaned by dry cleaning, but it is possible to iron a blouse, jacket, or dress using the right iron settings, the ironing board, and a hand towel.

Iron Settings for Raw Silk: Turn on your iron on low heat. Do not use the steamer to release water while ironing, as water will damage the silk. Unlike other natural fibres such as cotton and linen, water that comes in contact with heat on silk will cause a stain mark. Set the iron heat dial at 1 or 2, which are the two lowest settings. Do not turn the dial any higher than these when ironing silk. Ironing Raw Silk: Set the raw silk garment on the ironing board so that it lays flat. Place the unfolded hand towel over the garment, and lay the iron on top it. The towel will protect the fabric from coming into direct contact with the iron. Quickly move the iron across the towel without pressing hard on it. Set the iron upright on the ironing table and lift up the towel. Check and see if the wrinkles came out. If not, repeat the procedure a second time. Move the garment on the ironing board and continue to iron in this manner until all of the wrinkled areas are ironed out. When you finish ironing, turn off the iron and hang your raw silk garment in your wardrobe or closet.

REMOVE LINKS FROM A WRIST WATCH

If your wrist watch is too big on you, you can adjust the size by removing a few links. Follow these instructions to quickly and easily create a perfect fit for your watch.

- *Step 1:* Try on the Watch: In order to get the size you need, you need to wear the watch as normal. The best way to know what size you need is to pinch the middle of one of the arm bands. This will tell you exactly how many links to remove in order to make the watch fit correctly. Note that you will not remove the exact links you pinched. Instead, you will remove an equal amount of links from each band so that the watch will not look lopsided.
- *Step 2:* Locate Removable Links: On either side of the clasp, every watch has about 3 links that can be easily removed. These are characterized by a small hole on either side of the link. Count out how many holes there are on your watch to determine if there are enough removable links.
- *Step 3:* Remove Links: To remove links, use the jewelry punch. This will easily fit into the small hole of the watch. When you push the punch into the space where the hole is, you will notice a peg going out the other end. This is the peg that holds the unit in place. Divide the number of links being removed by 2. This is the number of links you will remove. Count down the links and remove the second peg to remove only the links you need for the perfect fit.
- *Step 4:* Reattach Links: Use the same peg you pushed out to connect the links to the other end that you removed. Repeat the same process on the other side. Make sure to try the watch on to see if the right amount of links have been removed. The watch should be somewhat loose, but if the watch can easily turn on your wrist, the band is still too loose. You can remove one link at a time in order to make sure you have a perfectly fitting watch. Hold on to the links in case you sell the watch or pass it on to a family member.

IRON TAFFETA

Taffeta can be extremely difficult to deal with. This is not to say you cannot do anything about wrinkles. By following a few simple and easy steps, you will be to get rid of wrinkles on your taffeta clothing.

- *Step 1:* Preheat Iron: Plug in your iron and turn the dial to the lowest setting. This is usually the silk setting on most irons. If there is not silk setting, simply turn the dial to the lowest possible setting.
- *Step 2:* Cover and Iron: Use a thin, damp, cotton cloth to cover the area you are looking to iron. Iron gently in order to avoid creating shiny spots in the fabric. Move the cloth as you get rid of all the wrinkles in the fabric. Hang up the garment as soon as you are done.
- *Step 3:* Use a Steamer: The steamer is the best tool to use when getting rid of wrinkles in taffeta. Simply wave the steamer wand in front of the garment and remove all wrinkles. Use your hands to smooth out any dificult patches.

IRON VISCOSE

Knowing how to iron viscose shirts will help to save you money at the dry cleaners. There is no reason why you should not be able to iron your own shirt at home. You just need to follow some quick and easy steps in order to get the best results.

- Step 1: Wash Your shirt: For the best results, you need to start with a clean shirt. Do not put the shirt in the dryer as the material does not respond well to high temperatures. Instead, transfer the shirt immediately to the ironing board, The wetness will help in ironing out any wrinkles.
- *Step 2:* Preheat the Iron: Plug in your iron and set the temperature gauge to rayon. If your iron does not have a rayon setting, it may read as silk, or low. Turn off the steam function as you will be using the water in the shirt for steam.
- *Step 3:* Iron and Hang: Viscose does not respond well to direct heat. Place a cotton cloth over the shirt before ironing in order to avoid shiny material and iron spots on the shirt. Lift the iron to check the status of the wrinkles. When the shirt has been completely ironed, hang to finish drying.

REMOVE YELLOW STAINS CAUSED BY BLEACH

Yellow stains caused by bleach are notoriously difficult to remove, but there are some simple ways to restore clothes and carpets in no time! While yellow stains on carpeting can be relatively easy to clean, stains on certain clothing fabrics may be a little more challenging.

- *Step 1:* Prepare the Stained Area: For fabrics, blot the bleach-stained area with a cloth dipped in sodium thiosulfate. This is surprisingly easy to find and is sold as a chemical fixing agent for developing photographs. Depending on how long the bleach has had to sink in, you may need to rub stained areas thoroughly for up to five minutes. Rinse with cold water, and repeat if necessary. It is advised that you wear rubber or latex gloves for this task. For carpets, begin by rinsing the yellow-stained area with cold water and blotting at it repeatedly.

- *Step 2:* Remove the Stains: For yellow stains on fabric that have already settled, saturate a clean white cloth with distilled white vinegar and blot the stain until it has soaked through. Next, simply rinse with cold water and repeat if necessary. Remember not to use a coloured cloth as this may intensify the stain and remember that extensive application of vinegar to fabric may degrade and weaken the fibres.

For carpets, mix ¼ tablespoon of washing liquid and 250ml of warm water together. Blot this into the stain repeatedly, working from the edge of the stain to the center. Repeat until the stain has been lifted before adding another application of the mixed solution the remainder of the stain for 5 to 10 minutes.

Continue this process until there is no more bleach being transferred onto the cloth that you are using. The fading smell of bleach will act as an indicator as to how much longer it should take. Finally, rinse extensively with cold water until your carpet is fresh once more.

- *Step 3:* Lay Them Out to Dry: This step is very important and dictates how well removal of the yellow stains will work. For fabrics, it is best to wet them first before laying them outside to dry in the sun. The sun's rays and oxygen given off by grass and plants counteract bleaching and will help provide a better overall stain removal. The optimum time for drying to take is between 4 to 6 hours. After this, the fabric should be restored to its original quality.
- *Step 4:* Drastic Measures: Occasionally, you will come across a yellow stain caused by bleach that cannot be removed by the above methods. In these situations, there are only a few tactics you could take to help avoid throwing away a much-loved piece of clothing. First, you may be able to cover a tiny stain with a permanent marker if you can find a closely-matched colour, but make sure that you are happy with making such a bold move before committing to it.

Alternatively, you could buy sodium hydrosulfite from local cleaners' stores and strip the entire garment of colour. Once done, you are free to re-dye the garment in any colour you wish!

IRON VELVET

Velvet is an extremely temperamental fabric. If you use direct heat on the material, you will end up damaging the plush fibres. The best way to get rid of wrinkles is through the use of steam. Here are three different ways you can get rid of wrinkles in velvet

- *Step 1:* Use a Steamer: The absolute best way to get rid of wrinkles is to use a steamer. Wave the steamer over sections of the material which have wrinkles. This will loosen the fibres and encourage them to flatten out with gravity on your side. You can also use your hands in order to smooth wrinkles out of the material.
- *Step 2:* Use Your Iron: Though you cannot use your iron to actually iron the fabric, your iron has steam which pours out of it. Turn your iron to the hottest temperature with the steam turned on. Pass the iron in front of the fabric in order to steam it. Many models will come with a steam button to inject extra steam. Use this on difficult patches.
- *Step 3:* Take a Shower: Hang up the velvet in the bathroom with you while you take a shower. The steam from the shower will permeate the fabric and help to loosen wrinkles. After you dry off, use your hands to smooth out the wrinkles.

IRON FLAT FRONT PANTS

Ironing flat front pants creates a vertical crease in each leg only to the bottom of the zipper placket. Use these tips to press casual or flat front dress pants.

Press Above the Pant Legs First: Open the zipper of the flat front pants, and slide the pants onto the ironing board's narrow end from the waistband to the bottom of the zipper placket. Press the entire waistband, including belt loops, turning the pants around the ironing board. Press beside the zipper from the waistband towards the pant hems. Press inside the pocket facings. Turn the pants to the right side seam and press it down smoothly. Continue around the rear of the pants, pressing down all pocket edges and flaps, and press down the left side seam.

Press Pant Leg Creases: Remove the pants from the ironing board. Match the inseam and outseam of each leg at the hem, and lay the pants on the board with the pant legs together. Press the front crease into the top pant leg, then the rear crease, then press the seam. Fold the pressed leg back over the waistband. Press the lower pant leg, front crease first, back crease, then the seam. Press the creases again on the opposite sides of each pant leg.

REMOVE SILICONE CAULK FROM CLOTHING

Silicone caulk is a handy substance to have around the house, useful for any number of sealing jobs. Unfortunately, it sticks to clothing even more easily than most other substances.

Luckily, there are a number of different methods you can use to remove it.

- *Step 1:* Freezing: Instead of trying to wipe the caulk off the piece of clothing, put it in the freezer, making sure the caulk is exposed. You could just wait for it to dry, but freezing it is quicker.
- *Step 2:* Removing the Bulk: Once the caulk is solid, carefully peel it off the article of clothing. The biggest chunk should come off in a glob.
- *Step 3:* Removing the Remainder: There will usually be some caulk residue left in the fibres of the cloth. Saturate that area with WD-40 or a similar degreaser (making sure whatever you use won't harm your clothing). Then use the flat-edged tool, scrape off the residue. Apply more WD-40 as needed. Continue this process until all the residue has been removed from your clothes, then run through the wash cycle as usual.

REPAIR YOUR IRON

An iron is used to straighten out the wrinkled clothes and to kill any microbial activity occurring inside the clothing. Very little repairing is needed in a well-made iron. Most repairs are needed for handles, faulty cords and clogged holes from where steam is released. You can easily repair your iron by following the steps described below.

- *Step 1:* Identify the Problem: Read the manual provided with your iron. Know what sort of problem exists and what is required before starting with the repairs. Check thermostat and electric cord if the iron does not heat or heats up exceedingly high when the power is switched on. If the steam is not coming out properly or the water is being spat out check the bottom of the iron (sole plate) and holes from where steam is released. Last but not the least, check the sole plate if the clothes are clinging to it. Now that you know the problem, follow the required steps.
- *Step 2:* Take Appropriate Precautions: Switch off or disconnect the iron and leave it to cool off properly. If you start repairing the iron while it is still plugged to the circuit, you might get an electric shock.
- *Step 3:* Repairing the Power Cord: Remove the cover panel using appropriate screw driver. Replace the power cord if it is faulty. Check if the thermostat is calibrating properly. If not, replace it too. Screw the cover panel back on. Switch the iron back on to check the iron is heating properly.
- *Step 4:* Cleaning the Sole Plate: Use a damp cloth with salt on it and rub the bottom of the iron or simply use a nylon pad with water and soap. If, however, the stain is a stubborn one, some toothpaste can

be rubbed with a soft cloth on the stain. If the bottom iron has starch build up on it use white vinegar. You can also mix equal amount of vinegar and salt and use it on the sole plate after heating the solution. Do not employ wire gauze pads or any other kind of pads that may scratch the surface of the non-stick iron. Also, remember not to use abrasive cleaners as they will damage the non-stick coating on the iron. Once the cleaning of this part is done, move towards cleaning the water container or reservoir of the iron.

- *Step 5:* Remove Burn Marks: Cover the whole iron with paper except bottom of the non-stick iron. Take the iron in open air so the oven cleaner fumes do not spread inside the house. Now directly sprinkle oven cleaner on the bottom. Leave it for three minutes, and then wash the bottom with cold water and remove the paper.
- *Step 6:* Cleaning the Water Container: Fill 1/4 of the container with white vinegar. Now empty the container by steaming the iron. The fumes of vinegar will open the holes that were earlier clogged by mineral deposits. Fill the container again with vinegar and repeat the process. Continue repeating the process until the holes are totally devoid of the deposits. After ensuring the complete removal of deposits, fill the container with distilled water and wash it thoroughly making sure no vinegar remains in the reservoir or the holes.

MAKE YOUR IRON NON-STICK

The hot under-surface of your iron goes through a lot of wear and tear through normal operation. The high temperature and the friction provided by the clothes greatly increase the chances of it getting scratched. A scratched and rough iron not only damages clothes, but also performs poorly. If you have an old or damaged iron, you should coat the underside with a Teflon-based non-stick coating. Your iron, as a result, will not only press clothes more efficiently, but will also use less electricity. Follow the simple steps given below to coat your iron with non-stick material.

- *Step 1:* Buy Teflon Base for Iron: Find a Teflon-based iron shield from a local store or online. Some iron shields have holes in them to allow steam to pass through. These are generally superior in quality to those with steam vents.
- *Step 2:* Take Necessary Precautions: When you receive the package containing the iron shield, open it and read the instructions. Once you are ready to start installing the iron shield, you should switch off the power supply to iron before attaching Teflon to the iron to avoid any chance of an electric shock.
- *Step 3:* Attaching the Iron Shield: The attaching method is different among brands but mostly it involves slipping on the shield on the

iron. Make sure that the iron surface is clean before covering its surface or simply clean the iron surface using salt on a damp cloth. The iron shield is manufactured using polytetrafluoroethylene, simply known as Teflon in the market. It is a plastic based product. Scratches can damage it so be sure not to use it on a very rough surface.

- *Step 4:* Putting it to the Test: After you have installed your iron shield, put it to the test by using your iron to press your clothes. You will not only see a marked difference in the quality of ironing but will also be able to finish the job quicker. Your iron now will not have to be set to high temperatures to get the job done thereby reducing electricity consumption.

CLEAN A NON-STICK IRON

Cleaning a non-stick iron is a relatively simple process. An Iron is used for the sole purpose of straightening the rumpled and wrinkled clothes and to kill microbial activity, if any, in the clothes. Two areas of iron need cleaning. These include the bottom non-stick plate of the iron (sole plate) and the container that holds water (reservoir). Usually detergents, starch etc., can get stuck to the sole plate. Also, minerals from water clog the holes from where the water in the form of steam is released by the iron. In order to deal with these issues, follow the simple steps described below and easily clean you non-stick iron.

Tools and Materials Required: To clean the non-stick iron you will need baking soda, distilled water, oven cleaner, salt, soft cloth and white vinegar.

- *Step 1:* Take Appropriate Precautions: Switch off or disconnect the iron and leave it to cool off properly. If you start cleaning the iron while it is still plugged to the circuit, you might get an electric shock.
- *Step 2:* Cleaning the Non-Stick Sole Plate: Use a damp cloth with salt on it and rub the bottom of the iron or simply use a nylon pad with water and soap. If, however, the stain is a stubborn one, some toothpaste can be rubbed with a soft cloth on the stain. If the bottom iron has starch build up on it use white vinegar. You can also mix equal amount of vinegar and salt and use it on the sole plate after heating the solution. Do not employ wire gauze pads or any other kind of pads that may scratch the surface of the non-stick iron. Also, remember not to use abrasive cleaners as they will damage the non-stick coating on the iron. Once the cleaning of this part is done, move towards cleaning the water container or reservoir of the iron.
- *Step 3:* Removal of Burn Marks: If there are burn marks on the sole plate of the iron, cover the whole iron with paper. Do not cover the bottom of the non-stick iron. Take the iron in open air so the oven cleaner fumes do not spread inside the house. Now directly sprinkle

oven cleaner on the bottom. Leave it for three minutes. Now wash the bottom with cold water and remove the paper

- *Step 4:* Cleaning the Water Container: Fill 1/4 of the container with vinegar. Now empty the container by steaming the iron. The fumes of vinegar are typically strong enough to open the holes that were earlier clogged by mineral deposits. Fill the container again with vinegar and repeat the process. Continue repeating the process until the holes are totally devoid of the deposits. After ensuring the complete removal of deposits, fill the container with distilled water and wash it thoroughly making sure no vinegar remains in the reservoir or the holes.

You should now be all set to use your iron again.

13

Table Setting, Skirting and Napkins

SETTING THE TABLE

The following guide is a basic set of rules for setting the table. It can be used for setting a formal as well as an informal one.

An attractive table adds to the enjoyment of a meal. To set the table, you need a "place setting" for each person. A place setting is all the items each person needs for eating. This includes the following appointments (any item used to set a table):

- Dinnerware (plates, cups, saucers, and bowls);
- Glassware (glasses of all shapes and sizes);
- Flatware (forks, spoons, and knives);
- Napkins;
- Centerpiece; and
- placemats or tablecloths, optional.

How a table should be set is determined in a large part by the serving style. Every family has its own eating style. There is really no right and wrong way to serve a meal, but there are three traditional serving styles:

- Family,
- Formal, and
- Buffet.

For the Foods Level C Guide, the family style table setting is most appropriate. Food is either:

- Passed around the table for everyone to serve themselves, or
- Portioned out by the head of the family and full plates are served to each family member.

The following rules for setting a table correspond to the numbers seen in the table setting.

1. The flatware, plate, and napkin should be one inch from the edge of the table.

2. The plate is always in the center of the place setting.
3. The dinner fork is placed at the left of the plate.
4. If a salad fork is used, it is placed to the left of the dinner fork.
5. The napkin is placed to the left of the fork, with the fold on the left. It can also go under a fork, or on top of the plate.
6. The knife is placed to the right of the plate with the sharp blade facing in towards the plate.T
7. he teaspoon is placed to the right of the knife.
8. If a soup spoon is needed, it is placed to the right of the teaspoon.
9. The soup bowl may be placed on the dinner plate.
10. The drinking glass is placed at the tip of the knife.
11. If a salad plate is used, place it just above the tip of the fork.
12. The cup or mug is placed to the top right of the spoons.

TIPS FOR SETTING THE TABLE

- The table should be clean; it can be left bare or a table covering can be used as the background for the food and appointments placed on it. A table covering helps protect the table and muffles the noise of clanking glassware and dishes.
- Placemats or tablecloths can be used for special occasions.
- Choose dinnerware and flatware appropriate for the occasion and that compliment the other table appointments. Match or blend colours and textures in the dishes or contrast with something different.
- Use appointments that match the meal or food to be served. That means, a snack can be served on a paper plate with paper napkins while a home-cooked dinner should be served on attractive dishes to show off the meal. On the other hand, party food may use the family's best dinnerware and cloth napkins.
- Only the utensils necessary for the meal need to be placed on the table.
- Put down the correct number of placemats or a tablecloth, if these are being used.
- If there is room, serving utensils and dishes can be placed in the center of the table or on a nearby counter or server.
- The centerpiece should be attractive. Simple ones such as fresh flowers, a plant, or fruit can be used. If candles are used, they should be lit with the flame above eye level. Be sure that the centerpiece is:
  - low, so that people at the table can see over it,
  - colourful and blends with the colours of the tablecloth and dishes;
  - fresh and clean looking.

Learn the following tips that deal with eating manners so you won't be embarrassed!

- Try some of every food served even if you don't like it or don't think you will.
- Avoid playing with foods on your plate.
- Ask to have foods passed to you, rather than reaching in front of someone else or across the table.
- Eat quietly with your mouth closed. Wait to speak until you have swallowed any food in your mouth.
- Take small bites. Eat all that you take on your fork or spoon in one bite.
- Look neat and talk about cheerful topics to make mealtimes pleasant.
- Pass food at the table to the right with your left hand. Try not to blow on soup to cool it - it is not polite.
- Cut salad with a knife if the pieces are too large to fit in your mouth.
- Use a small piece of bread as a "pusher" to help guide food onto your fork.
- Break off a whole piece of bread or roll into 2 or more small pieces.
- Leave your silverware on the plate or saucer under a bowl when you have finished.

SIMPLE RULES FOR TABLE SETTING ETIQUETTE

Table setting etiquette is the proper placement of eating utensils on a table, with the intention that the diner will have everything they need in within convenient reach. When you are planning a dinner party, social gathering or simply setting your own table for the family dinner, follow some basic table setting etiquette to ensure that everyone will have what they need to completely enjoy the meal.

When it comes to place settings, proper attention should be paid to plates and napkin. The base plate is the center of the setting and the main focus. A side plate, if any, should be set to the left side of the base plate. For a formal dinner, the napkin can be placed in the center of the base plate. For less formal settings, fold the napkin and place it on the left side of the base plate and forks. Don't place the forks on top of the napkin-a common error.

Move to cutlery. Cutlery generally consists of a fork, knife and spoon. However, depending on the courses of the meal, there can be salad forks, soup spoons, tea spoons and even shellfish utensils. Table etiquette dictates that forks will always go on the left, while knives and spoons are on the right. When it comes to cutlery placement, work from the outside in. This concept means that the utensils on the outside of the setting will be used first, such as the soup spoon and salad fork. A typical setting might look like this, from far left to far right: salad fork, entrée fork, base plate with napkin, dinner knife and soup spoon. Glassware finishes off the basic table setting. Most meals will consist of a water glass and wine glass.

Position the water glass right above the knife, with the wine glass to the right of that. If there is no wine glass, the water glass alone is fine. There are more rules for additional glasses, such as for sherry or when there are two wines, but these are basics for place settings, proper enough for everything but the most formal of dinners.

Table settings get increasingly complicated if you are serving additional courses or foods, such as soup, seafood and dessert. For seafood, place the seafood fork on the far right, after the spoon. This is the only exception to the fork-on-the-left rule.

Dessert cutlery should be set perpendicular to the other utensils, above the base plate. A bread or dessert plate should be set in the upper left, above the forks. A soup bowl should sit on the base plate, and then be cleared away when the soup course is finished.

Finally, all pieces of a proper place setting should be spaced evenly-the same space between cutlery, the same space between glasses and so forth. When the place setting looks balanced and symmetrical, it further enhances the appeal of a proper place setting.

FORK ETIQUETTE

When used in conjunction with a knife to cut and consume food in Western social settings, two forms of fork etiquette are common. In the *European style*, the diner keeps the fork in his or her left hand, while in the *American style* the fork is shifted between the left and right hands. The *American style* is most common in the United States. but the European style is considered proper in other countries.

Originally, the traditional European method, once the fork was adopted as a utensil, was to transfer the fork to the right hand after cutting food, as it had been considered proper for all utensils to be used with the right hand only. This tradition was brought to America by British colonists and is still in use in the United States. Europe adopted the more rapid style of eating in relatively modern times.

EUROPEAN STYLE

The European style, also called the continental style, is to hold the fork in the left hand and the knife in the right. Once a bite-sized piece of food has been cut, it is conducted straight to the mouth by the left hand. The tines remain pointing down.

The knife and fork are both held with the handle running along the palm and extending out to be held by thumb and forefinger. This style is sometimes called "hidden handle" because the palm conceals the handle.

AMERICAN STYLE

In the American style, also called the *zig-zag method* or *fork switching*, the knife is initially held in the right hand and the fork in the left. Holding food to the plate with the fork tines-down, a single bite-sized piece is cut with the knife.

The knife is then set down on the plate, the fork transferred from the left hand to the right hand, and the food is brought to the mouth for consumption. The fork is then transferred back to the left hand and the knife is picked up with the right. In contrast to the European hidden handle grip, in the American style the fork is held much like a spoon or pen once it is transferred to the right hand to convey food to the mouth. Though called "American style", this style originated in Europe.

HYBRID STYLE

Though not endorsed by most etiquette guides, in the United States, a hybrid of the American and European styles is becoming prevalent. In this style, the fork is held in the dominant hand while cutting with the knife in off hand. The tines of the fork are normally kept up for use as a scoop.

SOUTHEAST ASIAN STYLE

The South East Asian style is similar to the European style, wherein the fork is held in the left hand throughout consumption (except with certain dishes when a fork is more suitable). The difference is that a spoon is often used in the right hand and knives are rarely used. Rice and soups are a staple of the diet in South East Asian countries, so using a spoon would be practical in such dishes.

The spoon is the main utensil in bringing food into the mouth, in tandem with using a fork. The spoon could also be used for manipulating food in the plate and as an alternative for a knife. Often dishes require slicing before serving or sliced into small portions before cooking to relinquish the use of a knife.

PLACEMENT OF FORKS

Tables are often set with two or more forks, meant to be used for different courses; for example, a salad fork, a meat fork, and a dessert fork. Some institutions wishing to give an impression of high formality set places with many different forks for meals of several courses, although many etiquette authorities regard this as vulgar and prefer that the appropriate cutlery be brought in with each course.

It should not be necessary for the diner to distinguish between types of forks; forks are used in order from outside to inside, with the exception of oyster forks, which are placed on the right side, the tines nested in the bowl of a spoon.

CUTLERY ETIQUETTE

In western countries, such as Australia and the United States, there are a variety of ways to signify that one has completed their meal. Of these, most often used is placing the fork at the 5 o'clock position, with the knife either in the top right corner or together with the fork at the 5 o'clock position. If one is still eating their meal the fork is to be placed at the 8 o'clock position and the knife at the 4 o'clock. In European countries such as Germany, the placement of these utensils is at the 4 o'clock position. The placement of the utensils in this position also serves as an indicator to the waitress/waiter that your plate can be removed.

FORMAL TABLE SETTING

This is the table setting for festive family dinners, holiday celebrations, weddings and semi-formal events. A variety of specialty pieces are used depending on the formality of the occasion or event and meal plan.

Formal table setting includes dinner plate and fork; salad plate and fork;knife; bread and butter plate; butter knife; spoon; water and wine stemware; and linens.

- To the left of dinner plate (outside in): individual salad fork (when salad is served before the main course), and dinner fork.
- Above salad fork and dinner fork is bread and butter plate and butter knife.
- A salad plate is not set. If salad is served before the main course, the salad plate is placed on top of the service plate.
- At the center: service plate, with napkin or soup bowl at the center. Appetizer or other first course is placed on top of the service plate.
- When it is time for the main course, the used appetizer, soup or salad plate is removed along with the service plate. The entree is immediately served on the dinner plate.
- To the right of dinner plate (outside in): soup spoon (if serving an appetizer in lieu of soup, place cocktail or oyster fork to the right of knife), place or dinner knife.
- Dinner spoons and forks may be placed horizontally above the place setting, with spoon facing right and fork facing to the left, or may be brought in on the dessert plates.
- To the right above knife (from left to right forming triangle): water goblet, (white) wine glass, and champagne flute.
- Cup and saucer with teaspoon may also be brought in with dessert, or served separately.

CASUAL TABLE SETTING

This table setting is designed for everyday use and is suitable for any meal.

Casual table setting includes dinner plate and fork; salad plate and fork; knife; spoon; water and wine glasses; and linens.

- To the left of the dinner plate: napkin, salad fork, place fork. Napkin can also be placed on top of the plate.
- At center: Dinner plate with salad plate or appetizer - if one is to be served - should already be in placed.
- Set bread and butter plate to the upper left of a dinner plate. Lay butler spreader horizontally across bread and butter plate with handle to the right.
- To the right of dinner plate (outside in): teaspoon (can be placed on the table or brought in later with dessert), dinner knife.
- To the top of dinner knife and teaspoon: water goblet and wine goblet may be placed.

BUFFET TABLE SETTING

This table setting is based on your needs and space limitations. Food are arranged down the table in succession. Using your creativity, you can work with what's best for the situation.

A buffet table setting includes flatware, multiple dinner plates, stemware, and linens (number of settings will depend on number of guests expected).

- Buffet table style is the easiest to serve a large number of guests.
- The food being served and the logical sequence of serving yourself usually determine the layout of the buffet table.
- Dinner plates should come first followed by entree and serving pieces.
- Napkins should be large enough for placement on guest's laps and, along with flatware, should come last so that they need not be carried the entire length of the table. It is also helpful to guests to have flatware wrapped in napkin or tissue.
- Leave enough room between serving bowls so that guests can rest their plates as they move through the line.
- Set up a side table for coffee, tea, and other beverages.
- Dessert can also be set at a side table or the main buffet can be cleared and reset for the dessert.

The type of table setting as well as the food being served can make a meal a success. However, proper table etiquette will set the mood for a comfortable and enjoyable meal experience.

THE TRADITIONAL TABLE SETTING AND COVERS

Table Covers: The first step in setting the table is deciding on the table covering. Conflicted about using a tablecloth or placemats? If you have a beautiful table, consider using placemats instead of a tablecloth. Mats can be plain or patterned, woven or made of rush, as long as they're heatproof. If your table surface needs to be protected or is already damaged, use a tablecloth. The cloth should be big enough to drape 6 inches over each side of the table. Some tablecloths need a heatproof protective mat laid under them to prevent spills from penetrating through to the table surface.

White tablecloths are traditional for formal meals, but you can also use lace or plain-coloured cloths. Patterned cloths are okay, as long as they don't make the table look too cluttered once it's set. If a tablecloth is wrinkled or creased, throw it in a clothes dryer set on "Fluff" or "Air" along with a damp towel.

Cutlery: Don't let the fork run away with the spoon! Forks go on the left, spoons and knives on the right. They should be placed in the order in which they will be used, with the first utensil on the far end from the plate, the second utensil closer towards the plate and so on. Knife blades should be turned towards the plate.

Bring out specialty utensils, like grapefruit spoons or shellfish forks, with the course. Do the same with forks or spoons for dessert.

China: The side plate goes to the left of the place setting. If the first course is a cold one, such as a salad, set the dish at each place before guests sit. If you're serving finger foods that might get messy, set out finger bowls with warm water and a lemon slice. Glasses: If there is one wineglass, place it at the tip of the main-course knife. If there is more than one glass, arrange them in the order they will be used, outermost first. Bring liqueur glasses or brandy balloons to the table with the liqueurs. Napkins: If you are using a fancy fold, place the napkin on top of the main plate. Otherwise, place it on the side plate or underneath the knife and spoon.

Place Cards: Using place cards avoids awkward moments when guests seat themselves and wards off potential problems if a fussy aunt sits next to a sloppy child or a fur-loving fashion slave sits next to a social activist. You can make place cards by simply folding in half an unlined index card and writing in calligraphy.

SERVING OPTIONS

The Buffet: Place the plates, flatware and napkins close to each other on one side of the table. Use large 12-inch plates instead of 9-inch entree plates so diners have enough space to pile on the fixings. Check the table occasionally to refill certain dishes and to rearrange serving platters that are messy.

Of course, make sure you have enough chairs and eating surfaces. Avoid benches and stools without backs if you have elderly guests or toddlers.

For a compromise between a formal dinner and a buffet, set the dishes in the kitchen and have the guests serve themselves. Then serve seconds and dessert at the dining table. The Kids' Table: You may remember as a kid how wearisome adult dinner conversation can be. Setting up a separate table for the kids is a tradition worth upholding. Use brightly coloured paper or plastic plates. The Sunday funny papers make great table covers, as do informal, plain-coloured tablecloths. Buy laundry markers so kids can write on the cloth during the meal. Set out a new cloth the next Thanksgiving; then years down the road you can reminisce and read the cloths. Whichever you choose, use padding to protect the table.

You could also take a tip from restaurants by setting out paper place mats and crayons. Colouring books with a Thanksgiving theme or other activity books can be placed on the kids' table as well.

TABLE AND PLACE SETTINGS SYSTEM

In most traditional Chinese dining, dishes are communal. Although both square and rectangular tables are used for small groups of people, round tables are preferred for large groups, particularly in restaurants, in order to permit easy sharing. Lazy Susans are a common feature.

A basic place-setting consists of a small teacup; a large plate with a small, empty rice bowl; a set of chopsticks, usually on the right of the plate; and a spoon. Additions may include a chopstick holder; a large water or wine glass; and a smaller glass for *baijiu*. At homes and low-end restaurants, napkins may consist of tissues or rolls of toilet paper on the table or need to be provided by the diner. High-end restaurants often provide cloth napkins similar to western dining as part of the place-setting. In all settings, toothpicks may be provided at each setting or in a communal holder.

COURSES

Wide variations exist throughout China, but the vast majority of full-course dinners are very similar in terms of timing and dishes.

SNACKS

Snacks are the first items presented. Two or more small dishes are brought to the table, holding boiled unsalted peanuts, salted roasted peanuts, pickled vegetables, or similar dishes. These may be consumed while ordering or while waiting for other dishes to arrive.

BEVERAGES

Tea is almost always provided, either in advance of the diners' being seated or immediately afterwards. It can be consumed at leisure throughout the meal. (Water is sometimes served, but tea is the default beverage.) A verbal thank you may be offered to the server pouring the refill or, if in the middle of a conversation where it would be rude to interrupt the speaker, the table may be tapped twice with two bent fingers instead. Other drinks are not typically ordered in advance of the food and are usually served by the pitcher or large bottle, to be poured into the glasses on the table. Bottles of beer and *baijiu* will similarly be opened and left on the table among the diners, to be shared among their glasses. In many areas, it is common to offer alcoholic beverages only to the adult men among the diners, although women may request to be served as well.

MAIN COURSE

This typically consists of many dishes, usually roughly one dish per person. White rice is provided in small bowls and food is often consumed over it, flavouring it with their sauces. The rice is consumed little by little along with the other dishes and not separately, unless the diner remains hungry after the last dish has been removed.

A soup may also be served as one of the dishes. At small meals, especially at home, it may replace the diners' beverage entirely.

DIM SUM

Dim sum refers to a style of Cantonese food prepared as small bite-sized or individual portions of food traditionally served in small steamer baskets or on small plates. Dim sum is also well known for the unique way it is served in some restaurants, whereby fully cooked and ready-to-serve dim sum dishes are carted around the restaurant for customers to choose their orders while seated at their tables.

Eating dim sum at a restaurant is usually known in Cantonese as going to "*drink tea*" (yum cha, ò˜6*f*), as tea is typically served with dim sum.

HISTORY

Dim sum is usually linked with the older tradition from *yum cha* (tea tasting), which has its roots in travellers on the ancient Silk Road needing a place to rest. Thus teahouses were established along the roadside. Rural farmers, exhausted after working hard in the fields, would go to teahouses for a relaxing afternoon of tea. At first, it was considered inappropriate to combine tea with food, because people believed it would lead to excessive weight gain. People later discovered that tea can aid in digestion, so teahouse owners began adding various snacks.

The unique culinary art of dim sum originated with the Cantonese in southern China, who over the centuries transformed yum cha from a relaxing respite to a loud and happy dining experience. In Hong Kong, and in most cities and towns in Guangdong province, many restaurants start serving dim sum as early as five in the morning. It is a tradition for the elderly to gather to eat dim sum after morning exercises. For many in southern China, *yum cha* is treated as a weekend family day. More traditional dim sum restaurants typically serve dim sum until mid-afternoon. However, in modern society it has become common place for restaurants to serve dim sum at dinner time, various dim sum items are even sold as take-out for students and office workers on the go.

While dim sum (literally meaning: touch the heart) was originally not a main meal, only a snack, and therefore only meant to touch the heart, it is now a staple of Cantonese dining culture, especially in Hong Kong. Health officials have recently criticized the high amount of saturated fat and sodium in some dim sum dishes, warning that steamed dim sum should not automatically be assumed to be healthy. Health officials recommend balancing fatty dishes with boiled vegetables without sauce.

CUISINE

A traditional dim sum brunch includes various types of steamed buns such as *cha siu baau*, dumplings and rice noodle rolls (cheong fun), which contain a range of ingredients, including beef, chicken, pork, prawns and vegetarian options. Many dim sum restaurants also offer plates of steamed green vegetables, roasted meats, congee porridge and other soups. Dessert dim sum is also available and many places offer the customary egg tart.

Dim sum can be cooked by steaming and frying, among other methods. The serving sizes are usually small and normally served as three or four pieces in one dish. It is customary to order family style, sharing dishes among all members of the dining party. Because of the small portions, people can try a wide variety of food.

DISHES

Dim sum brunch restaurants have a wide variety of dishes, usually several dozen. Among the standard fare of dim sum are the following:

MAIN

- *Gao*, or *Dumpling*: Jiao zi is a standard in most teahouses. They are made of ingredients wrapped in a translucent rice flour or wheat starch skin, and are different from *jiaozi* found in other parts of China. Though common, steamed rice-flour skins are quite difficult to make. Thus, it is a good demonstration of the chef's artistry to make these translucent dumplings. There are also dumplings with vegetarian ingredients, such as tofu and pickled cabbage.
- *Har gow* (shrimp dumplings): A delicate steamed dumpling with whole or chopped-up shrimp filling and thin wheat starch skin.
- *Teochew-style dumplings*: A dumpling said to have originated from the Chaozhou (Teochew) prefecture of eastern Guangdong province, it

contains peanuts, garlic, chives, pork, dried shrimp, and Chinese mushrooms in a thick dumpling wrapper made from glutinous rice flour or Tang flour. It is usually served with a small dish of chili oil.

- *Guotie* (pot stickers): Northern Chinese style of dumpling (steamed and then pan-fried jiaozi), usually with meat and cabbage filling. Note that although potstickers are sometimes served in dim sum restaurants, they are not considered traditional Cantonese dim sum.
- *Shaomai*: Small steamed dumplings with either pork, prawns or both inside a thin wheat flour wrapper. Usually topped off with crab roe and mushroom.
- *Haam Seoi Gaau*: deep fried oval-shaped dumpling made with rice-flour and filled with pork and chopped vegetables. The rice-flour surrounding is sweet and sticky, while the inside is slightly salty.
- *Dumpling soup*: soup with one or two big dumplings.
- *Bau* : Baked or steamed, these fluffy buns made from wheat flour are filled with food items ranging from meat to vegetables to sweet bean pastes.
- *Char siu baau* : the most popular bun with a Cantonese barbecued pork filling. It can be either steamed to be fluffy and white or baked with a light sugar glaze to produce a smooth golden-brown crust.
- *Shanghai steamed buns*: These dumplings are filled with meat or seafood and are famous for their flavour and rich broth inside. These dumplings are originally Shanghainese so they are not considered traditional Cantonese dim sum. They are typically sold with pork as a filling.
- *Mantou* : plain steamed bun like *cha siu baau* without filling stuff.
- *Phoenix claws:* These are chicken feet, deep fried, boiled, marinated in a black bean sauce and then steamed. This results in a texture that is light and fluffy (due to the frying), while moist and tender. Fung zau are typically dark red in colour. One may also sometimes find plain steamed chicken feet served with a vinegar dipping sauce. This version is known as "White Cloud Phoenix Claws".
- *Steamed meatball* : Finely ground beef is shaped into balls and then steamed with preserved orange peel and served on top of a thin bean-curd skin.
- *Spare ribs*: In the west, it is mostly known as spare ribs collectively. In the east, it is Char siu when roasted red, or when roasted black. It is typically steamed with douchi or fermented black beans and sometimes sliced chilli.
- *Lotus leaf rice* : Glutinous rice is wrapped in a lotus leaf into a triangular or rectangular shape. It containsegg yolk, dried scallop,

mushroom, water chestnut and meat (usually pork and chicken). These ingredients are steamed with the rice and although the leaf is not eaten, its flavour is infused during the steaming. *Lo mai gai* is a kind of rice dumpling. A similar but lighter variant is known as "Pearl Chicken".

- *Congee* : Thick, sticky rice porridge served with different savory items. The porridge one will see most often is "Duck Egg and Pork Porridge"
- *Sou* : A type of flaky pastry. Char siu is one of the most common ingredient used in dim sum style sou. Another common pastry seen in restaurants are called "Salty Pastry" (yž4lÒ‰ "haam4 seoi2 gok3") which is made with flour and seasoned pork.
- *Taro dumpling* : This is made with mashed taro, stuffed with diced shiitake mushrooms, shrimp and pork, deep-fried in crispy batter.
- *Crispy fried squid* : Similar to fried calamari, the battered squid is deep-fried. A variation of this dish may be prepared with a salt and pepper mix. In some dim sum restaurants, octopus is used instead of squid.

ROLLS

- *Egg roll* : a roll consisting of various types of vegetables — such as sliced carrot, cabbage, mushroom and wood ear fungus — and sometimes meat are rolled inside a thin flour skin and deep fried.
- *Rice noodle rolls* or *coeng fan*: These are wide rice noodles that are steamed and then rolled. They are often filled with different types of meats or vegetables inside but can be served without any filling. Rice noodle rolls are fried after they are steamed and then sprinkled with sesame seeds. Popular fillings include beef, dough fritter, shrimp, and barbecued pork. Often topped with a sweetened soy sauce.
- *Tofu skin roll* : a roll made of Tofu skin

CAKES

- *Turnip cake* : cakes are made from mashed daikon radish mixed with bits of dried shrimp and pork sausage that are steamed and then cut into slices and pan-fried.
- *Taro cake* : cakes made of taro.
- *Water chestnut cake* : cakes made of water chestnut. It is mostly see-through and clear. Some restaurants also serve a variation of water chestnut cake made with bamboo juice.

SWEETS

- *Chien chang go:* "Thousand-layer cake", a dim sum dessert made up of many layers of sweet egg dough.

- *Egg tart:* Composed of a base made from either a flaky puff pastry type dough or a type of non-flaky cookie dough with an egg custard filling, which is then baked. Some high class restaurants put bird's nest on top of the custard. In other places egg tarts can be made of a crust and a filling of egg whites and some where it is a crust with egg yolks. Egg tarts now come in a variety of different flavours, taro, coffee, and strawberry for example. a„»d (po taat) is a Portuguese styled egg custard, common in Hong Kong, with origins in Macau, and has a layer of burnt sugar on the surface.
- *Jin deui* or *Matuan* : Especially popular at Chinese New Year, a chewy dough filled with red bean paste, rolled in sesame seeds, and deep fried.
- *Dou fu fa*: A dessert consisting of silky tofu served with a sweet ginger or jasmine flavoured syrup.
- *Mango pudding* : A sweet, rich mango-flavoured pudding usually with large chunks of fresh mango; often served with a topping ofevaporated milk.
- *Sweet cream buns*: Steamed buns with milk custard filling.
- *Malay Steamed Sponge Cake* : A very soft steamed sponge cake flavoured with molasses.
- *Longan Tofu*: almond-flavoured tofu served with longans, usually cold.

THE HISTORY OF TABLE SKIRTING

The history of table skirts seems to consist of bits and pieces of information as well as a great many educated guesses about the origin of covering the front of a table. Such seemingly unrelated bits of information, some without documentation, are difficult to call a definitive history, yet evidence of table skirts in the past does indicate that the custom existed before the 20th century.

DEFINITION AND FUNCTION

Without much exception, a table skirt in any setting is a fabric or paper drape which covers the front and sides of a table from the surface down nearly to the floor. Occasionally, a skirt covers also the back of the table. A table skirt commonly does not cover the table top which must be draped first with a tablecloth. The skirt is attached to the tablecloth by some temporary means such as Velcro, snaps or basting. The purpose of the skirt is to shield all the legs under the table from view. A table skirt creates an uninterrupted visual impression as well as provides complete modesty for those people seated at the table.

RECENT HISTORY

In 20th century history and in 21st century custom, a banquet or conference table is nearly always skirted especially if it is on a dais or raised platform. This custom probably grew from the inclusion of women in ceremonial or business occasions. A desire to preserve modesty and aesthetic uniformity made the table skirt a welcome addition to a well-dressed table.

KINDS OF TABLE SKIRTS

When the custom of table skirts began, the skirt was always made of fabric. The style of early table skirts is unknown but in 2010, there is no limit to style possibilities. Traditional fabric skirts may be plain, pleated in several ways or shirred. They may be decorated with lace, ribbons and bows or left unadorned. Modern designers have created table skirts in plastic materials, metallics, tissue fabrics, even raffia. It would be possible to find or create a table skirt to lend to any party theme or add to any special occasion.

EARLY DOCUMENTATION

While it was not a dining table but a dressing table that Thomas Chippendale designed in 1762, he did include a fancy fabric skirt that concealed the legs of the table according to The Providence Journal. That table which included a mirror and resembled some contemporary vanity tables apparently set a style that has endured in feminine settings for centuries. The table skirt is no longer associated only with femininity, but the desire to preserve the continuous flow of design below a tabletop is still a consideration.

SPECULATIONS

Little of the Victorian English preoccupation with sex can be firmly documented, but there is ample evidence that the upper class and #039;s need to preserve absolute modesty was nearly an obsession. Ladies, young, old, and elderly, were never to allow a man to glimpse an ankle lest he be engulfed with lust. The devotion to modesty carried into the language which termed human legs as limbs and into decor which sometimes required shielding furniture legs from view.

TABLE SKIRTING TECHNIQUES

Table skirts are an inexpensive and versatile way to add pizzazz to your decor and can provide storage solutions by hiding objects underneath a table. Table skirts can even conceal unattractive plumbing beneath bathroom sinks. Many table skirt techniques involve only a few items and no sewing whatsoever.

ASSEMBLED ITEMS

Measure your table height from the edge to the floor, and select fabric big enough to cover the table. Add on at least 2 inches for hemming. You'll find your material at a fabrics or crafts store. The fabric can be silk, cotton, felt or even raffia. Using fusible table, hem the top and bottom edges of the fabric (with the exception of raffia). Using Velcro strips, attach one side to the top of the fabric edge and the other to the table's edge. Instead of Velcro, you can use a staple gun and simply staple the edges to the table. The gun can also be used to staple a decorative trim over the top fabric edge for a more finished look. Using a staple gun or furniture tacks will make it easier to create pleats with the fabric.

Using a bathroom shower curtain, measure an appropriate length to cover your vanity or bathroom sink, cutting away the excess, or fold the curtain in half and iron a crease. Use any cut excess to add a second layer of skirting, and angle it away from the center front to form a faux pleat.

If the top of your table is on the shabby side, cover it with wrapping paper in your chosen design (the sturdier, the better), and use a product such as Mod Podge glue to decoupage and seal the paper. Use the Velcro or staple-gun technique above to add the skirting around the table edges.

READY-MADE OPTIONS

For inexpensive, ready-made table skirts, stores such as Party City have plastic skirts in a variety of styles. These come with their own sticky backing to attach to the table and are perfect for children's rooms, parties or other temporary situations.

For an elegant look suitable for weddings and receptions, purchase pleated paper fans in either white or a desired colour. Fold them out halfway, and use double-stick removable tape to attach the straight edge of each fan to the underside of the table, leaving the round pleated side hanging down. Use several fans arranged end-to-end to cover the length of your table.

STEPS IN TABLE SKIRTING

Table skirts offer more coverage than typical tablecloths that leave the legs and space under the table exposed. They are an inexpensive solution for covering weathered, damaged or unattractive tables. From start to finish, a lot of work goes into making table skirts to custom-fit table sizes and shapes.

MATERIAL

Table skirts can range from formal and decorative to simple and casual, depending on the fabric you choose. Satin, embroidered upholstery fabric and bright white fabric of any material usually creates a more formal look. Floral patterns, neutral cottons, and solid or patterned polyester fabrics can be used for everyday table skirting that can be washed as needed and requires little upkeep.

MEASURING

Measure your table from the floor on one side to the floor on the opposite side with a tape measure. If your table is circular or square, this is a sufficient measurement. If your table is rectangular, measure the other way across from the floor on one side to the floor on the opposite side. This will give an accurate size for the amount of fabric your table skirting requires.

PREPARATION

Mark your fabric with fabric chalk, according to the measurements you took of the table, adding 1/2 inch to each side. To create straight lines, use a straightedge or yardstick. To create a circular line, pin one end of a string that is half the length of the circular table measurement to the center of the fabric, and tie a piece of chalk to the other end. Press the chalk onto the fabric and draw a circle by rotating the string around the center where the other end of the string is pinned in place. Cut the fabric along the chalk lines with sewing scissors.

FINISHING

Fold the edges around the table skirt 1/2 inch, and pin them in place all the way around with straight pins to prepare to sew a hem. Sew along the hem by hand with needle and thread or with a sewing machine, using matching thread to finish the table skirt, then remove the pins. Consider adding braided trim, lace or beading for an extra decorative touch. Center the finished skirt over the table and adjust the bottom so that it touches the floor all the way around.

SHIRRED TABLE SKIRT

A shirred table skirt is a gathered length of fabric that reaches from the edge of a table to the floor, hiding the under-table area and giving the table and its surrounding setting a more formal, finished look. Shirred table skirting is used to finish the appearance of tables from conferences and banquets to birthday parties. Don't be afraid of the volume of fabric making your own shirred table skirt requires. The project moves quickly and once finished you have the perfect table finisher for all your future gatherings.

Instructions:

- Measure the circumference of your table, and the distance from the table edge to the floor. Choose a fabric that is wide enough on the bolt to reach from the table edge to the floor, plus 5 inches for the elastic channels at the top, and for bottom hemming. Purchase a length of fabric twice as long as the table's circumference. For example, a standard adjustable folding table used at conferences and banquets is 30 inches wide and 60 inches long, and adjustable from 24 to 30 inches high. At its tallest, this table requires fabric that is at least 35 inches wide, and a length of fabric 360 inches (30 feet) long.
- Cut two lengths of 1/2-inch elastic that are both 2 inches shorter

than the table's circumference. In the previous example, both lengths of elastic would be 178 inches long. Join lengths of the fabric end to end if you couldn't buy a single length of fabric twice the circumference of your table, until the length of the fabric meets your required dimensions.

- Fold the top 4 inches of the fabric over and machine sew at the bottom edge of the fold-over to create a 4-inch-wide pocket down the entire length of the fabric. Iron the top of the pocket all the way down the length of the fabric to create a crisp top fold.
- Skip down 1 inch from the top fold of the pocket and stitch a line down the length of the fabric. Stitch through both layers of the pocket. Sew another line down the length of the pocket 2 inches down from the first, or 3 inches down from the top crease.
- Pin a safety pin to the end of one of the elastic lengths and thread the elastic through the top 1-inch channel between the top crease and the first line of stitching, using the safety pin to move the elastic through the channel. The fabric gathers onto the elastic as you pull it through the channel. Pin or stitch the ends of the elastic together. Thread the second piece of elastic through the bottom 1-inch channel at the bottom of the 4-inch-wide pocket. Pin or stitch the ends of the elastic together.
- Stitch the ends of the fabric length together, catching the ends of the elastic in the seam. Hem the bottom of the fabric to the appropriate length for your table. Turn the shirred table skirt right-side out. Fit the shirred table skirt onto the table by placing the edge of the table between the two lines of elastic.

TABLE SKIRTS AND ITS MANY USES

Table skirts are the best solutions to cover your table beautifully. They are also called as "table covers" or "convertible table throws". They are mainly used as decorative clothing. They do not only cover the top but table skirts are wrapped around the tables.

Table skirts hide the unpleasant look of the table thus giving your table a good look. They also protect the table from stains. The two parts of the table skirts are the top cloth and the skirt. The latter can be attached to the table by using clips or tacks. There are plastic clips that have hooks to attach the skirt on the table. If you want your work to be fast and easy, you can use the sticky-back hook-and-loop fastener.

Table skirts usually cover up bad curves and displays on tables. They are getting widely popular nowadays that is why there are a lot of new styles and designs that are being introduced in the market. When choosing a table skirt, the most important thing to consider is the fabric and its quality. The colours of the skirts are also important. Most of these table skirts are made from several fabrics that can be easily washed, handy and versatile. They are also available in very affordable costs. Some of the commonly used materials are cotton, linen, silk, satin and polyester.

Polyester is a less expensive skirt and is made synthetically. It does not absorb anything especially if there are spilled food and liquids. Plastic can lasts longer and it is cheaper compared to other materials. Linen fabric is flexible and stretchable. This is very helpful if you cannot find a perfect skirt for your table. Fitted are not ready made skirts.

You need to buy a piece of cloth and leave the work to the tailor. This is somewhat customized because you choose your own design, style and colour. Pleated skirts use of two types of fabrics. The first one is to cover the table the other one is to cover the first cloth to give a more beautiful look. Overlays are additional pieces of cloth for decorations. Overlays usually add more colours and styles to the table.

Table skirts are ideal for any special occasions such as wedding receptions, banquets, meetings, birthdays and a lot more. Table skirts come in many sizes too. They are available in rectangular, square and round fits. Most of these table skirts are intended to cover all four sides of the table. In most cases, the usual length for a table skirt is 29 inches. You can buy or rent skirts from clothing companies, retailers and from those who sell linens. Table skirts that completely cover the table and go to the floor are very pleasing especially in special events. A plain table can totally change its look into a more beautiful one with a table skirt.

TABLE SKIRTING FABRICS

100 per cent polyester is a versatile choice for many manufacturers for fabricating skirting for tables, counters, stages and any other custom application. Polyester knit is a rich looking fabric that has the appeal of satin, without all the care and maintenance headaches. Poly-satin has been developed as a low-cost alternative to the traditional rayon taffeta decorating fabric. Linen fabric is typically used in more formal areas such as banquets, meeting rooms, and offices. All skirting fabrics are machine washable and dryable.

TABLE SKIRT DESIGNS

TABLE SKIRTING

There are various table skirt designs available which we are discussing below:

ROUND TABLE SKIRTS

This design is a simple circular fabric which is used on the round table and the fabric exten from extend from the edge of the table to the floor.

GATHERED OR SHIRRED TABLE SKIRTS

In this design, a fabric drape is drawn together using threads along the top hem. This offers an extra body to the skirt. With a tighter gather, a full, ruffled appearance is seen on the table skirt.

KNIFE PLEAT TABLE SKIRT DESIGN

Another popular design is the knife pleat design, where a number of narrow, sharp creases of the fabric are folded in the same direction. They create smooth, precise lines down the length of the table skirt. This is considered to be the least expensive of the table skirt design.

KIDNEY TABLE SKIRT DESIGN

This table skirt is used in the kidney table, the table whose shape is often similar with an arc shape like that of a human kidney. Kidney table skirts are designed to fit into these type of tables and the pleats are tapered to follow the design of the table.

TYPES OF TABLE SKIRTING

Table skirting can add decorating pizazz to any party or social function. Relatively inexpensive, skirting is used instead of table linen and is available in a wide variety of colours and materials. From plastic to lace, to metallic to paper, table skirting can enhance a theme or carry out a colour scheme. Attached around the edges of the table and draped to the floor, table skirting can be a cost-effective way to decorate for banquets or other social events.

PLASTIC SKIRTING

Plastic table skirting is available in just about any colour and comes in lengths of around 14 feet. Roughly 30 inches tall, the skirting is attached to the edges of banquet tables with ordinary tape.

METALLIC SKIRTING

For a more festive appearance, metallic fringe skirting can be found in a variety of bright colours.

TISSUE SKIRTING

Tissue fringe skirting that trims the edge of the table but does not extend to the floor can be a less expensive alternative.

RAFFIA SKIRTING

Table skirting that is made of raffia or artificial grass-like material can add an element of fun to luaus and events with a more tropical theme.

DECORATIVE WRAP SKIRTING

A slightly more expensive example of table skirting is decorative wrap skirting. This skirting is generally constructed of theme-printed, card stock weight paper. At around $30 per 25-foot roll, this product offers a theme or holiday-specific alternative to traditional plastic skirting.

PRICE

The price of table skirting will depend on the type of skirting that is selected. Basic plastic skirting will generally cost around $7 for a 14-foot length. Raffia and metallic fringe skirting may cost as much as $20 for a 9-foot length.

TABLE SKIRT - AN IMPORTANT ACCESSORY FOR YOUR DINING AREA

Table skirt is the material that is used on your table to make it look complete and beautiful. It is basically used to take your attention from the tables' legs by hiding them with a cloth. Table skirts are used in home, hotels and restaurants on normal days and also during special occasions. Let us now see the benefits of using this accessory.

1. It hides the unnecessary things that could be kept under the table.
2. It gives the table a very good look.
3. If you are dining with your family, there are chances of your children spilling the juice on the table. If your table has a skirt, it would protect the table from not getting stained by those spilled juices.

Let us now look at the different types and varieties of table skirts and clothing available in the market and how they are unique from each other:

1. Polyester: It is a less expensive skirt and is synthetically made. It does not absorb anything so it is good if you have a polyester table for your children.
2. Plastic: It has a long lifetime and it is cheap too. It would not dig a hole in your pockets.
3. Linen: Linen is a very flexible and stretchable fabric. So if you find a linen skirt which is not a perfect size for your table, then you can probably stretch them up at the corners to compensate for the short size.
4. Fitted: These are basically not ready made skirts. You buy a piece of cloth or any other material suitable for the table and tailor make it to exactly fit your table.
5. Pleated: It is a kind of skirt which uses two fabrics, one to cover the table and keep it secure and the other is used to cover the first cloth and give the table a trendier look.
6. Covers: These covers are more flexible in nature and are basically used to cover the table. It is firmer, flat and once fitted does not

move like skirts. The cover is fitted by folding the cupping of the cover at the corners below the table. It is very easy to put it on but it does not cover the legs of it which gives your dining area a better look.

7. Cloth: Is basically used to cover up the dining place and is available in various fabrics, size and shape.
8. Overlays: It is basically the additional piece of decorative cloth that goes on the top of the table cloth. It is used basically to add more colour and style to a dining area. These overlays could be used in different styles and come in different colours.

Thus, these are the different types of skirt available for your dining area and their uses too. After going through all the above information, one thing is for sure that a table without a skirt would look like a man without his pants.

TABLE SKIRTS AND HOW TO CHOOSE THEM

Table skirts are considered to be one of the most effective ways to dress up your table. They resemble tablecloths in the sense that they do not cover the top of the table but wrap around its edge. Properly selected table skirts can go a long way in imparting a stylish and demure look to your room. They have become an unavoidable constituent of any grand occasion. The decorative trim of table skirts can be enhanced by integrating additional trims, embroideries and borders. They are also known to have other uses rather than just for decoration.

The skirt usually consists of two parts, one is the table topper cloth and the other is the skirt which can be fastened to the edge of the table using snaps or clips. They tend to drape to the floor and therefore bring about a smart cozy look to the table. They are mainly used as a decorative equipment, but it also offers certain other functions. Since they wrap the whole perimeter of the table edges, equipments which are stored under the table for easy access are well concealed. Hence, they are mainly used for social gatherings like marriage parties, birthday parties, banquets and so on.

Since they are widely popular, several new styles are being introduced regularly. The four generally accepted styles are runners, covers, drapes and stretch covers. Table runners are laid over the table cloths. They are comparatively smaller pieces of fabric. Since they are plain in colour, logos and designs can be printed on them so as to give them a more attractive look. There are experts who can do this printing work in a professional way. They are highly customizable and therefore can be used for various occasions.

The stretch table skirting style was introduced very recently. They can be completely stretched over the table thereby leaving no wrinkles on the table top. After laying the stretch table skirting, one can zip the rear to give a wrinkle free tight appearance. Since the zipper can conceal items underneath the table, they are widely used for business conventions, birthday parties, etc. Designers make use of several fabrics to make the table skirting. Some widely used materials are poly linen, cotton, poly silk, satin, linen and polyester poplin. In some cases, plastic table skirts can also be employed. They lack the attractiveness of other table skirt materials.

There are certain other things that should be kept in mind while selecting table skirting for your room. The primary thing to consider is the type of the fabric and its quality. The colour of the table skirt should also be given high priority. The fact that they are intended to improve the overall appearance of your room should always be kept in mind. Certain colours might appear catchy, but one should also consider the wall colour and the colour of your table before selecting that table skirt.

Due to such wide possibilities, these items are used in exhibitions, business conventions, libraries, malls, banquet halls and for similar events.

ELASTIC TABLE SKIRT

When storage options are limited, or if you need a quick, decorator-look table covering for an inexpensive table, an elastic table skirt is a simple option that works well on a limited budget. These table skirts are versatile and offer a quick way to transform a folding plastic table into an organized, tailored landscape of coordinated fabric pleats. Additionally, when storage is in short supply, you can use an elastic table skirt elegantly to cover unsightly boxes under your tables, leaving your rooms pretty and organized.

INSTRUCTIONS

- Measure one side of your table from corner to corner. Write down this measurement and double it to allow for your gathers. For example, if one side of your table is 42 inches, double that number to 84 and write it down. Complete for all four sides of your table. Add all of these numbers together and add two inches. This is your width measurement.
- Measure the length from the table to the floor. Add two inches to this measurement and write it down. This is your length measurement.
- Cut out your skirt piece. Your skirt piece will be as wide as the width measurement you wrote down and as long as the length measurement you wrote down.
- Hem the bottom edge of your elastic skirt. Turn up 1/4 inch of the bottom raw edge towards the wrong side and iron into place. Turn up an additional 1/2 inch and iron into place. Pin into place and hem using a 1/4-inch seam allowance around the entire lower edge of the fabric. Repeat with the top edge of your elastic skirt.

- Measure the original circumference of your table around the edges. Cut a width of elastic 1 inch longer than this width. Pin one short raw edge of elastic to the top short edge of the elastic skirt; pin the other short, raw edge of the elastic to the opposite side of the elastic skirt.
- Pin the elastic to the top edge of the skirt, stretching the elastic as you go. The stretch of the elastic will create gathers in the fabric, and it is helpful to use as many pins as you feel necessary in this stage. Adjust the elastic and the fabric so that the gathers and the elastic are even from edge to edge.
- Change your sewing needle to a ballpoint sewing needle. Sew the top edge of the elastic to the fabric with a 1/4-inch seam allowance, taking your tie and stretching the elastic as you go so that the fabric is smooth and tight. Backstitch at the beginning and ending of your seams. Repeat on the lower edge of the elastic. Remove your pins.
- Change your sewing needle back to a standard sewing needle. Pin the short edges of the fabric with the right sides together and stitch with a 1/2-inch seam allowance to close your elastic skirt. Backstitch at the beginning and ending of your seam to lock in the stitching. Turn right side out and press. Place over your table with the elastic lined up at the top edges of the table.

SEWING PROJECTS: BANQUET TABLE SKIRT

A table skirt is a piece of sewn fabric that goes around the edges of a banquet table. The table skirt helps to cover up an otherwise ugly table and hide its legs. A table skirt can also be used as part of the decoration for any event that you are planning. Sewing a table skirt will take only a few hours, but can transform tables.

FABRIC

Choose from a variety of fabrics such as cotton, decorator fabrics, tapestries and even a lightweight vinyl. The fabric you choose depends on the type of event you are having. For more formal events, choose a more formal fabric. For casual events where you may want to use the same table skirt over and over again, use a more serviceable fabric, such as a cotton blend. Cotton blends can be washed over and over again and need little ironing. When using 100 per cent cotton, plan on ironing every time you use it. If there is going to be food served at the table, a washable fabric will be much better.

RUFFLES/PLEATS

The amount of fabric you need to sew your banquet table skirt depends not only on the size of the table, but also whether you want to add ruffles or pleats. When sewing a table skirt that just fits around the table, you only need that amount of fabric plus a few extra inches for hemming and overlap. However, when you want to add ruffles or pleats, you will need at least double the fabric of the table perimeter measurement.

LENGTH

Finding the length necessary for your table skirt is as simple as measuring from the top edge of the table to the floor. Add 2 extra inches for a hem.

CUTTING AND SEWING

Figure the amount of fabric necessary for the table skirt using the length and perimeter measurements. To cut the fabric, cut from selvage to selvage edge, which, on average, is 44 inches wide. Cut as many pieces as you need to go around your table, cutting them to the proper length of the skirt. Sew the pieces together end-to-end. Hem the top of the table skirt by folding down the fabric 1/2 inch and then another 1/2 inch to hide the raw edges. After hemming the top, add your ruffles or pleats. To make sure that you hem the skirt to the right length, hold it up to the table and pin the fabric at the bottom of the skirt.

ATTACHING THE SKIRT TO THE TABLE

One of the most efficient ways to attach the table skirt to the table is by using hook and loop tape. Look at your fabric store for adhesive hook and loop tape. Attach one side of the tape around the upper hem of the skirt and use the other piece to attach to the edge of the table.

NAPKIN FOLDING

Napkin folding is a type of decorative folding done with a napkin. It can be done as art or as a hobby. Napkin folding is most commonly encountered as a table decoration in fancy restaurants. Typically, and for best results, a clean, pressed, and starched square cloth (linen or cotton) napkin is used. There are variations in napkin folding in which a rectangular napkin, a napkin ring, a glass, or multiple napkins may be used.

HISTORY

Napkin folding has a centuries old history and dates back to the times of Louis XIV of France.

COMMON NAPKIN FOLDS

- Bishop's Hat
- Buffet fold (rectangular pocket)
- Candle
- Diagonal pocket

- Dress Shirt
- Envelope
- Fan
- Fleur-de-lis
- Iris
- Lotus (water lily)
- Rose

A BRIEF HISTORY OF NAPKIN FOLDING

The use of the napkin in Europe began in 1400 on the tables of royalty, where they started to use napkins made from warm or even perfumed cloth.

At the beginning of the 1800s, napkins became part of the bourgeois lifestyle, mostly to protect the sumptuous dresses of the period during meals. This is the era when the folding of napkins as decoration for dining tables began. The art really took off around 1880 with the incoming prosperity of the Industrial Revolution.

Mrs Beeton's book of Household Management, published in 1861, had an extensive reference section on napkin folding. These designs have now become classics and are still used today. Some of them, with modified instruction are featured in Luigi's book.

The First and Second World Wars were periods of interlude in terms of the development of these decorations.

At the beginning of the 1950s, with the war over, decorations and creativity flowed again reviving the art of folded napkins as a means of expression. This is when the development of very elaborate and complex napkin folds took place.

The James Ginder book on Napkin Folding, first published in 1978 by Virtue in over 54 languages, has been my inspiration and my guide through my career — not always very easy to follow but the only one available at the time.

Since the early 1980s we have become more reluctant to use napkin folding as part of the table preparation on the grounds of hygiene. With no practice there is no training and napkin folding has seen a decline in application in favour of a new style of table setting. A new trend of minimalism has been embraced. Elaborate napkin folding went out of favour and a new term "simplicity in style" has been has adopted. This new minimalist trend is very popular today with many fine dining operations.

Even so, we still use fancy napkin folds — particularly for weddings and special occasions where the "Fare la bella figura" is of great importance and considered a valuable asset.

There is no doubt that the development of napkin folding has been greatly influenced by Origami, the ancient Japanese art of paper folding. I would go as far as saying that it is an extension of this noble art, after all it does give the same pleasure and satisfaction to the creator.

NAPKIN RINGS

We must not overlook the Napkin Ring although it has no bearing to the Art of Napkin Folding but it has played a considerable part in table enhancement.

The usage of a napkin ring or a serviette holder started in Europe during the Napoleonic period. Mostly used by bourgeoisie's family as a mean to identify who each napkin belonged to. The practical use of the napkin ring soon spread throughout the western world and it is still widely used today and well integrated as part of the table setting — a good alternative to napkin folding.

A NEW APPROACH TO BEAUTIFUL TABLE SETTING

THE NAPKIN

The good point about the napkin, unlike the other items of the table setting, is that it allows itself to be customised just the way you like it. A touch of creativity on your part is all that it is required. It allows you to develop your own individual style and you can alter the design as often as you like.

THE CREATIVE ART OF NAPKIN FOLDING

Every time you fold a napkin in any particular style or fashion you are involving yourself in an Art form of self expression resulting in stimulating your mind giving you the pleasure of achievement and satisfaction for the individual to whom the folded napkin is dedicated.

THE LANGUAGE OF NAPKIN FOLDING

The first part of this web site will give you an insight about your host, the history of napkin folding, different type of napkins available and best applications plus an array of digest of information to help you create your own design with the napkin you already have or you intend to purchase.

The second part, covers the book Luigi's Language of Napkin Folding. With step by step instruction, under Luigi's expert guidance, you too can create beautiful designs with stunning results that you can call "your own creation". Napkin folding is an art which is within everybody's capabilities.

NAPKIN FOLDING PROBLEM

The napkin folding problem is a problem in geometry and the mathematics of paper folding that explores whether folding a square or a rectangular napkin can increase itsperimeter. The problem is known under several names, including the Margulis napkin problem, suggesting it is due to Grigory Margulis, and the Arnold's rouble problemreferring to Vladimir Arnold and the folding of a Russian ruble. Some versions of the problem were solved by Robert J. Lang, Svetlana Krat, Alexey S. Tarasov, and Ivan Yaschenko. One form of the problem remains open.

Formulations: There are several way to define the notion of folding, giving different interpretations. By convention, the napkin is always a unit square.

Folding along a straight line: One can consider sequential folding of all layers along a line. In this case it can be shown that the perimeter is always non-increasing under such foldings, thus never exceeding.

It is still unknown if there is a solution using a sequence of foldings, such that each is a reflection of a connected component of folded napkin on one side of a straight line.That is whether a solution can be folded using some combination of mountain folds, valley folds, reverse folds, and/or sink folds (with all folds in the latter two cases being formed along a single line). Also unknown, of course, is whether such a fold would be possible using the more-restrictive pureland origami.

Where only the result matters: One can ask whether there exists a folded planar napkin (without regard as to how it was folded into that shape).

Robert J. Lang showed in 1997 that several classical origami constructions give rise to an easy solution. In fact, Lang showed that the perimeter can be made as large as desired by making the construction more complicated. However his constructions are not rigid origami because of their use of sink folds and related forms; although no stretching is needed in sink and unsink folds, it is necessary to curve facets and/or sweep one or more creases continuously through the paper in intermediate steps before obtaining a flat result.

In 1998, I. Yaschenko constructed a 3D folding with projection onto a plane which has a bigger perimeter. This indicated to mathematicians that there was probably a flat folded solution to the problem.

The same conclusion was made by Svetlana Krat. Her approach is different, she gives very simple construction of a "rumpling" which increase perimeter and then proves that any "rumpling" can be arbitrary well approximated by a "folding". In essence she shows that the precise details of the how to do the folds don't matter much if stretching is allowed in intermediate steps.

Folding without stretching: One can ask for a realizable construction within the constraints of rigid origami where the napkin is never stretched whilst being folded. In 2004 A. Tarasov showed that that such constructions can indeed be obtained. This can be considered a complete solution to the original problem.

SOLUTIONS

Lang's solutions: Lang devised two different solutions. Both involved sinking flaps and so were not rigid origami. The simplest was based on the origami bird base and gave a solution with a perimeter of about 4.12 compared to the original perimeter of 4.

The second solution can be used to make a figure with a perimeter as large as desired. He divides the square into a large number of smaller squares and employs the 'sea urchin' type origami construction described in his 1990 book, *Origami Sea Life*. The crease pattern shown is the $n = 5$ case and can be used to produce a flat figure with 25 flaps, one for each of the large circles, and sinking is used to thin them. When very thin the 25 arms will give a 25 pointed star with a small center and a perimeter approaching $N/(N$ " $1)$. In the case of $N = 5$ this is about 6.25, and the total length goes up approximately as N.

HISTORY

Arnold states in his book that he formulated the problem in 1956, but the formulation was left intentionally vague. He called it 'the rumpled rouble problem', and it was the first of many interesting problems he set at seminars in Moscow over 40 years. In the West, it became known as Margulis napkin problem after Jim Propp's newsgroup posting in 1996. Despite attention, it received folklore status and its origin is often referred as "unknown".

THE PYRAMID NAPKIN FOLD

This classy napkin folding technique is simple, fast, and can be made easily with most napkins. If the napkin being used is thin and flops easily then iron it with light starch prior to folding.

1. Lay the napkin face down in front of you.
2. Fold the napkin in half diagonally.
3. Rotate the napkin so the open end faces away from you.
4. Fold the right end up to meet the far corner, ensuring the edge of this new fold lays on the centreline.
5. Repeat the last step with the left side, folding the left tip up to the far corner, creating a diamond shape with a seam running down the centre.
6. Turn the napkin over, keeping the open end facing away from you.
7. Fold the napkin in half by bringing the farthest point of the diamond up and back to the nearest point.
8. Turn the napkin over again, this time keeping the open end facing towards you.
9. Fold the napkin along the centre seam and you have a neat, sturdy pyramid. If your napkin won't stand neatly then you may need a little starch.

THE BISHOP'S HAT FOLD

This particular fold can be a bit tricky when it comes to lining up the corners in the cap. Again, some starch and an iron make it easier to be precise while folding this one.

1. Lay the napkin face down in front of you.

2. Fold the napkin in half so that the open end is towards you.
3. Fold the far-right corner diagonally towards you, resting the point in the centre of the side closest to you.
4. Fold the near-left corner diagonally away from you, resting it so that it lies right next to the previous fold.
5. Flip the napkin over and orient it so it points to the far-left and to the near-right.
6. Fold the bottom half of the napkin up and away from you, laying it so the far edges run on top of one other.
7. Reach underneath the napkin and pull out the flap on the right, making the near-side come to two points.
8. Gently roll the left half of the left triangle over and tuck its end underneath the right triangle.
9. Flip the napkin over, points pointing away from you.
10. Fold the right-triangle to the left, tucking its end into the other triangle.
11. Open up the hat and press the material inside down to fill it out so that it becomes circular, this may take a little cajoling.

THE BIRD OF PARADISE FOLD

This technique will require a stiff napkin. If you don't have any dinner napkins made of stiff linen then a light starching should work.

1. Lay the napkin face down in front of you.
2. Fold the napkin in half.
3. Fold the napkin in quarters.
4. Fold in half diagonally, creating a triangle.
5. Arrange the triangle so the open tip is facing away from you.
6. Fold the right corner diagonally towards you – laying it down along the centreline of the triangle, making a new tip pointing towards you. An iron can make this important fold a whole lot easier.
7. Do the same with the left corner, fold it diagonally towards you and press it down next to the previous fold.
8. Fold the two "wings" that you just made in folds 6 and 7 under so that you have your original triangle shape back. Once again an iron can make a world of difference.
9. Fold the triangle in half by bringing the centre seam towards you and allowing the ends to fall.
10. While holding the base firmly to keep your folds together, pull up the four 'flaps' created by the napkin's corners.

TABLE SETTING: THE ART OF NAPKIN FOLDING

For an especially polished table, cloth napkins can be folded into appealing shapes to add to the décor of your table. Napkin folding works particularly well on freshly starched napkins. Here are some common folding techniques:

THE TRIFOLD NAPKIN

- Place the unfolded napkin in front of you in the shape of a diamond
- Bring the top corner down to meet the bottom corner (fold it in half diagonally) creating a triangle with the point facing down
- Fold the left and right corners down to the center point
- Fold the top point down to meet the bottom
- Lift the napkin from the center, allowing it to stand alone on the two folded sides

Windmere's Fan

- Place the unfolded napkin in front of you in the shape of a square
- Fold the napkin in half either vertically or horizontally
- Starting at the shorter end of the resulting rectangle, begin making ½ inch accordion pleats, stop when there are approximately 4 inches left to fold
- Fold the accordion section in half so that the folds are on the outside with the remaining 4 inches at the center
- Make a stand by folding the 4 inch section towards the base of the fan, allowing the pleats to fan out

The Rose

- Place the unfolded napkin in front of you in the shape of a square
- Fold each of the four corners into the center of the napkin
- Again, fold the four new corners into the center of the napkin
- Carefully turn the folded napkin over, and fold the four corner into the center one more time
- Holding the folds together, slide the folded napkin into a diamond shape
- Use one hand to hold down the bottom two points and use the other hand to reach under the two points to pull out a flap
- Repeat this step with the remaining 3 corners
- Hold the center point to access and reveal the additional "petals"

Bibliography

Aikens, Charlotte Albina.: *Hospital Housekeeping.* Detroit Mich: D.T. Sutton, 1906.

Angela Wadia.: *Broadcast Management in India : Major Guidelines and Policy Frameworks*, Kanishka Publication, Delhi, 2007.

Arvind Gautam.: *Accommodation Operation Management*, Navyug Publication, Delhi, 2008.

B B Vidyarthi.: *Management of Hotel and Catering Industry*, Pearl Books, Delhi, 2007.

B.K. Chakravarti.: *Hotel Management Theory, Vols. I and II*, APH Publication, Delhi, 2009.

C.P. Yadav.: *Management of Hotel and Catering Industry*, Anmol Publication, Delhi, 2001.

D.K. Aggarwal.: *Housekeeping Management*, Aman Publication, Delhi, 2006.

D.K. Sharma.: *Perspectives of Hotel Management*, Pearl Books, Delhi, 2012.

Dahl, Crete M. and Grace H. Woolley.: *Housekeepers' Guide to Selecting and Training Employees.* Stamford Conn: Dahl Pub. Co., 1949.

Dahl, Crete M.: *Housekeeping Management and Organization for Hotels and Institutions.* Stamford, Conn.: The Dahls, 1945.

G. Raghubalan and Smritee Raghubalan.: *Hotel Housekeeping : Operations and Management*, Oxford University Press, 2009.

Gagandeep Singh.: *Global Aviation and Hospitality Management*, Book Enclave, Delhi, 2008.

Gaurav Gandhi.: *Hotel Management Food and Food Services*, Random Publications, Delhi, 2012.

L.K. Sharma.: *Hotel and Catering Management*, Surendra Publications, Delhi, 2012.

Lalita Sharma.: *Tourism and Hospitality Management*, Centrum Press, Delhi, 2011.

M C Metti.: *Catering : Housekeeping and Hotel Management*, Anmol Publication, Delhi, 2008.

M C Metti.: *Customer Service and Hotel Management*, Anmol Publication, Delhi, 2008.

M C Metti.: *Hospitality and Facilities in Hotel Management*, Anmol Publication, Delhi, 2008.

N N Dahalia.: *Fundamentals of Hotel Management and Operation*, Pearl Books, Delhi, 2007.

Neeta Mehta.: *Fundamental of Hotel Management and Operations*, Random Publications, Delhi, 2012.

Nirmal Dubey.: *Hospitality Tourism and Hotel Management*, Sonali Publications, Delhi, 2011.

O.P. Kandari and Ashish Chandra.: *Hotel, Tourism and Catering Management*, Shree Publication, Delhi, 2004.

Ravindra Verma.: *Hotel Management and Tourism*, Centrum Press, Delhi, 2010.

Rubina Joseph.: *Modern Hotel Management*, Alfa Publication, Delhi, 2006.

S.K. Singh.: *Fundamental of Hotel Management and Operations*, Centrum Press, Delhi, 2010.

Sonia Rahul Sharma.: *Text Book of Computers for Hotel Management*, Aman Publication, Delhi, 2010.

Sujit Kumar Dwivedi and Simran Kaur Julka.: *Principles of Hotel Management*, Naman Publication, Delhi, 2011.

Varinder Singh Rana.: *Catering Hospitality and Tourism*, Centrum Press, Delhi, 2012.

Varinder Singh Rana.: *Catering Management*, Centrum Press, Delhi, 2011.

Vijay Kaushik.: *Management and Functions of Housekeeping*, Book Enclave, 2006.

Vijender Singh.: *Hotel Housekeeping with Video CD*, Tata McGraw Hill, 2012.

Index